Critical Youth Studies
A CANADIAN FOCUS

Critical Youth Studies
A CANADIAN FOCUS

James E. Côté
University of Western Ontario

Anton L. Allahar
University of Western Ontario

PEARSON

Prentice
Hall

Toronto

Library and Archives Canada Cataloguing in Publication

Côté, James E., 1953–
    Critical youth studies: a Canadian focus / James E. Côté, Anton L. Allahar.

ISBN 0-13-127590-9

1. Youth—Canada—Textbooks. I. Allahar, Anton L., 1949– II. Title.

HQ799.C3C68 2006   305.235'0971   C2005-903521-8

ISBN 0-13-127590-9

Vice President, Editorial Director: Michael J. Young
Acquisitions Editor: Patty Riediger
Signing Representative: Carine Pierzchalski
Executive Marketing Manager: Judith Allen
Associate Editor: Paula Drużga
Production Editor: Kevin Leung
Copy Editor: Ann McInnis
Proofreader: Maryan Gibson
Production Coordinator: Janis Raisen
Composition: Carolyn E. Sebestyen
Art Director: Mary Opper
Cover Image: Stockbyte Teenage Kicks

Statistics Canada information is used with the permission of the Minister of Industry, as Minister responsible for Statistics Canada. Information on the availability of the wide range of data from Statistics Canada can be obtained from Statistics Canada's Regional Offices, its World Wide Web site at www.statcan.ca, and its toll-free number 1-800-263-1136.

2 3 4 DPC 09 08 07

Printed and bound in Canada.

*This book is written for the thousands of young people
we have taught in our courses since the late 1970s.
We hope your voices and concerns are represented in our words,
even if we do not shine spotlights on your individual cases.*

Brief Contents

Contents

About the Authors

Dr. James E. Côté

James Côté received his Ph.D. from York University in 1984, after completing an M.A. at the University of Western Ontario, and an Honours B.A. at Trent. He is a Full Professor in the Department of Sociology at Western. He is the founding editor of *Identity: An International Journal of Theory and Research* and Past-President of the Society for Research on Identity Formation (SRIF). Dr. Côté is also on the Executive Board of RC34 (Sociology of Youth) of the International Sociological Association, and Editor of the *International Bulletin of Youth Research*. He and has authored or co-authored five books in Youth Studies and Identity Studies, including *Adolescent Storm and Stress* (Erlbaum, 1994), *Generation on Hold* (Stoddart, 1994; New York University Press, 1996), *Arrested Adulthood: The Changing Nature of Identity and Maturity in the Late-Modern World* (New York University Press, 2000) and *Identity Formation, Agency, and Culture: A Social Psychological Synthesis* (Erlbaum, 2002). He has also published several dozen journal articles and book chapters, and made numerous conference presentations around the world in these fields.

Dr. Anton L. Allahar

Anton Allahar completed his M.A. and Ph.D. in Political & Economic Sociology at the University of Toronto and is currently a Full Professor of Sociology at the University of Western Ontario. Dr. Allahar's principal areas of interest are economic development, the politics of globalization & democracy, and ethnic and racial relations, as these apply to the Caribbean and Central America. His books include: *The Sugar Planters of Colonial Cuba* (Two-Thirds Editions, 1982); *Class, Politics and Sugar in Colonial Cuba* (Mellen, 1990); *Is there Life after Debt? The Latin American Debt Crisis* (IOHE, 1993); *Sociology and the Periphery: Theories and Issues* (Garamond, 1995); *Generation on Hold: Coming of Age in the Late 20th Century* (Stoddart, 1994; New York University Press, 1996); *Richer and Poorer: The Structure of Inequality in Canada* (Lorimer, 1998, with James Côté). He has also edited *Caribbean Charisma* (Ian Randle Publishers, 2001) and *Ethnicity, Class and Nationalism: Caribbean and Extra-Caribbean Dimensions* (Lexington Books, 2005), along with two Special Issues of *Identity: An International Journal of Theory and Research:* (i) *Diasporas and Transnational Identities* (2001), and (ii) *Diasporic Identity: Myth Culture and the Politics of Home* (2002). In addition, he has written over 60 refereed articles and book chapters on related themes and has won three major teaching awards at Western.

Acknowledgments

We would like to thank the staff at Pearson Education Canada for bringing this book to life, from initial discussions about its potential for the Canadian market to the final production process. In particular, we thank Jessica Mosher for signing the book and Paula Drużga for her patient and expert stewardship in taking it through two review processes. We are also grateful to the reviewers who gave their valuable time, and provided their expert advice, to help shape the book to its current form: Helen Douglas, Okanagan University College; James Penner, University of Lethbridge; Doreen L. Smith, University of Winnipeg; and Anne Wagner, Nipissing University. Of course, we take full responsibility for any errors or misstatements that might have survived the extensive reviewing and editing this book has received.

An Introduction to
Critical Youth Studies

In 1994, we published the book *Generation on Hold: Coming of Age in the Late Twentieth Century*, speaking on behalf of the young people in Canada and the United States who were among the first cohorts experiencing the prolonged transition to adulthood that is now commonplace. We argued that the primary root of this longer transition was a decline in their workplace opportunities that had gained momentum in the 1980s. These diminished opportunities had many ripple effects in their lives, especially in delaying their assumption of independent adult roles—hence the title *Generation on Hold*.

During the publicity tour for that book, we encountered wide support from the public, especially among those who called in to the various radio and television phone-in shows in which we participated. In Canada, a number of the journalists who interviewed us also sensed that something had changed in the fortunes of the young. Both the public to whom we spoke and the journalists who took on the story seemed to appreciate the fact that we had evidence for what they had only sensed. Internationally, the book has also been influential and stands as one of the first to identify the global decline in the status and fortunes of young people coming of age in advanced industrial societies. At the same time, in Canada and the United States, there unfortunately continues to be reluctance in certain quarters to accept the possibility that young people constitute a disadvantaged group in need of special academic and policy attention (cf. Krahn, Lowe, & Lehmann, 2002).

Some ten years later, although the statistics are in need of updating, much of what we wrote in *Generation on Hold* has been empirically supported, both in terms of our account of the conditions at the time and what we predicted the future would hold. Indeed, many of the conditions we documented either have continued at generationally high levels or have worsened. The clearest trend we identified was the increasingly prolonged transitional period between the dependency of childhood and the independence of adulthood caused by the diminished workplace opportunities available to the young. Not only is the existence of this trend no longer in dispute in Canada (e.g., Lowe, 2001), but there is clear evidence that it is occurring in virtually every advanced industrialized country in the world, such that the full cohort transition now spans the ages of 15 to 35 in some countries (Cook & Furstenburg, 2002; International Labour Office, 2004). In the present book, we fully document this international trend with the results of numerous studies that have been undertaken over the past decade. Young Canadians should take a particular interest in these studies because they show how their experiences are shared by others around the world, and how other countries have responded in ways that provide examples for how Canada can better deal with this situation.

Youth Studies is now a rapidly growing area worldwide, prompted by the increasing concern over the above-mentioned sweeping economic changes associated with globalization. However, in comparison with Europe and Australia, in Canada (and the United States) there is a conspicuous absence of deep concern among policy-makers for the new challenges now confronting young people. In addition, comparing Canada with some other industrialized countries, most notably the Scandinavian countries and the United

Kingdom, there is little academic research conducted on youth (see Gauthier & Pacom, 2001, for a review). And, unlike these other countries, Canadian policy-makers rarely call upon academics for consultations about what research should be conducted to illuminate problems and what measures need to be taken to address them. A possible consequence of this inactivity is the remarkable complacency among much of the Canadian public and many politicians regarding youth issues (cf. Hollands, 2001).

With respect to the limited attention given youth issues in Canada, most of this attention has been paid to the upper end of the spectrum of young people—those who go on to higher education—and little heed is given those on the lower end, those who complete high school or less. This may relate to the public's false belief that everyone can gain a higher education if they try hard enough, thus personalizing and individualizing blame for the shortcomings of our economic system. Accordingly, there seems to have been an attempt to "naturalize" a situation that has been socially engineered (i.e., to view it as inevitable and therefore acceptable), while in other countries there have been concerted public debates and government-sponsored research programs aimed at addressing the problems of youth marginalization and exclusion, particularly at the lower end of the income and education spectrum (these are described in the United Kingdom by Catan, 2004, and Jones, 2002, as discussed in the final chapter of this book). Perhaps because of this complacency, Canada has not developed a clear policy to address the mounting difficulties faced by youth in making the transition to adulthood (e.g., Gauthier & Pacom, 2001; Lowe, 2001). To provide a comparison, this complacency in Canada regarding youth issues stands in stark contrast to widespread concerns here over racial and gender inequalities among academics and government policy-makers.

Although our attempts to bring youth issues to light among the general public have been successful to some extent, we have been disappointed in our lack of widespread impact on the people most affected—young people themselves. In spite of having their economic prospects and citizenship rights seriously altered by the changes we documented ten years ago, there seems to be a lack of a critical understanding of what lies behind the growing inequities among the age cohorts that ostensibly share equal citizenship rights. Certainly there is disaffection among some young people stemming from their disadvantages, and concern among some adults about youth disadvantages, but the disaffection and concern are often diffusely directed because there is not a firm appreciation of the nature of the problem. We find this year after year in our classes when we discuss youth issues with our young students. When the sources of their disadvantages are pointed out to them, many students finally grasp the meaning of their malaise and are very thankful to us for raising their consciousness, as we hope students reading this book will be. As is the case in general with respect to human adaptation, current conditions constitute a "new normal" that is simply taken for granted as inevitable. In other words, there is a tendency to accept the world one grows up in as natural and inevitable; many people are not stimulated to contemplate what actually created that world.

In general, then, whether we are speaking about young people or adults, the seriousness of the situation facing many young people has not led to attempts to understand its root causes. There are several reasons for this neglect that are explored in this book. For the moment, however, we shall briefly identify three sources of bias here.

First, people can find it difficult to develop a critical awareness of complex social problems, like those that have altered the transition to adulthood, because, in an individualistic society such as ours, individualistic explanations for societal problems are preferred. Accordingly, people are more likely to learn to see the causes of societal patterns in the concrete behaviours of observable individuals, rather than in patterns of interaction, much as it is easier to observe the actions of specific automobiles than it is to sort out patterns of traffic flow. The danger in viewing things only from an individualistic perspective is in "blaming the victim," namely, mistakenly attributing a person's social or economic misfortune to him or her personally, when it is clear that many others share the misfortune for reasons beyond their control.

Second, it is more comforting to believe that Canadian society is simply "evolving" according to some underlying, indisputable logic than it is to look at evidence that aspects of our society might be the product of the workings of self-interested groups in search of power and wealth. This tendency relates to the fact that many people, especially those who are politically conservative, "need" to believe that the world, as it is, is fundamentally fair and just (e.g., Dittmar & Dickinson, 1993; Mohr & Luscri, 1995). To believe otherwise— to identify injustices and unfairness affecting others—can make people feel anxious, dissonant, and less deserving of their own good fortunes. It is simply easier psychologically to believe that there is some sort of "grand plan" that is unfolding (whether it be the "invisible hand" of the market, or the will of a god) and that this plan is kinder to some people than others. When combined with the first bias of viewing social problems in individualistic terms, the need to believe in a just world creates a blind spot among those with a conservative outlook, because casting social problems as systemic threatens to upset the status quo from which they personally derive material benefits and emotional security.

And, third, most people do not possess the historical perspective and knowledge to see how present-day Canadian society has been shaped and formed by self-interested groups of people acting over long periods of time, in this case decades and even centuries. To develop that historical perspective requires levels of study and sustained interest that many people are apparently unwilling to undertake. Some young people may view history as something best left in the past, and is therefore irrelevant and inconsequential to their current lives. With limited real-life experience and a short historical memory, it is understandable that many young people might be confused or mistaken about the social and historical forces that have affected not only the current circumstances faced by their cohort, but also how previous cohorts have faced different prospects.

As we argue below, these three biases can also be identified among some social scientists as manifested in their theories and research. The public might assume that all social scientists critically attend to the complex causes and consequences of social problems, but this is not always the case, as we show later on in the text when we discuss various issues affecting young people. In this regard, we separate social scientists roughly into two groups: conservative and critical.

Conservative social scientists tend to see contemporary societal arrangements—the status quo—as fair and well functioning, and therefore they oppose significant social change. Like conservatives in the political realm, they favour what are now "traditional" ways of doing things and resist calls to change the established ways of thinking and behaving.

Critical social scientists, on the other hand, tend not to accept the fairness and legitimacy of the status quo at face value. Instead, they seek to identify whom societal arrangements favour and whom they disadvantage, and they advocate social and economic changes to remedy any unfairness in such arrangements. From the outset, it is crucial to understand that taking a critical perspective does not simply mean to find fault (as in one definition of the word "critical"), but to use logic and evidence to carefully evaluate and judge, as in a critical appraisal of art. To illustrate this point, one would not immediately label *movie critics* as "troublemaking radicals," but this can be a knee-jerk reaction to *social critics*, who are then dismissed as such by those who are defensive about the status quo. Two critical approaches are adopted in this book: the political-economy approach, which looks at the material basis of people's living conditions; and the late-modernist approach, which focuses more on the symbolic meanings that people use to make sense of their world.

It is within this context of prevailing conservative postures bolstered by underlying biases that we offer in this book a Critical Youth Studies that is intended both to help young people recognize their common interests and to prompt adults to live up to their intergenerational obligations. Our aim is to provide the knowledge base and perspective for all Canadians to better understand the changing life chances of the young and their altered relations with older age groups. We are building this approach by refining and updating what we wrote in *Generation on Hold* in conjunction with (a) the myriad studies published since the publication of that book, (b) considerations of criticisms about what we wrote in *Generation on Hold*, and (c) the growth of our own thinking on these matters.

In order to ensure that some common misconceptions do not interfere with the ability to critically evaluate the arguments presented, we ask readers to think of the transition to adulthood in three ways. First, at 18, Canadians reach the age of majority, which entitles them to the same rights and responsibilities as all other citizens of legal age. Second, as with other species, reaching maturity means that humans have fully developed according to their potentials (think of a flower growing according to its innate potential, but being influenced by the environmental conditions while it grows). And, third, adulthood involves integration into society through direct participation with other citizens in mainstream institutions.

Taken together, all citizens over 18 are entitled to full citizenship rights in Canadian society in ways that allow them to reach their full potentials or "humanness" through participation in mainstream institutions. We alert readers to this now because, as we see in the final chapter of this book, we can take lessons from countries like Sweden that recognize these ideas as the starting point for informing public debate and policy-making on a range of issues, like the direction that societal change should take in ensuring that their citizens' age, race, and gender do not interfere with their life chances.

Finally, several additional points need to be made to put this book into context.

First, this book presents a focused argument; as such it is not a textbook covering all aspects of youth studies. For the reasons just discussed concerning the widespread conservatism taken toward youth issues, we see the need for a book that directly challenges the complacency associated with it and provides a model for critical thinking on these issues. Our book might be used as a supplement to Lerner, Brown, and Kier's (2005) textbook *Adolescence: Development, Diversity, Context and Application*, Canadian Edition. While that textbook is written from a psychological perspective and focuses only on adolescence, the approach taken is a critical one that advocates significant change to address the issues facing young Canadians. Moreover, Lerner, Brown, and Kier lay out the basis for instituting many of those changes through private and public programs. Accordingly, we refer readers of our book to that source if they wish to find more information on certain topics, such as summaries of research on the family, peer groups, and sexuality, but also to see how policy-based action can be taken on many of the problems we discuss.

Second, the focused argument in this book concerns the changing nature of the transition to adulthood that is creating an increasing source of disadvantage for those in the "youth" age status. Not only is "youth" associated with increasing material disadvantage in relation to adult status, but this period of disadvantage is growing, such that people are finding themselves at a disadvantage for longer periods of their lives. In order to maintain the focus of this argument on the dimension of age status (i.e., youth), we do not delve in detail into other social statuses of advantage-disadvantage like race/ethnicity, gender, sexuality, ability, and so forth. The reason for this is twofold. On the one hand, youth status cuts through each of these other statuses, potentially placing younger members of each status at a disadvantage in relation to older members. So regardless of their other sources of disadvantage, young people have a greater chance of being disadvantaged than those with adult status. At the same time, the sources of disadvantages often simply multiply, producing double and even triple jeopardies, as in the case of "youth × race × gender" resulting in young, black females having the poorest economic opportunities and prospects compared to older white males. On the other hand, while these experiences are real and serious in their consequences, if we were to attempt to document each and every combination and permutation of disadvantage that compounds with youth status, we would be writing an entirely different book that would constitute an encyclopedia of disadvantage rather than focused analysis of youth and the changing nature of the transition to adulthood. The fact that youth is consistently overlooked as a source of disadvantage makes it even more important that we maintain our focus on it.

And, third, in developing our argument and analysis we draw on the writings of other social scientists whose commentaries on adolescence and youth have dealt with the psychology of adolescence, cultural anthropology, demography, workplace economics, the history of education, criminology, the sociology of the family, and so forth. Our aim, however, is to go beyond such approaches, which generally focus on one isolated aspect of the picture to the exclusion of other aspects. What we do that is different is to portray the "big picture" in which a broad-strokes understanding of the problems is presented, *and* in which we undertake the risky tasks of diagnosing the problems and recommending solutions. Although we call our approach "critical materialist," it is interdisciplinary to the extent that we draw freely from anthropology, demography, history, psychology, psychoanalysis, economics, and sociology in our attempt to understand the challenges and opportunities youth face today, and the implications of these conditions for Canadian society.

In some respects, therefore, specific details of what we have to say are not new, for there are now some 15 000 keyword listings for books dealing with various aspects of youth and adolescence in our university library. Those books, however, appear to have had little impact on the problems we identify and discuss. Our hope with this book, therefore, is to reach the audience that needs to know what is happening to their world: young people themselves who will likely read this in a course, and who we hope will take this information to their parents, community leaders, educational policy-makers, and even government ministries.

chapter one

Youth in Historical and Societal Context

As noted in the introduction, public consciousness of youth issues does not include a disciplined understanding of the history of youth as a period in the life course. Indeed, as we will see later in this book, misconceptions abound about the fundamental nature of the transition to adulthood, some of which were created by certain social scientists who first worked in this area. Accordingly, this chapter provides three useful ways of looking at the history and nature of the transition to adulthood: (a) a view of youth–adult relations in terms of historical changes in the conceptions of youth, (b) a historical perspective on youth in Canada, and (c) an account of young people in the context of the current Canadian political economy. Then follows the plan of this book, which has been designed to systematically build a Critical Youth Studies that is informed by empirically supported sociological theory.

A BRIEF HISTORY OF YOUTH–ADULT RELATIONS

Throughout the millennia, adults have periodically left records expressing their concerns about the members of their community who had yet to "come of age." Records of complaints about recalcitrant youthfulness date as far back as the eighth century B.C. with the Greek poet Hesiod's warning that he saw no future if it depended "on the frivolous youth of today, for certainly all youth are reckless beyond words" (as cited in

Manning, 1983, p. 824). Similar laments can be found in other writings through the ages, including those of William Shakespeare and George Bernard Shaw. Shakespeare, in *The Winter's Tale*, crafted a character who wished that youth could be bypassed because between the ages of 16 and 23 men do nothing other than "getting wenches with child, wronging the ancientry, stealing, fighting" (as cited in Springhall, 1986). More recently, George Bernard Shaw is noted for complaining that youth was wasted on the young, although he actually wrote, "youth is a wonderful thing. What a crime to waste it on children," so his quip was not likely meant as a put-down of those in the age ranges now associated with "youth."

Although some people use such anecdotal evidence to argue that there have always been negative attitudes among "adults" toward "youth," all it really proves is that we can find some evidence that some adults have at times expressed negative views about the "younger generation." However, such evidence is not proof that (a) all adults throughout human history held such negative attitudes, (b) the few views represented in these rare archives represented typical behaviours of those times (Manning, 1983; in fact they could be more indicative of curmudgeon tendencies among just a few older adults), (c) the transition to adulthood was structured in the same way in the past as it is now (especially as in contemporary Canadian society), or (d) that youth or adolescence are "essential" stages marked off from other life stages in terms of biology or genetics. In fact, this point about negative adult attitudes is sometimes offered as part of conservative arguments that we do not need to be concerned about negative stereotypes about young people, with the implication that, because they were held in the past, they are justified in the present. To provide an analogy that exposes this faulty reasoning, negative views toward women were held in the past, but this does not justify their continued use.

However, regardless of how accurate such characterizations were of youth as a whole, or how representative they were of adult attitudes at the time, such prejudices do exist today and have become part of the "common-sense" view—the view of the average person—taken toward young people. Characteristically, a common-sense view is nonreflective in the sense that the full complexity of a problem is not considered. For example, operating on the basis of common sense, we could preempt further consideration of the focus of this book with one of several conclusions. We could conclude that when young people appear to be acting immaturely, they must be inherently that way. Or, we could infer that when young people do not seem to be able to handle responsibilities, there must be something about them that makes them irresponsible.

These are "essentialist" views of youth, namely, assumptions that there is something in the essence of being "young" that produces inevitable results like immaturity or irresponsibility. Such views are the basis of stereotypes that generalize expectations to all members of a group, in this case all young people. Consequently, when put together with common sense, laypeople might conclude that all youth are essentially "immature" and "irresponsible," and therefore that the youth segment of society must be closely watched and regulated by adult authorities. This negative stereotype about young people so permeates contemporary Canadian culture that it is difficult to even raise the issue for discussion.

Furthermore, the current common-sense view of "adolescence" and "youth" casts them as natural and necessary stages or phases of life-course development. People in the rather fuzzy age ranges representing the phases of adolescence and youth are believed to be biologically and/or emotionally immature, and therefore unsuited for admission as full-fledged members of a "complex" society. If young people do not accept the conditions of this phase of the life cycle, it is believed that there must be something wrong with them, something inside them that makes them unable to control themselves and accept what everyone else accepts—the inevitability of a slow and prolonged coming of age.

Many people believe that the "adolescence" they see in contemporary society is as inevitable as old age and death. As we shall see, several social scientific perspectives seem to share this common-sense view of young people. However, this view is specific to contemporary Western societies. Before the twentieth century, young people in Western societies were thought of quite differently, primarily because there was not a sharp distinction between being an adult and a non-adult. Under the right circumstances teenagers could assume many adult roles without interference, including work, marriage, and military duty (e.g., Steinberg, 1990).

An examination of the etymology and meaning of the word *adolescent* (e.g., from the Oxford English Dictionary) explains why young people in past eras, and still in some cultures, could have taken on such tasks and been "allowed" to accomplish at early ages what are now considered "adult" tasks. The term itself came into English usage only in the 1400s, taken from the Latin *adolescere*, meaning, "to grow up, mature." The word *adult* did not come into usage for another 50 years, but is derived from the same Latin root as adolescent (the past participle *adultus*, meaning "grown up").

Many other languages have either borrowed from English or still do not have a specific word that is comparable to *adolescence*, essentially because there is no equivalent period of life in need of a word to describe it. Among the Inuit in Canada's Arctic, the word *inuhaaq* roughly meant "becoming a person" and referred to those in early puberty, while the term *inirniq* designated "fully grown," and was given to males when they could grow a beard and to females when they had fully developed breasts (Condon, 1987). However, as a result of Western influence, the first term now translates as "teenager." Commenting on this issue in reference to cultures around the globe, Brown and Larson (2002) observe the following:

> In some cases, there is simply no term to describe adolescence, a certain sign that the society does not regard it as a distinct and important stage of the life cycle. Until recently, this was the case in many East Asian societies. . . . Often, such societies were organized so that children take on major adult responsibilities at an early age; in their activities, young people are not commonly segregated from adults. (p. 4)

In point of fact, the scientific identification of adolescence as a distinct stage of life was proposed only around 1900 by a social scientist—G. Stanley Hall, about whom we will be hearing more below—to give a name to what was increasingly defined as a "problem" believed to be associated with the transition to adulthood (Hall, 1904). The adoption of the term *adolescence* into the social sciences was accompanied by the notion of adolescent "storm and stress," which evolved into the notions of "adolescent turmoil" and "raging hormones." These ideas persist today, with many people believing that all adolescents are prone to often-uncontrollable biological impulses. Consequently, many adults maintain the belief that adolescence is a rather distasteful and tumultuous stage of human development, which everyone must pass through in order to learn how to manage impulses and emotions in a mature fashion. Instead of looking to social causes, like the disruptions then associated with urbanization and industrialization that made teen labour redundant in the later part of the 1800s (leaving many idle, without structure), the "deviance" associated with being "adolescent" in an industrial society was attributed by Hall to a "developmental period" that he believed to be an inevitable time of storm and stress—an oscillation between opposing emotional states.

Such ideas were and are popular both in terms of their simplicity and by the fact that they let policy-makers off the hook: Policies can be made to "fix" the individual rather than to remedy the societal conditions producing individual problems. At the same time, because of Hall's influence, many adults came to believe that attempts to intervene in "adolescent turmoil" are largely ineffective because of its biological inevitability. From this stereotype has come the belief that it is better to leave young people to themselves—segregated from adult society—until the turmoil passes. Although informed social scientists have rejected the notion of universal storm and stress, it is not hard to find stereotypes perpetuated by that notion. For example, as recently as March 2004, CBC television aired a two-part documentary titled *Raging Hormones*, in which conflicts between teenagers and their parents were filmed among several highly selected families. All this documentary proved was that some families experience difficulties (a mundane fact); no evidence was presented that "hormones" or "biology" are responsible for these conflicts, yet this is the implication made by the title, and therefore likely what had the greatest impact on the public's consciousness of youth issues.

Hall's storm and stress argument has informed not only public opinion and public policy, but also much theorizing about the young, particularly among psychologists and psychiatrists. Unfortunately, assumptions derived from his argument are dying a slow death as scientific studies have demonstrated that adolescent "turmoil" is not culturally universal and therefore cannot be an inevitable part of human development (Arnett, 1999; Lerner, 2004; Muuss, 1996). Indeed, some social scientists still favour biologically oriented views of adolescence as part of a genetically valenced view of human nature. In addition to Hall's influence, this biological view of adolescence emerged from the "nature" position on the "nature–nurture" debate—the "great debate" of twentieth-century social science in which the relative importance of genetic and environmental causes of behaviour are contested (see Hellman, 1998). The fact that this larger debate is relevant to the study of adolescence complicates matters significantly, because it carries with it serious political implications that polarize the discussion of social issues, as we will see in Chapter 2.

The opposing view, which is widely embraced among anthropologists, sociologists, and other social scientists, holds that adolescence, and the difficulties associated with it, are largely a product of certain cultural conditions. The pioneering anthropologist Margaret Mead was the first to advance this argument in a study carried out in the 1920s and published in *Coming of Age in Samoa* (for discussions of Mead's work and the controversy surrounding it, see Côté, 1992, 1994). Since then, considerable historical and cross-cultural evidence supports her conclusion that adolescence is a product of culture: It does not exist in some cultures and its structure changes over time in those cultures where it can be found (e.g., Aries, 1962; Schlegel & Barry, 1991).

This anthropological, historical, and cross-cultural evidence suggests that social expectations determine how the transition to adulthood is structured in a given culture, and therefore even whether or not periods akin to Western adolescence can be found. Moreover, when such periods emerge, how they are experienced by the person passing through them depends upon whether these social expectations provide a meaningful environment as well as whether the adult community is welcoming and provides suitable guidance (cf. Benson, 1997; Damon, 2004; Males, 1996). Mead's study suggested that several conditions are important to produce a transition that is relatively stress-free. Of particular cross-cultural relevance is the importance of the adult community providing a set of consistent beliefs and clear roles for the young. In the face of inconsistent beliefs and ambiguous roles, people experience conflicts that can stimulate the types of emotional difficulties to which Hall and others identified with the transition to adulthood (cf. Condon's, 1987, study of Inuit youth in the Canadian Arctic). In light of this evidence, strictly biological arguments evaporate.

In terms of the implications of her research findings, Mead realized that the conditions found in small, homogeneous societies cannot be easily replicated in large, heterogeneous ones. The key difference between her Samoan adolescents and those in Western societies is the amount of choice available to them, and hence the amount of choosing they must do on an ongoing basis. Mead therefore recommended that part of the coming of age in Western societies should include an "education for choice," whereby the young person comes to understand the nature of choice in his or her society, including the illusion of limitless choice, the capacity for critical thinking, the necessity of tolerance, and the hazards of prejudice. In spite of their simplicity, we can take from Mead's insights a sense of what the transition to adulthood can be like if it is benignly structured. Too often, it is not; when it is not, the young may not receive an adequate "education for choice." Ignoring the young as if some "condition" will pass is exactly the wrong thing to do.

A BRIEF HISTORY OF YOUTH IN CANADA

If we take the year 1900—a mere century ago—as a point of reference, we see that the teen years and twenties were structured quite differently than they were in 2000. For example, only a small number of teens attended secondary schools, almost half were employed in the agricultural sector, and the rest were employed in clerical, manufacturing, and service industries—with young men often making a living wage or close to it (according to Synge, 1979, young men earned about twice as much as young women, and women would typically take a job in their early teens, but continue working only until married). While many young people lived with their families, there was paid work available for them (without many of the age-prejudices we now witness), and considerable financial contributions were made to the household or family unit (cf. Modell et al., 1976, for a comparable account for the United States). In fact, working-class families would typically encourage their young adult offspring to remain at home because it was the norm at the time that they would hand over a good portion of their pay to their parents, making this the most affluent period of the parents' lives (cf. Darroch, 2001; Katz, 1975; Lapsley, Enright, & Serlin, 1985).

By the year 2000, the vast majority of teens attended secondary schools, and about two thirds of secondary-school graduates went directly to post-secondary institutions in the year following high school graduation (Montgomery & Côté, 2003). Canada is now a world leader in education according to Statistics Canada (2003a), which reports that Canada ranks fourth worldwide in terms of "the proportion of its working-age population with a university degree" (p. 10). The agency also reports that Canada now ranks first when community college and university graduates are combined. According to Statistics Canada, "in 2000, 41% of Canada's population aged 25 to 64 had either a college or university education, compared with 37% in the United States, 36% in Ireland, and 34% in Japan" (2003a, p. 10).

However, only a minority of those in their teens and early twenties is now engaged in employment that is sufficiently well paid to afford them independence from their parents, which helps explain why so many young people now stay in school well into their twenties. Only one third of those in their early twenties live out of their parents' home, and only two thirds of those in their late twenties do so (Boyd & Norris, 1999). The rate of co-residence of young people with their parents has steadily increased since the early 1980s. Aside from this increase in intergenerational co-residence, a primary change in family norms is that those who stay with their parents are usually not expected to contribute financially or to significantly participate in household labour (although young females do more housework than young males), leaving them free to pursue various leisure activities (cf. White, 1994). Instead, their parents often subsidize them with free or cheap room and board, sometimes with allowances, and their mothers often provide what amounts to free domestic services. One result of these changes is that those aged 15 to 24 gained an extra hour per day of time in the 1990s to spend on leisure activities, regardless of whether they were working or going to school (Fast, Frederick, Zukewich, & Franke, 2001). Almey and Normand (2002) report that those "aged 15 to 19 devote less time than older adults to productive activities, including paid and unpaid work as well as educational activities, while they have more free time and spend more time sleeping."

Over the late twentieth century, something happened to transform young Canadians from productive citizens into relative dependents on their families and the government, and from valued citizens to second-class citizens who have minimal participation in the mainstream economy. What happened? Was this a positive development for young people, or does it set them back in terms of their life chances? Was this inevitable, or is it traceable to the deliberate actions of certain groups and individuals with something to gain from these changes?

In answering these questions, we can look primarily to changes that occurred during the 1980s and 1990s, but there was also a building of factors earlier in the century leading to these changes. Three earlier changes are notable. First, there was the identification of the "teenager" as a consumer, with the word *teenager* coined by marketers in the 1930s (Quart, 2002; note that it was also marketers who coined the more recent term *tweens* in the late 1990s). Second, there was the rise of mass education, which gathered momentum from the 1940s through 1970s, institutionalizing the segregation of the teenager from adult society. And, third, a youth-oriented popular culture emerged that was distinct from adult popular culture (from the 1960s on; Owram, 1996). However, it was the collapse of the youth labour market of the late 1970s and early 1980s that set in motion circumstances that have created the most severe difficulties for many young people, suggesting that some of the changes to the transition to adulthood have set back the life chances of many contemporary young Canadians. The most serious difficulty, which is the focus of this book, was to transform the "twenties" of the current generation into a variant of what the "teens" was for the previous generation—a period of prolonged dependency on adult society and drawn-out preparation for fully productive adult roles.

In light of the fact that the twenties age range is now structured differently than in the past, and is in some ways similar to what the teens used to be, it is useful to adopt terminology to distinguish the two age periods as they are currently structured in Canadian society. Accordingly, as undesirable as it may be to adopt terms that can take on a life of their own (by becoming reified, as the word *adolescence* did in the twentieth century), it is useful to distinguish those in their twenties (or roughly those 18 through 30), the so-called "emerging adult" (Arnett, 2000) from those in their teens, the so-called "adolescent."

Distinguishing between adolescence and emerging adulthood accomplishes several things. First, we can avoid continually repeating the more general terms *young people* or *youth*. Second, those roughly 18 and over are legal adults in Canada, yet are increasingly treated as if they were teenagers. This is a primary thrust of *Critical Youth Studies*—to point out the injustice of this form of infantilization. Thus, if we were to mix everyone from 12 through 30 into the same pot, it would be difficult to focus on the relevant issues, because 12-year-olds and 25-year-olds are not facing the same circumstances, and are not in need of the same policies. And, third, the literature on emerging adults has been written mainly from a perspective that assumes a natural social evolution and that is in need of a corrective. This corrective looks at this new stage of life in more critical terms, as a social rather than a psychological stage. Viewing it as a social stage helps one to see more clearly how the status of the young has been diminished and certain rights of adulthood have been undermined.

The main question explored in this book concerns just what happened to undermine the status of the young in Canadian society, especially in terms of the diminished citizenship rights for equal access to Canada's affluence. Before presenting answers to this question, it is useful to give further background to contemporary problems, by showing their interrelations.

YOUTH IN THE CONTEXT OF CONTEMPORARY CANADIAN SOCIETY

This book is written by two Canadians for all Canadians, as well as for others around the globe with an interest in Youth Studies. We are well travelled, so we also draw on our experience outside Canada, and on youth research undertaken there. We have extensive international research experience, including involvements with the International Sociological Association (Research Committee 34 on the Sociology of Youth). Accordingly, we draw on Youth Studies as conducted internationally, especially in Europe (notably the United Kingdom and Sweden), to supplement the research available in Canada. In addition, we draw on research conducted in the United States, as necessary, to provide a useful point of comparison for Canadian findings. We also draw on U.S. research findings because some aspects of the youth situation are studied more thoroughly there (e.g., the experiences of emerging adults while in colleges and universities), just as other aspects of the youth situation are more completely studied in Canada (e.g., the experiences of university graduates).

Most observers agree that, with the emergence of industrial society a century and more ago, something dramatically changed in terms of how young people came of age. The teen years increasingly became a period of dependency and increasing leisure, and new issues developed between adults and their offspring (e.g., Gillis, 1974). What is now widely accepted is that more has changed in the way young people come of age as we have moved into what has been called, variously, advanced industrial society or late-modern society. These changes are most evident in terms of the occupational and educational experiences associated with the transition to adulthood.

Changes in the occupational and educational structures of Canadian society appear to be affecting the transition to adulthood in several ways. As of the 1990s, these changes became increasingly obvious and public attention again turned to the young "not-yet-adult" members of society. Unfortunately, this attention was mainly directed toward the consequences of the changes we discuss here, not the causes. For that reason, throughout the 1990s we saw increasing media attention to youth violence, from the random and gang violence on the street to the shootings and bullying in high schools, increasingly featuring females. We also saw concerns about precocious sexuality, including an earlier age of first sexual intercourse, casual oral sex, the spread of sexually transmitted diseases, and teenage pregnancies. Academics in the United States sounded the alarm much more loudly than their Canadian counterparts. For example, in the United States, Dryfoos (1998) and Lerner (1995) raised concerns among policy-makers about the level of risk engagement that can diminish life chances (high school failure and dropout) or create higher-than-acceptable mortality and morbidity rates (like violence and substance abuse).

Unfortunately, what we do not see to a great extent in Canada is an analysis of the root causes of these problems (for discussions of various aspects of research on young people in Canada, see Gauthier & Pacom, 2001). On the one hand, it is pedestrian to say that it is essential to identify the root of a problem if one hopes to alleviate the problem; we are all told this in terms of taking care of our own health, for example. Indeed, looking for root causes is the key to an effective critical analysis. On the other hand, we do not find the same extent of critical analysis among Canadian social scientists with respect to youth issues as we find in other countries, especially in the United Kingdom and Sweden, as we will see in the concluding chapter of this book. Indeed, it appears that we have much to learn from our European counterparts in terms of approaches both to incisive research and effective public policy.

In fact, in Canada, we can learn more about youth issues from the press than from published academic research, in part because there are few academic outlets in Canada (readers will note the number of references we use from magazines, newspapers, and government reports). However, as informative as journalistic reports can be, they are rarely methodologically sound or theoretically informed, and therefore do not provide a comprehensive overview and diagnosis of the problems facing young Canadians. This book provides this comprehensive perspective along with a sense of the "big picture" of the status of young people in Canadian society, focusing primarily on the age range of 18 to 25—what is now called emerging adulthood. At the same time, issues on either side of these age limits are examined where appropriate.

The Structure of the Critical Perspective

This book is about the changing circumstances facing people as they mature, and attempt to come of age in advanced industrial societies. These changing circumstances include facing an increasingly prolonged period between the time when someone becomes biologically mature and when they are considered to be socially mature "adults." This increasing delay is experienced by a significant proportion of young Canadians as economic exploitation in low-paying jobs, financial dependence on parents, social marginality as second-class citizens, sequestration into age-segregated groups in schools, and concerted attempts by corporations to influence their identity formation.

The remainder of this book provides the building blocks of a Critical Youth Studies. Each chapter builds on the previous one to increase the reader's awareness of the knowledge and issues associated with understanding how young Canadians now come of age, and the new challenges and opportunities they face. In order to understand the position of "youth status" in relation to "adult status" one needs to use a building-block approach to knowledge where an understanding is multi-layered, reflecting increasingly complex appreciations of the circumstances facing people as they come of age. Each chapter in this book represents an additional block of this understanding, as follows:

- First, in Chapter 2, after sorting through the various social-scientific theories that can be brought to bear on the topic, we accept the argument that the period we call "adolescence" took its prolonged form as a result of industrialization, and the legislation developed to "stabilize" industrial societies, such as child labour laws and compulsory education. However, we propose that as we have moved into the most recent phase of industrial capitalism—corporate capitalism—the prolongation of adolescence has stretched from the teens into the twenties for recent cohorts, creating a new period in life that has been optimistically called "emerging adulthood" (Arnett, 2000), but which for many is experienced as a form of "arrested adulthood" or "youthhood" stretching into the 30s and beyond (Côté, 2000). With less need for youth labour in general, except in the more exploited sectors of the labour force, emerging adults have lost a "franchise" previously accorded them. Now they participate less in the labour force, and when they do participate, it is in more subordinate positions.

  With fewer people in their twenties achieving adult status economically, it is easier for employers to justify using them as a reserve of cheap labour in the service sectors in the same way that teenagers of past generations were used. Accordingly, a cycle has been established where young adults have fewer and fewer de facto rights and privileges of citizenship, and each cohort has had to wait longer and longer before being granted the full citizenship rights of adult status. In addition to being denied meaningful participation in the economy, adolescents and emerging adults have been increasingly encouraged to remain in schools, foregoing potential income and incurring increasing debt loads, while often maintaining a dependency on their parents and adult-run businesses and institutions.

  In order to account for how and why the transition to adulthood changed in the late twentieth century to produce more inequities in Canadian society we adopt a political-economy perspective. We also discuss developments in other critical perspectives, adopting them to explain the "hows" and "whys" of aspects of the transition to adulthood not readily explained by the political-economy one. Accordingly, in addition to the materialist assumptions of the political-economy approach, we expand the critical approach taken to Youth Studies in this book in ways that represent the "symbolic" assumptions of other critical approaches, notably the "late-modernist" approach (some prefer to call this a "postmodern" approach). By looking at both material and symbolic conditions affecting youth historically and in the present, we feel that we can present a more complete and convincing perspective that will sound less conspiratorial. In this way, we explore both the material changes undermining youth status and power to the advantage of other age groups (from the political-economy approach) and the symbolic changes resulting from the destructuring of important aspects of the transition to adulthood that reduce the normative direction and personal meaning in young people's lives, requiring more individualized behaviour from them (the late-modern approach).

- The consequences of the diminished status of the young in relation to the adult have not been neutral. In Chapter 3, we document the various challenges these changes have introduced to the transition to adulthood. Together, these new challenges have altered educational opportunities and occupational possibilities, prolonging the transition to first adult roles, and introduced new liabilities to youth status.

- There is now much evidence with which to demonstrate that many of the economic and social changes affecting young Canadians, for better or worse, have been "steered" by certain adult interests. At the same time, the "individualization process" has become more obvious, requiring young Canadians to be the architects of their own destiny more so than in the past, as we will see in Chapter 4. This process requires that each person now function more or less independently of the old collective supports that once provided clearer pathways to adulthood. A result of these changes is that the lives of young people are increasingly dictated by conditions in the "market," the more corrosive workings of which can be seen in the attempts at identity manipulation undertaken by corporate marketers. The key to this manipulation is captured in the term "the conquest of cool" (Frank, 1997a). Working on the basic human desire to fit in and be accepted, marketers have learned how to produce a form of conformity to what appears to be an autonomous youth culture. However, much "youth culture" can be seen as little more than a strategically planned form of consumer culture that makes the young feel like they can display their "individuality" by "resisting" attempts to make them conform to the demands of mainstream society (Heath & Potter, 2004). In reality, however, this form of individualistic youth culture is now crucial for the profits and wealth of some of the more self-interested members of adult society that constitute a new "élite," largely made up of the top 20% of wealth holders. This manipulation of youth resistance to authority works well for the wealthy adults running, working for, or owning stock in corporations, but we submit that it is ultimately corrosive for society and diminishes the futures of those young people who get taken in by it.

- With these building blocks of understanding laid out as a foundation, we then go into more depth regarding how the youth segment has been manipulated to co-operate in its own exploitation. As argued in Chapter 5, this can be understood in terms of the manufacture of consent, effected through major social institutions like the mass media and mass educational systems. The consent-manufacturing mechanism involved includes the use of ideologies that obscure aspects of social reality, especially who benefits and who suffers from certain political economy arrangements. Language is crucial in maintaining these ideologies. We also note that the manufacture of consent has unintended consequences, namely, the manufacture of "dissent," where the frustrations of some young people emerge in various forms of internalizing and externalizing deviance. However, it is usually young people themselves who suffer the negative consequences of this dissent, not those in charge of the social and economic forces stimulating the dissent. As such, these manifestations of dissent are not a threat to the system, and so they often go unaddressed.

- The principal mechanism for the manufacture of consent is illustrated in Chapter 6, namely, the use of "complementary conditions" to further the interests of the élites who stand to gain from steering the consumption behaviours and productive roles of young people. This principle illustrates how certain interests, like corporations, expend a great amount of effort and expense to ensure that the attitudes and behaviours of those they want as customers are carefully shaped to reap high levels of profit. This chapter is devoted to showing how the principle of complementarity can be used to elicit conformity, and either co-opt or defeat resistance and rebellion. This principle is illustrated in reference to the use of ideologies to elicit mass conformity with respect to the mass media, mass education, gender relations, and political (non)participation. These analyses help us to understand that, while historically the youth segment of a society is the source of revolutionary foment and resistance to adult authority, recent cohorts are so accepting of their manipulation, and even protective of it when it is pointed out.

• The youth trends we describe and analyze are occurring on a global basis in some form or degree. But, not all young people in all countries are experiencing the same things as young Canadians to the same degree. Although there are global shockwaves associated with changes in the labour-market experiences of the young, different countries have reacted differently to these changes. In the concluding chapter we focus on how Sweden has handled these changes. Just as it was the case that Sweden was the world leader in youth policy in the 1980s, so it continues to be in the 2000s. We report on another decade of policy initiatives undertaken by the progressive Swedes, and on how these initiatives have buffered young Swedes from some of the deleterious effects of corporate-dominated advanced industrial economies. With these insights added to the critical understanding developed in this book, we end with a set of recommendations for individual young people in terms of how to deal with the challenges and opportunities in their lives.

This last chapter shows how youth agency can be rescued from the corporate attempts to subvert it in the name of materialism, consumerism, and high profits for the élites. There must be no confusion on this point: The contention is not that all young people are the same (i.e., a homogeneous group), that they are all easily duped, are not capable of agentic self-direction, or in need of control. The argument is much more complex and nuanced than that, as it derives from a macro analysis of the overall patterns of youth behaviour and youth culture, while recognizing the importance of individual, micro-level behaviours in perpetuating or transforming the current age-status system of economic relations.

Race and Black Youth Inequality

Finally, before we proceed to unfold the argument outlined above, a statement is in order regarding the scope of the critical perspective adopted in this book. As noted in the introduction, the focus of this book is on youth as a central axis of analysis. As an analytical category, "youth" is unlike any other. For while socially constructed categories like gender and "race" are more or less stable, and class has a certain persistence across generations, age cohorts change constantly. Thus, today's old are yesterday's young, and today's young are tomorrow's old. For this reason it is best to regard "youth" more as a social status than as a set age range (cf. Tyyskä, 2001). Further, given the broad cast of this category, "youth" transcends different "races" and ethnic groups, genders, and classes. Moreover, when dealing with structured social inequalities in contemporary capitalist society, "race," ethnicity, gender, and class may overlap and shade into one another. They are separable, however, for analytical purposes; depending on a given set of circumstances, exploitation may involve the vehicle of class, "race," gender, immigrant status, or age.

In the present volume, which deals with the sociology of youth *per se,* we want to highlight the broad connections across these demographic divides rather than pay specific attention to ethnicity, gender, class, and other social-analytic categories. We have already written that book (Allahar & Côté, 1998), where we employed a political economy approach to inequality in Canada with a view to bringing class back into the picture. We did so because in much of contemporary scholarship, issues of "race" and gender have trumped class, and relegated class inequality to the sociological back burner.

This notwithstanding, "race" and gender inequalities are undeniable. Indeed, given the relentless pursuit of the so-called bottom line, all manner of capitalist entrepreneurs and manufacturers are ever cognizant of the need to cheapen costs of production and gain the economic upper hand over their competitors. As is well known, historically two of the most tried and tested ways of cheapening labour costs have been by taking advantage of cultur-ally condoned sexism and racism: Women, ethnic minorities, and people of colour can be made to work for less because of their status disadvantages and accepted prejudices against them. Thus, to the extent that Canada is a nation of immigrants, it is to the recent immi-grants, who are overwhelmingly people of colour from the developing world, to which employers look for cheap labour. This situation is facilitated by the fact that, since the con-solidation of the European Union, European immigrants are no longer flocking to Canada; consequently, countries and regions such as the Philippines, China, India, the Middle East, Southeast Asia, East and West Africa, the Caribbean, and South America now supply over 75% of Canada's immigrants (Isajiw, 1999, p. 92).

That there is patterned racial inequality in Canada is beyond dispute. Some compara-tive data from the 1991 Canadian Census illustrates this point, showing this as a long-standing problem. Although Canada prides itself as a country in which education is the main means to mobility, Black/Caribbean people in Canada do not fare as well as Italians, Greeks, Portuguese, and other "White" groups when compared along lines of education, income, and managerial positions. For example, while 20.5% of Black/Caribbean immi-grants have a university education, their average income in 1990 was $17 613 and only 8.1% of them held managerial positions. This compares with White Canadians, who had a marginally lower level of university education (20.2%), but whose average income was $23 607, and who held 12.6% of managerial positions. While traditional Black/White dif-ferences are not necessarily startling, the position of French, Italians, Greeks, and Portuguese is. As far as university education is concerned, compared to Blacks/Caribbeans these four groups all had lower levels of university education, yet they all had higher aver-age incomes and higher representation in the category of management positions (Isajiw, 1999; Allahar & Côté, 1998). This unfortunate situation has continued, with the latest Census showing that immigrants are still at a disadvantage in the Canadian labour force; in fact, the most skilled immigrants have been hardest hit (Statistics Canada, 2003b).

It is also the case that special circumstances can be found among certain ethnic groups that do not apply to other groups. For example, with respect to the disadvantages faced by Black youth, one only has to look at the debates over community policing and the all-too-frequent and deadly confrontations between Black youth and the police. The high rates of arrests and criminal convictions of Black youth underscore the existence of serious prob-lems within the Black community. For, independently of charges of police harassment, racial profiling, and dirty police tactics, Black youth suffer from high rates of unemploy-ment and underemployment, school dropouts, teen pregnancies, Black-on-Black gang vio-lence, drug trafficking and drug use, and so on. And while these problems are by no means unique to the Black community, they are nevertheless real.

Of particular relevance here is the question of education and whether the Toronto school system fairly and adequately meets the needs of Black youth. For researchers such as George Dei and Carl James the answer is a clear "no!" Their concerns are well captured in the recent debate over segregated or Black-focused schools, which has involved such high-profile Black Canadians as Lincoln Alexander (former Lieutenant-Governor of Ontario) and Zanana Akande (former Member of Parliament and President of the Urban Alliance on Race Relations). In the words of Akua Benjamin, Director of Social Work at Ryerson University, "We need more Black teachers, more Black principals and a plethora of Black social workers." Extolling the benefits of a Black curriculum for building Black self-confidence among Black youth, Dei favours the establishment of "alternative schools for Black students," while James thinks it is time to start "experimenting with a Black-focused school" (Heath-Rawlins, 2005, p. A15). In sum, then, instead of the simplistic view which sees Black students as failing, leading voices in the debate charge that it is more appropriate to see the Toronto school system as responsible for failing Black youth. This is tied in with the presence of prejudiced teachers, Eurocentric curricula, insensitive administrators, and a general lack of positive Black role models.

As stated above, however, while acknowledging the great disadvantages faced by minority and female youth, that is not the central focus of the present work. Those disadvantages are well researched and documented by many competent scholars (e.g., Anisef & Kilbride, 2003; Dei, 1996; Li, 2003; Fleras & Elliott, 2002). The main aim is to examine "youth" more as a generic category—as a social status (cf. Tyyskä, 2001). For while young people may be divided by ethnicity, sex, class, religion, and national origin, etc., they are united or connected by their common position vis-à-vis capital, which knows no race, sex, colour, or religion. Capital will exploit where it can, when it can, whomever it can. And at a time when certain ethnic minorities and women have made significant gains in the workplace in terms of recruitment, salary, security, and promotions, young people remain highly vulnerable and exposed to the vicissitudes of global capitalism.

chapter two

The Discovery of Youth: Social-Scientific Attempts to Explain Coming of Age Processes

INTRODUCTION

As noted in the last chapter, the human life course has changed dramatically in industrialized societies over the last couple of centuries. This book deals with changes in how people become fully functioning human beings, otherwise known as adults. These changes have been so pervasive that in the past 100 years alone a number of terms have emerged in the social sciences to describe developments in this maturation process, including *adolescence* and *youth*. More recently, we hear marketers referring to the "tweens"—a sort of pre-adolescence—and psychologists referring to "emerging adulthood," which is an apparently new "postadolescence/pre-adult" phase. These various terms represent a variety of conflicting interpretations regarding "youth" and its properties. To simplify matters, this chapter is concerned primarily with theories developed in the twentieth century regarding "adolescence," and with changing notions about the intrinsic nature of the transition to adulthood.

We can gain insight into the difficulties encountered by the social-scientific enterprise in studying something like the transition to adulthood by recalling the Hindu folktale regarding the three blind men who encountered an elephant while walking together down a path. Not realizing they were all touching the same entity, the first blind man touched only the tail, thinking the elephant was a rope; the second touched only the trunk, concluding the elephant was a snake; and the third, touching the leg, believed he had felt a tree. This folk tale suggests that how something is described depends in part on how one's approach helps one to grasp the totality of a given phenomenon. Similarly, the positions social scientists take regarding the period of life between childhood and adulthood can be generally classified in terms of their approaches. If they approach their subject assuming that human behaviour is biologically caused, they will draw certain conclusions about what humans "are," and if they assume that behaviour is socially caused, they will draw other conclusions. Although most social scientists do not explicitly speak in terms of extreme biological or social causes of behaviour, and will publicly state that behaviour is a combination of the two causes, often their underlying assumptions reflect one position over the other.

THE EARLY FOCUS ON BIOLOGY

Like people from all age groups, some young people sometimes experience emotional problems, and a minority experience chronic problems. However, unlike those in other age groups, the public now *expects* most adolescents to routinely experience chronic emotional problems. Following decades of social change based on this stereotype, we now have a veritable army of psychologists and psychiatrists, employed variously by the government, educational institutions, or parents, positioned to help young people when they need to deal with these real or illusory emotional problems.

To exacerbate this stereotype, many of these helping professionals have contact primarily with a minority of young people—young people who are seeing them precisely because they are emotionally distraught—leading to sometimes sensationalized reports of adjustment problems among all adolescents. These skewed encounters help explain why many helping professionals tend to think of all young people as inherently emotionally unstable (cf. Offer & Church, 1991). Indeed, it appears that focusing on either the psychological or psychiatric perspectives carries the risk of overestimating the extent to which adolescence is intrinsically a period of intense emotional distress.

What the psychological and psychiatric views have in common is that both focus on the mental operations of the individual—what people think and feel is used to explain how they behave. As we saw in Chapter 1, early thinking in this area, influenced by G. Stanley Hall's (1904) storm-and-stress theory, saw these mental operations to be in continual conflict and turmoil, ostensibly explaining the supposedly erratic behaviour of the person deemed to be an "adolescent."

More recently, the "positive youth development" movement emerged in psychology to view adolescents in more positive terms (e.g., Catalano, Berglund, Ryan, Lonczak, & Hawkins, 2002; Lerner, 2004; Lerner, Brown, & Kier, 2005; Rich, 2003). However, there remains in adolescent psychology a tendency to view adolescence as something that is "essential" or "constitutional," namely, a period during which certain developmental changes must occur if the individual is to become a "healthy" adult (e.g., Arnett, 2004). If certain changes do not appear to have taken place or if certain emotional problems emerge, psychologists generally advocate "fixing" the individual to make the changes happen, rather than addressing the societal conditions that might have created the problems in the first place.

Recent attention in psychology has also turned to incorporating "environmental" or social influences in order to direct policy initiatives, but detailed analyses of the societal conditions that might be creating widespread psychological difficulties are rarely undertaken by psychologists. Accordingly, the actual position taken by most psychologists tends to favour the biological (or "nature") side of the equation more than the social (or "nurture") side. With this bias, psychologists can underestimate the extent to which the behaviour of individual young people is socially influenced.

But, let's back up a bit here, to examine G. Stanley Hall's role in the sequence of events affecting how adolescence came to be understood by psychologists and psychiatrists.

The Legacy of G. Stanley Hall

G. Stanley Hall is most generally known as "the father of a scientific 'psychology of adolescence'" (Muuss, 1996, p. 1), for his "discovery" of adolescence as a unique stage of the life course. Hall published his theory in his two-volume tome, *Adolescence,* in 1904, and was influential in psychology and psychiatry through figures like Kurt Lewin, Sigmund Freud, (especially) Anna Freud, Peter Blos, and Erik Erikson.

In his work, Hall presented a "recapitulation thesis," which postulates that the life course of each person (ontogenesis) repeats (recapitulates) the evolutionary history of the human species (phylogenesis) because of the influence of human evolution on our genetic make-up. Using this logic, Hall claimed that adolescent "storm and stress" is universal because human ontogenesis is driven by phylogenesis, and there is something in human evolutionary history that drives everyone to go through a period of adolescent turmoil. Thus, for Hall, the root of "adolescence" did not lie in culture, but in individual genetic make-up.

Hall was quite emphatic in his designations of the symptoms of adolescent storm and stress. He defined storm and stress in terms of the emotional instability associated with swings between opposite feelings: "alternations between inertness and excitement, pleasure and pain, self-confidence and humility, selfishness and altruism, society and solitude, sensitiveness and dullness, knowing and doing, conservatism and iconoclasm, sense and intellect" (1904, p. 40). In the chapter in which he describes these in detail ("Evolution and the feelings and instincts characteristic of normal adolescence," pp. 40-94), Hall was clear in his assertions regarding their evolutionary basis and universality as part of human nature. For example, he contended that

> early adolescence is . . . the infancy of man's higher nature, when he receives from the great all-mother his last capital of energy and evolutionary momentum. Thus the child is father of man, far older and conditioning his nature . . . . The parent and teacher must understand that mother nature has again taken her child upon her knee and must stand off a little to see and make room for her more perfect education. These years again, like infancy, *should be sacred to heredity, and we should have a good warrant indeed before we venture to interfere with its processes.* (p. 71, emphasis added)

Thus, Hall was so convinced about the absoluteness of evolutionary influence over adolescents that he advised adults to stand back and let the processes see themselves through according to their inherent evolutionary logic. It is a matter for historians to debate just what influence Hall had outside these fields, but his influence in these fields was strongest among those who favoured evolutionary-biological views of human development, and his "views exerted a marked influence upon the study of adolescence for many years" (Rice, 1992, p. 71). However, even though his "ideas were strongly challenged by other prominent psychologists at that time (e.g., Hollingsworth, 1928; Thorndike, 1904)" (Petersen, 1991, p. 500), and have been shown to be faulty by anthropologists and sociologists since the 1920s (as we will see below), Hall's theory of inevitable storm and stress is still influential today in some circles, especially among the public and journalists (Rice, 1992, p. 72). Hall's legacy includes circular stereotypes about "raging hormones" that supposedly turn teenagers into emotional wrecks, and about misbehaviours among teens as ostensibly the result of these raging hormones. Indeed, this has been one of the most enduring, and difficult to eradicate, stereotypes the social sciences have produced (cf. Coleman, 1978).

From Storm and Stress to an Essential Stage

Proefrock (1981) has critically examined the history of the psychological model of adolescence and argues that the work of some psychologists has had the effect of shaping the way the general public views the person we call the "adolescent" and has therefore affected the very nature of adolescence as it is currently structured in Western societies. He argues that, based on views advanced by Hall and others, the psychopathology attributed to adolescence by psychologists came to be used as a legitimation for the juvenile justice system in the United States and the suspension of rights imposed by that system.

According to current law in Canada and the United States, if a case can be made that there is something wrong with an individual, especially if that individual is believed not to be responsible for his or her behaviour, custody and treatment can be ordered, even if the behaviour is a mere "status offence" (i.e., an offence by merit of being "underage," as in drinking before the legal age). Indeed, Melton notes "limitations on adolescents' rights have been premised on unsupportable assumptions about adolescents' competence as decision makers" (1991, p. 931). Developments in Canada regarding the age-based restriction of rights paralleled those in the United States.

Proefrock warns of the problems that can emerge when the psychological position is taken to the extreme. He argues "that the developmental period of adolescence does not exist outside of the social factors which caused its emergence," and we are therefore "in danger of making attributions to the adolescent which exist because of social conditions. These attributions . . . are not . . . intrinsic to the persons themselves. They are intrinsic to the person living under a particular set of societal constraints and dictates" (Proefrock, 1981, pp. 857-858).

While the idea that storm and stress is universally experienced has been debunked (Arnett, 1999; and in the following pages), it is still possible to find attempts to explain the behaviour of the young in biological terms, especially in the psychological fields that focus almost exclusively on human biology, like neuropsychology. Most recently, medical technology has been used to attempt to map the human brain, and some researchers are attempting to argue that the "adolescent brain" is different in significant ways from the "adult brain." This line of research has led to statements like the following: "Simply put, there is now biological evidence that adolescents do not have the same ability to make sound decisions and to prevent impulsive behavior" (Ortiz, 2003, Section 5, para 4).

This quote is from a brief, written for the Juvenile Justice Center of the American Bar Association, titled "Adolescent brain development and legal culpability." It echoes efforts from the early twentieth century to "protect" young people through the legislation described above by Melton, although at that time it was believed that the upper age limit for those in need of protection was 16 to 18. This brief actually argues for pushing the upper limit for diminished responsibility to an even later age. For example, it also quotes Ruben Gur, a neuropsychologist and Director of the Brain Behavior Laboratory at the University of Pennsylvania, who would raise this age-protection limit to the early twenties, the age now called emerging adulthood:

> The evidence now is strong that the brain does not cease to mature until the early 20s in those relevant parts that govern impulsivity, judgment, planning for the future, foresight of consequences, and other characteristics that make people morally culpable . . . . Indeed, age 21 or 22 would be close to the "biological" age of maturity. (Ortiz, 2003, Section 5, para 5)

Aside from the more extreme biological assertions like this, adolescent psychology is still dominated by an essentialist view: that adolescence is a necessary stage of development, during which certain changes must take place if the person is to become a fully functioning member of society (e.g., Arnett, 2004; Lerner, 2004). While there may be some truth to this claim, especially if it is couched in culturally specific terms (i.e., Danish adolescents need to experience certain things to become fully functioning adults in contemporary Danish society, as argued by Mørch, 1995), the claim loses its generalizability when adolescence is examined cross-culturally (below).

From Biology to Pathology

Psychiatrists share many of the assumptions associated with the psychological view discussed above. However, being based on the medical model, which is oriented to diagnosing and treating diseases, psychiatry has a history of seeing young people as being "afflicted" with the so-called "condition" of adolescence. In fact, as we will see, there is a tendency in psychiatry to view adolescence itself as a "disorder" with various sets of symptoms. In turn, various "symptoms" are taken as evidence that adolescence is in fact a "disorder." Such circular logic can ignore the extent to which the current prolonged adolescence is unique to modern industrialized societies, and that behavioural disturbances among adolescents can sometimes be a response to problems of living with limited rights and roles in these societies.

The traditional psychiatric view bears marks of Hall's biological-evolutionary influence, and may be generally summarized as recommending that young people "hang on" until their "condition" passes. Take for example the following recommendation, published as recently as the 1970s, in a leading psychiatric publication (*Adolescent Psychiatry*):

> There exists one real cure for adolescence, and only one, and this cannot be of interest to the boy or girl who is in the throes. The cure for adolescence belongs to the passage of time and to the gradual maturation process; these together do in the end result in the emergence of the adult person. This process cannot be hurried or slowed up, though indeed it can be broken into and destroyed, or it can wither up from within, in psychiatric illness. (Winnicott, 1971, pp. 40-41)

Such a statement appears naïve when considered against the more contemporary social scientific perspectives examined in this book. Yet, such views apparently informed psychiatric practice just 30 years ago and therefore guided the process of drafting social policies still affecting young people. More incredible yet is Winnicott's further statement, which holds that the crucial thing to be recognized "is the fact that the adolescent boy and girl do not want to be understood. Adults must hide among themselves what they come to understand of adolescence." These patronizing remarks do not reveal the type of compassion one would expect in a doctor-patient relationship, and while Winnicott is used here as an example, he was by no means alone among psychiatrists and their approaches to understanding and dealing with adolescents.

Fortunately, there has been a movement in this field to attempt to deal with the recognition that adolescence is largely a cultural phenomenon, not a biological one. For example, in their longitudinal study of a sample of American male adolescents, Offer and Offer (1975) classified about one quarter of teens they studied as experiencing a conflict-free, "continuous" growth. Another one third were classified as experiencing "surgent" growth—temporary, moderate difficulties in emotional adjustments. And only one quarter of their sample were classified as experiencing what they termed "tumultuous" growth—severe turmoil—corresponding to the storm-and-stress stereotype evoked by G. Stanley Hall.

The intention here is not to embarrass individual writers, but to point out how fatuous some experts can be when their expertise goes unchecked and uncriticized. Fortunately, these excessive psychiatric views have been challenged by social scientists who have taken the time to examine adolescence and youth historically and cross-culturally. For example, Hill and Fortenberry reviewed the psychiatric tendency to medicalize and pathologize adolescence, and concluded that adolescence "is neither a disease nor an epidemic." Indeed, they go on to argue that characterizing "adolescence as an age-based pathological condition serves to mask factors that threaten well-being in advanced societies. They contend that this view is based on the stereotype of young people that has emerged in Western societies, and that by looking only for disorders inherent in the young person

> adolescent medicine specialties may unintentionally draw attention away from more important bases of youth morbidity and mortality: racism, the juvenalization of poverty, underemployment, inadequate education and declining per-capita resources for dependent children and youth. (Hill & Fortenberry, 1992, p. 78)

THE LATER ATTENTION TO CULTURE
Anthropology

Margaret Mead was the first social scientist to directly study the validity of Hall's claims about the intrinsic nature of the transition to adulthood, publishing her findings in *Coming of Age in Samoa* (1928), which became the best-selling book ever in anthropology. She described Hall's influence in the following manner:

> A great mass of writing about adolescence is flooding the book shops; so the psychologist in America tried to account for the restlessness of youth. The result was works like that of Stanley Hall on Adolescence, which ascribed to the period through which the children were passing, the causes of their conflict and distress. Adolescence was characterized as the period in which idealism flowered and rebellion against authority waxed strong, a period during which difficulties and conflicts were absolutely inevitable. (1928/1973, p. 2)

To empirically test these claims, investigators would simply have had to present evidence that "adolescent turmoil" was not universally experienced within a culture. However, the object of Mead's study was to undertake a comparative analysis of adolescence, with an eye to seeing if, and how, adolescence in another culture differed from American culture in terms of manifestations of emotional turmoil. Mead reasoned that, because the biological processes of adolescence are the same among individuals in different cultures, the conclusion that adolescence is easier to experience in Samoa than in the United States would mean that difficulties experienced by American adolescents must be attributed to characteristics found in American culture, but absent in Samoan culture. Mead evaluated her research problem with a cross-sectional sample drawn from the teenaged girls on a remote island of Samoa (in the South Pacific), representing prepuberty, puberty, and postpuberty. In observing and interviewing these girls, she noted that there were no major characterological or emotional differences among these three groups suggestive of storm and stress as described by Hall. Accordingly, Hall's claim of universal adolescent storm and stress was refuted by Mead's study. Mead did not deny that *some* adolescents experienced difficulties; rather, she found that only a minority of the Samoan girls experienced adjustment difficulties and she concluded that the higher incidence in the United States must have been due to the dramatically different social environment there that structured the period of adolescence.

As we will see below, the preponderance of research undertaken since Mead's study support her conclusion that societal factors are responsible for the types of widespread emotional turmoil found in Western societies, and biological factors play a role only in individual cases, as it does for any period of the life course (e.g., Condon, 1987; Offer & Offer, 1975). This more recent evidence is examined below, but in order to avoid misunderstandings, it must be stressed that, just like Mead, one cannot reject the notion that human behaviour has a biological basis. Such a position is clearly foolhardy, and ignores established scientific facts, like the basis of thought processes in brain structures and the role of hormones in sexual behaviour. However, there is a clear difference between the fact that we are biologically based creatures and the specific behaviours we act out in our day-to-day lives in cultural settings.

For example, our native ability to speak languages as humans has nothing to do with the specific language we speak. Likewise, the dialect each of us has with respect to the language we speak has nothing to do with our individual genetic make-ups; apart from speech impediments, how we speak is a matter of the language and dialect spoken around us as we grow up (i.e., our cultural influences and socialization experiences). On the other hand, genetics and (brain) biology do affect how well we speak our native language (there are well-established individual differences in verbal abilities, including gender differences; e.g., Mackie, 1991), how well we speak non-native languages, and so forth. But, even so, this effect is clearly mediated by our experiences as we grow up.

So, for those who strongly identify with biologically based positions, biological and genetic bases of human behaviour are readily acknowledged. The real question at hand is the strength of these effects in the transition to adulthood and when they become relevant in explaining the difficulties that young people have with this transition (see Lerner, Brown, & Kier, 2005, for discussions of genetic influences on adolescent behaviour, including gene-environment infusions). Answering questions concerning nature-nurture interactions is extremely difficult and beyond the capacity of the social sciences, as they are currently constituted in terms of ethical restraints.

Sociology

Over the decades, developments in sociology paralleled those in psychology and psychiatry, but with a crucial difference (e.g., Parsons, 1961; Eisenstadt, 1961). In the late 1940s,

Hollingshead made the following observations regarding how Hall's work was viewed at the time by sociologists:

> Hall's prestige as a psychologist . . . was so great and his influence over students so dominant that his theories were accepted widely . . . . Gradually, however, the weight of empirical information indicated that these views were largely doctrinal. But, even now, the idea that adolescence is a period of "storm and stress," . . . is held by many people, in spite of the fact that it has never been demonstrated to be true. (1949, p. 6)

In reference to the different perspectives taken by psychologists and sociologists on the intrinsic nature of adolescence, Hollingshead noted that "sociologically, adolescence is the period in the life of a person when the society in which he functions ceases to regard him (male or female) as a child and does not accord to him full adult status, roles, and functions" (1949, pp. 6-7). This means that, behaviourally, adolescence is defined by the roles the person is expected, allowed, or forced to play, by virtue of an ascribed age-status in a given society. Sociologically, then, adolescence is defined by culturally based behavioural norms, evidence for which is derived from the fact that the form, content, and duration of the transition to adulthood varies widely among societies; there is nothing intrinsic to adolescence in the biological make-up of the person (adolescence is often confused with puberty, but people in Western societies are still treated as adolescents long after puberty).

In spite of the extensive sociological undertakings on the transition to adulthood reported in publications like *Elmstown Youth* (Hollingshead, 1949), far less attention has been given these efforts by the media, perhaps because the media tend to see biological research as more "scientific" and therefore more legitimate. Consequently, the public and policy-makers have largely ignored the knowledge that has accumulated over the years concerning cultural influences on the transition to adulthood. Recently, however, with the emergence of conditions for those in the twenties (emerging adults) resembling those of teenagers (adolescents) of the past, it is beginning to dawn on people that biological explanations are insufficient: Those in their twenties are far beyond puberty, eliminating the pubertal-hormone thesis.

Sociologists, then, tend to view adolescence as a product of social expectations associated with the normative structure of a given culture. In spite of this common assumption, however, significant disagreements exist among sociologists, so it is useful to separate the sociological perspectives with respect to what is identified as being most important in structuring coming-of-age processes. As noted by Hollingshead, sociologists tend to be in agreement that adolescence and youth are social structures imposed on people by forces beyond their control. The differences among sociologists lie in how these social structures and their imposition are explained—whether they "evolved" out of historically inevitable social and economic forces and therefore are somehow morally justified, or whether they were orchestrated by self-interested parties who increased their advantage at the expense of the young and are therefore not morally justified. For the sake of simplicity, sociological approaches are grouped and discussed here in terms of this moral fault line regarding whether the new transition to adulthood has naturally evolved or has been politically orchestrated in some ways (cf. Hollands, 2001; Tyyskä, 2001).

CONSERVATIVE APPROACHES: SOCIAL EVOLUTION

Many sociologists prefer simply to describe the society around them and to assume that, because certain practices and institutions now exist they are performing some essential function for the society (cf. Andres, Anisef, Krahn, Looker, & Thiessen, 1999; Beaujot, 2004; Cook & Furstenberg, 2002; Galaway & Hudson, 1996; Milner, 2004; Shanahan, 2000). The general approach taken in sociology and anthropology corresponding with these assumptions is referred to as functionalism, or structuralism functionalism.

In general, functionalists see the prolonged transition to adulthood as an inevitable "function" of social and institutional changes associated with industrialization and modernization. Functionalists argue that, like other forms of inevitable social evolution, the human life cycle in Western culture has become increasingly differentiated, ultimately to accommodate a more complex adulthood associated with changes that increase the institutional complexity of societies (see Parsons, 1961, for the differentiation principle applied to American youth). In particular, they argue that the period between childhood and adulthood has increased significantly to allow the person to better prepare for the complexities of modern life. Accordingly, they conclude that the young need to remain dependent longer while preparing for adult roles (e.g., Parsons, 1961; see Hollands, 2001, for a discussion of Parsons's influence in Canada).

With respect to the lengthier transition, functionalists observe that adolescence became prolonged as a result of improvements in nutrition, sanitation, and health care, affecting basic human biological maturation: The onset of puberty apparently now takes place some 4 years earlier than it did in 1850 (Lerner, Brown, & Kier, 2005). In fact, since the 1850s, it appears that puberty has begun about 1 year earlier for every 25 years of improvement in these areas. In the present era, the average age for the onset of puberty in most Western countries is about 12 for females and 14 for males. During the 1850s, these figures would have been about 16 for females and 18 for males, respectively (Sprinthall & Collins, 1984). If this is true, then it is easier to see why premodern societies would have encouraged or required people to take on adult roles immediately following puberty—they were 4 years older than is the case today, and therefore more experienced. This is one reason why this book focuses on those in the late teens and twenties—it is the age range during which adult roles have been adopted throughout human history.

In reference to increased dependency, functionalists believe that industrialization has made it less necessary for the family unit to utilize the labour of the young, beginning first with children and then with teens. Young people have gone from being central to agricultural economies to being marginal to industrial economies; and they have gone from being economic assets to being economic liabilities for their families. Of course, they are not explicitly recognized as economic liabilities by most parents, but rather as wards in need of parental protection. It is not that the family as an institution has died or is dying, but rather its structure and function have changed in response to economic changes (e.g., Milner, 2004).

Combining these two factors—length of transition and need for dependency—the proposition has been offered recently that this lengthened dependency has an evolutionary logic because it allows parents greater opportunity to invest in their children, even while they are (legal) adults (Kaplan, 1997). Of course, the functional explanation for this is that this new arrangement promotes greater social integration and smoother social functioning.

Based on these assumptions, the functionalist account of the history of youth holds that, as a result of the shift from agricultural to industrial society, the belief grew that the young needed to be shielded from the evils and hardships of the adult world of work, and institutions were formed to protect them and educate them for industrial society. These new institutions thus began the process of life-course differentiation. And, as these institutions became more differentiated (e.g., primary, secondary, and tertiary education) young people could now capitalize on their freedom from labour obligations to undergo extensive socialization for the more complex skills required in industrial and advanced-industrial economies. Functionalists have continued to describe these changes in terms of social evolution and the inevitability of preparation for a more complex adulthood, especially in the workplace (see Galaway & Hudson, 1996, for a series of papers on Canadian youth that follow this logic, and Furstenberg, Cook, Sampson, & Slap, 2002, for an introduction to a series of papers using this logic in making international comparisons).

There is considerable evidence to support the functionalist view of adolescence. As noted in Chapter 1, many scholars argue that the notion of adolescence as a distinct stage of life is comparatively recent and the language used to discuss it in this way dates back only to the last century. For example, Cultice (1992) argues, "in a sense, there were no teenagers in early America. That is, there was no easily identifiable group of young people of certain ages who acted, dressed, and spoke in ways that were markedly different from those of other age groups" (p. 3). Indeed, Baumeister and Tice (1986) observe that, before 1800, "Americans did not think of youth as a period of personal indecision, awkwardness and uncertainty, or passive and helpless vulnerability. Rather, the general attitude was that puberty meant the young person was ready and able to do an adult's share (or almost) of work around the farm, shop, or house" (p. 186).

Implications of the Conservative Approach

While there is obviously much that is useful and convincing in what has been discussed as representing the functionalist perspective, this view of society has been criticized as too descriptive and as assuming too much of a natural evolution of society. Critics feel that the functionalist view assumes too much inevitability in the social order and social change. Moreover, in spite of their awareness of the importance of examining the historical antecedence of contemporary social structures, lessons of history seem to be forgotten, especially as they pertain to the "best practices" that we might learn from the past to apply to contemporary problems. In addition, many conservative sociologists blindly follow the scientific model, which requires data points for all conclusions (even though their own theories are often laden with "unobservables," as in the case of evolutionary theories). The pure scientific model is best suited for artificial laboratory-type research, but the real world is too big, complicated, and fast-moving for social scientists to gather data points for every conclusion. Instead, social scientists need to be able to use scientific methods as diagnostic tools and draw wider conclusions based on them in terms of theoretical frames of reference.

This problem is illustrated in the remarks of a sociologist who recently conducted an in-depth study of the consumption-based status relationships of American high-school students. Speaking to the issue of whether marketing to teens "works," he takes a "neutral" stance and simply says "there seems to be very little careful research on marketing to adolescents published in peer-reviewed journals or by academic presses," so he will not draw conclusions about the possible negative implications of marketing to teens (Milner, 2004, p. 158). He takes this position in spite of the mounds of data that he provides in his own book showing the corporate influence in the status-anxious lives of the high-school students he studied. The problem with waiting for the scientific "evidence" to appear in academic journals and books is that (a) conservative sociologists (who dominate the profession in North America) will not define the issue as a problem to be investigated in the first place, and

(b) the wheels of academia turn so slowly that by the time one marketing strategy is identi-fied and studied, another will have taken its place. Some things in the real world happen too quickly to use laboratory-type methods to study them. Instead, we need to use our powers of observation and our moral sensibilities, guided by theoretical frameworks.

As we will see next, other sociologists look to how conscious, human action shapes the social order and directs social change. This human action is often seen to be self-interested in nature, such that some groups benefit at the expense of others. Accordingly, it takes pur-posive human action to correct problems that have been created by other self-interested humans. (See Hollands, 2001, for a discussion of these types of approaches taken in Canadian youth studies.)

CRITICAL APPROACHES: MATERIAL INTERESTS AND SYMBOLIC MEANINGS

Critical sociologists pick up where functionalists leave off, using descriptions that func-tionalists have generated of social structures, institutions, demographics, the workplace, and the like as starting points. However, they feel that these descriptions tell only part of the story because they lack moral and ethical *inferences* concerning inequities in societies. For critical sociologists, who prefer to ask questions about the moral and ethical justifica-tions for societal structures and the inequities they perpetuate, what is important is not how youth behave, but rather what caused their (current) behaviour in the first place and who benefits from it (cf. Tyyskä, 2001). Thus, critical sociologists prefer to look beyond the moral "neutrality" of the functionalist perspective, with its assumption of evolution and the inevitability of inequities, while building on some of its descriptions of social organization to identify and explain inequities and what might be done about them (cf. Hollands, 2001; Wallace & Kovatcheva, 1998).

Changing Material Conditions

Some critical sociologists—political economists—look at the changing economic oppor-tunities of young people in relation to other age groups, noting that the relative material opportunities associated with the transition to adulthood have diminished over the past few decades. In countries that could be counted as "postindustrial," the youth labour market collapsed in the late 1970s and early 1980s as the relatively well-paying manufacturing sector gave way to the less well-paid service sector, caricatured in terms of the McJob (see Cook & Furstenberg, 2002, for a comparison of this in Italy, Sweden, Germany, and the United States; Furlong & Cartmel, 1997, for discussion of this in the United Kingdom; and Tannock, 2001, regarding Canada and the United States). During this period, youth partic-ipation rates in the workforce decreased dramatically while youth unemployment rates increased. At the same time, the major corporate restructurings of the labour force since the 1980s left many adolescents and emerging adults in a position of career disadvantage. Now, it is commonplace for them to have access mainly to dead-end, low-paying jobs (often part-time and/or contractual) that make it very difficult to attain financial self-sufficiency (e.g., Catan, 2004; Côté & Allahar, 1994; Jones, 2002; Schuller, Preston, Hammond, Brassett-Grundy, & Bynner, 2004; Tannock, 2001).

In the face of poorer entry-level job prospects, more adolescents and emerging adults sought postsecondary educational credentials, presumably in the hope of gaining an advantage in access to better paying jobs[1] by bypassing those attempting to climb internal career ladders. Consequently, higher-educational sectors in postindustrial societies expanded to include significant proportions of their youth populations. Countries like the United States and Canada now have almost one half of their citizens in their early twenties attending educational institutions full-time (e.g., Montgomery & Côté, 2003; Statistics Canada, 2003a), and the estimated duration of the cohort school-to-work transition in Canada is now 8 years and growing, 2 years longer than it was in 1985, beginning at 16 and ending at 23 (Bowlby, 2000).[2]

To give some historical context to the changing education-to-work aspect of the transition to adulthood, in 2000, some 40% of young Canadians aged 20 to 24 were attending school full-time (Statistics Canada, 2003a). In the 1950s, this was the approximate percentage of young Canadians aged 15 to 19 attending school full-time, while only about 5% of those in their early twenties were doing so (Normand, 1995). Accordingly, the educational experiences of those now in their early twenties resemble those in their late teens 50 years ago, suggesting that adolescence has undergone a metamorphosis into what may now be called emerging adulthood.

While those with higher credentials do in fact experience an advantage over the less educated in terms of workplace opportunities (higher salaries and less unemployment), it appears that much of this advantage is at the expense of those not fortunate enough to gain higher credentials, as detailed in Chapter 3. For example, between 1980 and 2000, while (inflation-adjusted) average incomes of young university graduates in Canada remained about the same, the incomes of high-school graduates dropped some 10 to 15% (Statistics Canada, 2003b). Similarly, Morris & Western (1999) estimate that in the United States between 1979 and 1994, baccalaureate graduate real earnings increased by only 5%, while those of high-school graduates fell by 20%. Looking at this time span in terms of gender differences, Hamilton and Hamilton (2005) report that in constant 2000 dollars, the experiences of young American men and women differed. Young women made gains in earning power (from their relatively lower level in 1971), while young men lost, reflecting a tendency toward income convergence. Between 1971 and 2000, female high-school graduates' median earnings increased by 6%, those with a bachelor's degree or higher earned 10% more, and high-school dropouts earned an additional 15%. However, the inflation-adjusted 2000 median earnings of males with a bachelor's degree or more was 6% lower than in 1971, while male high-school graduates lost 29%, and male high-school dropouts lost 38% in earning power (Hamilton & Hamilton, 2005). In the United Kingdom, this same trend is called the "youth divide" (Jones, 2002).

Referring to this often overlooked aspect of the transition to adulthood, Morris and Western (1999) argue that "it should be kept in mind that the 'rise' in the college premium was almost entirely driven by the *collapse* in the earnings of high-school graduates and dropouts. . . . This is what caused the doubling of the college premium" (p. 633, emphasis in original; the "college premium" is the salary and employability advantage that a university degree has over a high-school diploma).

In considering the changing nature of the transition to adulthood, then, we must be concerned with the experiences of *all* young people, not just the more fortunate ones. Indeed, noting a "generational divide" in the labour force, Statistics Canada (2003b, p. 11) interpreted the youth labour market trends for the 1980s and 1990s as follows:

> These [2001 Census] results are consistent with earlier Statistics Canada research showing that the earnings path of young men [in particular] has veered downward. The generation of men who

came of age during the late 1980s and 1990s started their careers making less than their counterparts who came of age in the 1970s, and made much slower progress for at least the first 10
years of their working lives . . . . A university education offers the young only a partial buffer to
this tendency.[3]

Adding to difficulties in the education-to-work transition is the disjunctive nature of
the link between the higher-educational sphere and the workplace. For example, many
high-school graduates have highly unstable work histories, including multiple, concurrent
part-time jobs (Tannock, 2001), while up to one half of higher educational graduates experience long periods of *under*employment where they are working at jobs that do not require
their level of earned credential (e.g., Nobert & McDowell, 1994; Frenette, 2000).

These developments are not readily explicable using the functionalist approach.
However, the central question for the political economist is just why the education-to-work
transition changed the way it did. While the above account is largely descriptive, it avoids
the functionalist implication that it was an inevitable evolution of social institutions.
Instead, it describes material changes in ways that political economists can readily analyze
in terms of shifting political power and economic status. For example, while the benefits
that accrue to young people from the above-described changes in the education-to-work
transition are highly questionable, those that accrue to Capital are unmistakable in terms
of the increase in the pool of cheap labour.

For political economists, the search for the roots of the contemporary structures in
society begins with "objective conditions" produced by the distribution of power, particularly economic and political power (e.g., Bailey & Gayle, 2003; Levitt, 1984; Rowntree &
Rowntree, 1968). In an early version applied to Youth Studies, young people were viewed
as constituting a "class" without power, disenfranchised economically, politically, and
socially. However, in order to mask this disenfranchisement and to ensure that young people do not mobilize as a reaction against their exploitation, it was argued that the State
needed to impose a long period of distraction and indoctrination, so it promoted mass education to later and later ages. The State did this, according to this view, because in capitalist societies the State directly serves the interests of Capital and the powerful groups and
people who control Capital. This indoctrination is accomplished mainly through the educational system, but other institutions such as the media are also complicit.

In this way, this political-economy view sees many young people as being "educated" into a state of "false consciousness," whereby they are cajoled, persuaded, or pressured to accept and support arrangements that work directly against their own interests.
Sometimes, this "education" can simply involve promoting ignorance and apathy by
avoiding some topics or teaching some subjects from a very limited point of view (like
not studying world affairs from the perspective of developing countries, or not teaching
history from a variety of perspectives). In particular, these arrangements engender a
form of alienation, especially from the "essence" of oneself as an agentic human being.
Thus, young people are taught in schools to believe that: society in general is benign; the
economy functions in the interest of the average person; they will be duly rewarded in
school if they have the ability; the educational system is based entirely on merit; they
will get the jobs they want if they behave themselves and "work hard"; and they will
"live happily ever after" if they adopt the conventional lifestyle. If they come to believe
these things, they may also accept that if something bad happens to them or to one of
their peers, those individuals are at fault, not the system. Thus, they are taught that their
alienation is "normal," and that any regrets they have about their lives are their own

doing. From a functionalist perspective, such attitudes indicate that the young person is well socialized; from the political-economy perspective, the young person exhibits false consciousness and alienation.

Political economists further argue that those who resent being pressured to accept existing social structures are usually subjected to additional pressures that compensate for their "inadequate" socialization and convince them to accept their circumstances without blaming the system. These additional "cooling-out" pressures come from counsellors, the police, the courts, social workers, psychologists, teachers, and so forth, all of whom are directly or indirectly paid by the State, and all of whom believe in what they are doing.[4] These pressures exist both inside and outside of the educational system, and from the political-economy perspective constitute an effective social control mechanism that quashes an oppressed group and protects the interests of the dominant economic interests, and all of its beneficiaries (cf. Bailey & Gayle, 2003).

Implications of the Political-Economy Approach To the extent that the bulk of young people are controlled financially in terms of the new cultural "agreement" that they should have access mainly to low-level jobs, thereby limiting their roles as productive contributors to adult society, it is easier to control them subjectively. Their subjectivity relates to how they define their sense of identity, and therefore their tastes and attitudes are affected, as are how they spend their money and leisure time. Thus, political economists argue that much of mainstream youth culture has come to constitute a special type of consumer culture, as recent cohorts have been enticed and cajoled to have their emotions, identity, and tastes defined and redefined for them by the massive industries that market fashion, music, art, and other consumer items. This early observation now finds strong evidence in the practice of "branding," commonly employed by major corporations (Klein, 2000; Quart, 2002). These products all have in common an identity-conferring quality. To be "someone," to be "cool," one has to have, wear, or consume that item and publicly display the labels and logos. Under these conditions, young consumers are perfect targets for such manipulation so long as they are kept "identity hungry." When identity is precarious among consumers, corporations change their products year after year, confident that consumers will follow the trends they arbitrarily set and announce through the media. From this political-economy perspective, the entire consumer-corporate system works in unison and is the perfect arrangement for capitalist enterprises that have as their primary objective profit maximization: Youth are both a source of cheap labour and a massive consumer segment (subsidized by their parents).

While the political-economy perspective appears to round out the functionalist view by specifying *why* the social order is the way it is and *how* it changes, like functionalism, it is primarily macro in orientation. As such, it does not provide the concepts by which we can understand things like the subjectivity of false consciousness and the micromanipulation of identities. Accordingly, it is useful to examine a complementary critical approach that helps us understand the changing nature of identity formation and the "normalcy" of false consciousness, namely, the late-modern perspective that focuses on the symbolic or meaning-structures in peoples' lives. As we will see, both the materialist and symbolic approaches share a concern with the disempowerment or disenfranchisement of youth, whether directly orchestrated by controlling interests in a society (cf. Lapsley, Enright, & Serlin, 1985) or allowed to happen because youth interests have been lost in the social disorganization created as economic changes have eroded normative structures.

Changing Symbolic Conditions

Another group of critical sociologists understands the changing nature of the transition to adulthood in terms of the meaning-structures that might guide young people during this transition. Meaning can be derived from the normative structures of a society associated with its culture, namely, the value-based patterns and standards of behaviour. In addition, people can develop meaning on the basis of their own subjective appraisals (associated with agency) and social commitments (associated with societal structure). From the perspective of the normative guidance of "Western culture," many sociologists believe that we have moved into a "late-modern society" that is increasingly anomic (or less normed) in certain respects (see Côté, 2000, for a discussion of this perspective and the distinctions between the concepts of late-modern and postmodern). This anomie seems to have affected the life courses of many people, who can find themselves (a) with little guidance from their families of origin or an organized religion, (b) compensating for fragmented institutional contexts (like education-to-work transitions), (c) coping with decoupled and erratic life-transition options (like family of origin to family of orientation), or (d) trying to meet the requirement to individualize their life plans (Côté, 2000). Faced with these challenges, adolescents and emerging adults more than ever need a repertoire of personal resources—identity capital[5]—to successfully integrate themselves into mainstream adult society, if they so wish.

At the same time, mainstream society is less insistent that everyone become an adult member, even in a timely manner, because their sustained economic participation is not as crucial as it was in industrial or pre-industrial societies, except as a reserve of cheap labour. Accordingly, there is little normative pressure for some people to "grow up" in terms of what would be considered a "traditional adulthood" defined in terms of commitments to lifelong roles and obligations based on identities embedded in community attachments and societal integration.

Under circumstances where well-structured socialization practices have diminished, adolescents and emerging adults find that they must compensate by engaging in what Heinz refers to as "self-socialization" (2002), an individualization process bound to be fraught with challenges requiring more time to enter even forms of "posttraditional" adulthood. Referring to the "loose coupling between social structure and the life course," Heinz proposes two principles for viewing development in terms of self-socialization:

1. Individuals construct their own life course by attempting to come to terms with opportunities and constraints concerning transition pathways and life stages.

2. Individuals select pathways, act and appraise the consequences of their actions in terms of their self-identity in reference to social contexts that are embedded in institutions and markets. (2002, p. 58)

Implications of the Late-Modernist Approach This new self-socialization requirement presents both risks and benefits to adolescents and emerging adults. While it provides greater freedom from traditional constraints, not all opportunities are the same, and not all choices made in the context of new freedoms are good ones or in one's best interest over the long term (cf. Schwartz, 2000, 2004a, 2004b). In the context of freedom without guidance, people can exercise the choice to pursue a life course totally devoid of traditional social markers, with or without exerting much mental effort. For those who elect not to exert much effort, they can simply select a number of "default options" now available in popular or mainstream youth culture, by which they follow paths of least resistance and effort, as in the imitation of the latest fashion and music trends. This type of individualization is referred to as "default individualization" because it involves little agentic assertion on the part of the person (Côté, 2000). It is exactly this form of development that corporate-driven consumer culture encourages.

Alternatively, more people are now freer to pursue life courses based on extensive agentic deliberations of the alternatives and opportunities now available—given increased educational opportunities in conjunction with the decline of (potentially stifling) social markers involving gender, sexuality, ethnicity, and social class—in pursuit of stimulating and liberating possibilities. This is referred to as "developmental individualization" because it involves a life course of continual and deliberate growth (Côté, 2000). Developmental individualization involves pursuing opportunities that lead to self-improvement in a variety of intellectual, occupational, and psychosocial areas, as well as selecting life courses based on extensive exploration of available alternatives. Therefore, because it implies the exercise of agentic capabilities, developmental individualization may help to prepare adolescents and emerging adults for making decisions and overcoming problems as they prepare to undertake adult roles.

The pursuit of developmental individualization can in many ways be socially structured relative to contemporary social and economic constraints and opportunities, but when the comparison is made between premodern and late-modern conditions (e.g., life in 1800 as opposed to 2000), the opportunities for self-development are obviously more plentiful now for more people, especially to the extent that people attempt to exercise personal agency. While some sociologists of youth may insist on the paramount influence of structural obstacles on life-course outcomes, unless some room is left for the prospect that at least some young people can overcome certain obstacles, these sociologists risk maintaining a patronizing view of the very people for whom they are attempting to advocate. One of the goals in this book is to point out some of the more insidious obstacles that interfere with the exercise of agency and reduce the extent of developmental individualization in the youth population (especially the interference of corporations in the lives of young people, as discussed in detail later, in Chapters 4 and 5).

At the same time, on the surface, the extended transition captured by the term *emerging adulthood* looks like a positive development, with late-modern societies giving people a greater amount of so-called choice and freedom. This was the same position taken on adolescence a century ago—that it was a positive development to nurture it in secondary schools and families, and for their own protection to keep them out of the labour force as long as possible. However, when we peel back the ideology of free choice (cf. Furlong & Cartmel, 1997), we often find that the absence of guiding structures and norms—anomie—presents serious challenges to some people. Without these guiding structures to give meaning to the potential choices people face, realistic and informed choices become burdensome for many young persons. This may be especially critical for those in their teens who may not have the personal agency to chart their own life course, especially teens from disadvantaged backgrounds, those with psychiatric challenges, and so forth. Indeed, Schwartz (2000, 2004a, 2004b) argues that Western societies now present many people with a tyranny of "freedom and choice" with their ideologies of individualism that can actually decrease their quality of life, and to some extent, diminishes their life chances.

SUMMARY OF THE CRITICAL APPROACHES

These two critical sociological approaches have in common the view that the declining fortunes of the young have roots in the shifting power structures of society. The first approach is concerned with the declining earning power of the young, identifying a redistribution of wealth and power toward older members of society. Chapter 3 elaborates this perspective, and examines how trends in the decline of the material conditions of youth in combination with the loss in symbolic meaning have created serious challenges that are creating emotional difficulties for many of those trying to negotiate their way through the increasingly hazardous passage to adulthood. The second approach is concerned with why societies have been normatively destructured in the ways they have, and who now benefits from the subsequent restructuring. Chapter 4 picks up this perspective, and examines how young people themselves have been trying to put meaning back in their lives while corporations have targeted their vulnerabilities in the quest for profits.

While the political-economy perspective may appear to overemphasize structural determinants in people's lives, the late-modern approach may also seem to overestimate the extent to which people can exercise agency. However, the perception of biases may be a result of differences in perspective vis-à-vis level of analysis, with the political-economy approach taking a decidedly macro approach that looks at broad patterns, and the late-modern approach taking a more micro one, where individual differences in people's behaviour receive more attention. Moreover, the late-modern approach highlights *the lack of structure* in certain areas of people's lives (i.e., the destructuring of cultural norms and practices that would have given their lives more meaning and direction), while political economists refer more to economic structures and other structures of opportunity that affect people's life chances. So, while these two critical approaches may appear on the surface to work at cross purposes sometimes, this is not the case.

CRITICISMS OF THEORIES

As readers may have concluded by now, Youth Studies is characterized by a number of internal divisions. Psychologists and psychiatrists generally hold views diverging from those of sociologists regarding the intrinsic nature of adolescence, along nature-nurture fault lines. And within each general position, there are also polarizing divisions: within psychology the fault line involves the pathologization of adolescence versus seeing its positive potential; within sociology, the division is in terms of the roots, functions, and moral implications of age-based inequalities associated with the transition to adulthood.

It is not likely that these divisions will be easily mended, because they go beyond the "data" to fundamental assumptions and ideological beliefs that the scientists themselves hold about the world, and these have far-reaching political implications. For example, the political implications of the nature-nurture debate are that the nature position justifies the status quo—economic and social privilege are given a genetic basis in the "natural order" of things—while the nurture position calls for social reform to deal with problems of human societies, because it is believed that the roots of those problems lie with inadequate societal structures (cf. Broad & Wade, 1982).

Still, it is worth examining what is behind these divisions if only to gain greater insight so that we might potentially develop more comprehensive theories without polarizing divisions.

The Limitations of Biology-Based Theories

Both the psychological and psychiatric perspectives developed into potent influences on public attitudes in Western societies, and both have been accused of having a stake in maintaining the view that the problems of young people can be addressed by "adjusting" them, rather than by adjusting social institutions. Critics argue that policy-makers want to hear that they can remedy social problems by adjusting people, because adjusting society to any great extent requires reform that acts against dominant interests. From a critical sociological view, dominant political and economic interests are protected when the individual is the source of concern, so the frustrations experienced by youth can be turned back on the individual, rather than directed at their sources in the wider society and economy.

On the other hand, as acknowledged previously, these "helping professionals" are well-intentioned and are working "in the trenches" trying to help young people with their personal struggles. Besides, individual psychologists or psychiatrists could do little to combat the problems facing young people as a group. However, to the extent that the burden of the problem is left with the young and to the extent that they are seen as the cause of that burden, the argument can be made that these professions engage in a form of "victim-blaming." For the critical sociologist, however, the ultimate solution to many of the problems facing the young lies with altering the social and economic circumstances to which they are subjected, and not with merely "fixing" the young victims of these circumstances.

As we will also see below, historical changes in the way the transition from "childhood" to "adulthood" has been restructured in Western culture constitute proof of the assumption that there simply is no one way that human beings make the transition to adulthood. Accordingly, the fact of historical variation in the structure of "adolescence" indicates that, despite the biological changes that take place during and following puberty, coming of age belongs to culture more than to the biological make-up of the individual. In other words, it is often less fruitful to look "within" the individual for an understanding of the causes of what happens during the coming-of-age period than it is to look at how a culture shapes the individual—pushing the individual toward the development of certain attributes and behaviours, and pulling him or her away from others.

Aside from these concerns, the fact is that when put to scientific tests, the common biological assumptions regarding adolescence have proven to be faulty. For example, after their close review of this literature, Petersen and Taylor (1980) conclude, "we have been overestimating the significance of biological factors because of the difficulty of dealing with some problems associated with adolescence. We tend misguidedly to equate 'biological' with 'immutable'" (p. 117). In fact, they argue that there is no evidence that behaviours associated with delinquency and various forms of "acting out" are biologically determined. Further, endocrinological research has found little association between hormonal activity and emotional difficulties among adolescents, and no direct connection of emotional difficulties with pubertal changes, just as Mead reported in the 1920s.

While some researchers have continued to look for the elusive link between biological factors and adolescent behaviour, such as the "hormone-delinquency link" (e.g., Buchanan, Eccles & Becker, 1992), these attempts require a considerable amount of argumentation and statistical manipulation to make their point. Even with these vigorous efforts, no one has been able to demonstrate statistically that biological variables are more important than social ones (cf. Paikoff & Brooks Gunn, 1990; Rowe & Rodgers, 1990). At best, such effects are either minor or indirect in that they are mediated by social experiences, which are culturally patterned. While biological factors may have had more of a direct effect on behaviour early in human evolution, humans have long since become an acculturated species for which instincts have become quite weakened and diffused.[6] Thus, biological influences now appear at best to be indirect in the sense that cultures have the capacity to both intensify and neutralize most biological tendencies and potentials. As argued by Sprinthall and Collins, "social and cultural standards, norms, and expectations and responses of others mediate the effects of physical changes" (1995, p. 80). Accordingly, experiences among those experiencing puberty, such as self-image and self-esteem, "are determined by sociocultural standards, norms, and expectations about physical characteristics that are widely held in a society or culture" (1995, p. 80).

Complicating matters further is the fact that behind many biological assumptions is an equating of puberty with adolescence. But, the term *puberty* most accurately corresponds to a number of biological changes that occur before and during the early teen years. As we just saw, behavioural correlates between emotional distress and puberty have been found to be non-existent, indirect, or minor. Thus, the belief in a biological inferiority among those coming of age is unjust, inasmuch as our treatment of them has been based on a false belief that the determinants of their behaviour are largely biological rather than social.

In any event, this book is not concerned primarily with what happens during puberty or early adolescence, but rather during the later teens and early twenties, the period now called emerging adulthood. These older age groups are clearly well past puberty, so any "hormone explanations" are at best weak. Unmistakably, the "biological immaturity argument" does not justify the suspension of rights of individuals in their late teens and twenties. For centuries, people in their late teen years and early twenties were seen to be capable of mature and responsible behaviour, including beginning their own families. Moreover, as noted, before the present century, puberty occurred at a later age than it does now. How is it then that we now impute less maturity to individuals of this age? Has something changed to make them constitutionally more immature, despite accelerated biological development? If so, what is it that has changed?

To provide an analogy, there is no direct link between, say, a sparsity of facial hair that might characterize an 18-year-old male and various types of competencies. Why not associate a lack of competency with a receding hairline or grey hair? In short, just because the body is still developing does not mean that the individual is any less capable of performing various adult roles than is an adult whose body is undergoing a gradual decline with aging. Rather, to deny the individual the chance to perform such roles in the first place is to maintain both immaturity and the self-fulfilling prophecy that physical appearance determines behaviour. We must all consider the prospect that, because of the way we treat young people, we are socially creating the very behaviours, like immaturity and emotionality, that we condemn among them (cf. Schultze et al., 1991).

CONCLUSION: THE LIMITATIONS AND ADVANTAGES OF CULTURE-BASED THEORIES

The cultural perspectives clearly add much to our understanding of the changing nature of the transition to adulthood. Some criticize sociological views because they are believed to be ideological, ranging from the conservatism of functionalism to the radicalism of the critical approaches. However, as we saw with the biological approaches, the same charge can be made of any perspective—all are imbedded in assumptions posed either for or against vested interests.

This book attempts to build a comprehensive explanation of why the transition to adulthood is now structured the way it is and who benefits from this arrangement. Perspectives should be judged on the evidence, not on whether they correspond with one's personal political preference or professional interests. The next two chapters lay out an array of recent evidence that helps us judge more thoroughly the usefulness of the critical perspectives. The functionalist perspective has been described as hegemonic (i.e., dominant, overshadowing opposing views; Hollands, 2001) and so thoroughly permeates contemporary thinking on youth issues among both sociologists and policy-makers that it does not need such an extensive elaboration. The same applies to the psychological approach to youth, as embodied in adolescent psychology and the stack of textbooks explaining that field. The same cannot be said for critical perspectives on youth; hence, the value of this book lies in its willingness to elaborate unpopular views that shed light on persistent problems confronting young people.

Sociological perspectives have also been criticized because they tend to reduce behaviour to social structural causes (e.g., Wrong, 1961), which some find to be too conspiratorial. While there may be some truth to this assertion, there are attempts within sociology to address this (e.g., Bailey & Gayle, 2003; Emirbayer & Mische, 1998), as with the late-modernist use of the concept of agency and individualization. At the close of the next chapter, after carefully examining the materialist conditions underlying the transition to adulthood in contemporary Canadian society, we will revisit the issue of whether sociological approaches amount to "conspiracy theories" or are simply useful in exposing the workings of self-interest that one would expect in a capitalistic economy governed by a neo-liberal philosophy.

ENDNOTES

1. See Lapsley, Enright, & Serlin (1985) for data from the early twentieth century supporting the argument that, historically, educational participation drops dramatically when good jobs are available to young people, and increases when youth labour is not needed.

2. The cohort school-to-work transition begins at the point where more young people are studying without working and ends at the point where the majority is working without studying.

3. The experiences of young women were similar, except that a university education did not have the same buffering effect as it did for men, and the generational dividing line is put at age 30 for females by Statistics Canada.

4. The term *cooling out* was introduced to sociology by Goffman (1952), who took it from street language to describe the final phase of a con game during which the person conned (the mark) is convinced not to go to the authorities, either because he or she will look stupid or is culpable. Goffman applied the phrase to a number of institutional spheres in which clients are not fully satisfied.

5. Identity capital resources have been identified as being both tangible and intangible (Côté, 1996). Tangible resources include the possessions, social networks, and behaviours of individuals, whereas intangible resources constitute their personality attributes. Tangible attributes comprise financial resources, educational credentials, group memberships, and parental social status, along with impression management skills and social skills. Intangible resources include psychological capacities such as ego strength, an internal locus of control, self-esteem, a sense of purpose in life, social perspective taking, critical thinking abilities, and moral reasoning abilities (Côté, 1997). The common

feature of intangible attributes is that they can afford the person the cognitive and behavioural capacities with which to understand and negotiate the various obstacles and opportunities commonly encountered throughout the late-modern life course with its decoupled and multi-faceted transitions.

6. Harris (1983) argues that genetics has not played a significant role in cultural evolution for many thousands of years, but most certainly not over the last 12 000 years, during which time there has been "an immense diversity of technological, demographic, ecological, economic, sexual, mental, familial, political, religious, philosophical, and ideological institutions and customs" (p. 21).

chapter three

The Changing Nature of the Transition to Adulthood

INTRODUCTION

Apart from the sexual division of labour, all societies divide tasks based on their versions of age-status. Generally, preindustrial societies assign children the simpler, more menial tasks. These tasks are then often divided again according to cultural conceptions of gender roles. As people grow physically and mature mentally, the tasks often become more complex and less menial. At the same time, rewards reaped from the community for individual efforts normally increase, but so do individual responsibilities to the community. This basic *quid pro quo* has bonded generations throughout human history: Younger members invest in their future adult roles, thereby contributing to community welfare; as adults, they later reap benefits from the new generation of younger members, but they are also expected to assume responsibility for the welfare of those younger members. As we see in this chapter, the intergenerational *quid pro quo* is now strained in Canadian society: Many younger members see less reason to participate in adult society, and many of the adult leaders of our society—from our economic and political élite—apparently see less reason to assume responsibility for the welfare of younger members.

When the history of age-relations in Canada is examined, marked changes can be seen, particularly with a delay in the age at which the person is (a) entitled to share equally in community rewards as a result of their efforts, and (b) expected to take on additional responsibilities. This is most clearly the case in terms of the young losing ground in the workplace and, as a consequence, having more difficulties gaining the economic independence traditionally associated with adulthood. At the same time, recent cohorts have spent increasingly longer periods in educational institutions ostensibly preparing for entry into a workforce that they are told demands increasingly higher levels of skill. On the one hand, those who make their way through higher-educational institutions generally find that they have surer and more direct routes to rewarding statuses. On the other hand, those who do not make it through the new credentialing institutions encounter significant difficulties in finding well-paying and rewarding jobs. Because we do not hear much about this latter group, researchers have referred to them as the "forgotten half" (e.g., Halperin, 1998; William T. Grant Foundation, 1988).

These changes in the means of achieving adult status have a variety of impacts on the lives of young people examined in this chapter. First and foremost, the notion of "starting at the bottom" has a different meaning for contemporary youth cohorts than it did for even their parents' cohort. As just mentioned, societies generally start children with the most basic and menial tasks, but as the person grows, the tasks often become more complex. In other words, "starting at the bottom" implies that there is somewhere above the bottom to move. In industrial societies, this meant that one could work "up the ladder of success" in factories, businesses, and government departments. However, as shown below, this no longer applies in many advanced industrial workplace settings. Many young people now start at the bottom and stay there for indefinite periods of time (Tannock, 2001), usually only advancing if they gain some outside, and sometimes arbitrary, credential. Young women and ethnic minorities have been accustomed to this for some time, but increasingly this applies to young white men as well. This chapter examines how we arrived at the current situation and what it means for the transition to adult status of young Canadians.

DEMOGRAPHIC SHIFTS AFFECTING THE FORTUNES OF THE YOUNG

Lavoie and Oderkirk (1993) provide an analysis of changes in the life experiences of the average Canadian woman and man over the past three centuries. According to their analysis, persons born in 1700 had life expectancies of between 30 and 35 years. This short lifespan was especially affected by a high infant mortality rate, but also relatively high rates of death due to disease, infection, and mishap. Over the next four generations this improved, but only to the point where, by 1831, men had a life expectancy of 40 years and women of 42. It took another four generations before life expectancies resembled those that we now take for granted. Of those born in 2002, females can expect to live about 82 years, and males some 77 years; this constitutes a 6-year increase in the lifespan for males just since 1979, and a 3-year increase for females (Statistics Canada, 2004a).

This new demographic reality appears to have had direct consequences for the relative position of the age-statuses making up Canadian society, especially as related to the transition to adulthood. In the twentieth century, an increasing proportion of the population lived well beyond their twenties and thirties—what came to be called young adulthood and then emerging adulthood during that century, but which in prior centuries would have been the prime years of adulthood. As Table 3.1 shows, while the median age of the Canadian population was only about 18 in 1861 (Bureau of Agriculture and Statistics, Census Department, 1863), by 2001 it was more than double that, at 37.6 (Statistics Canada,

TABLE 3.1	The Competition Ratio: The Proportion of "Youth" to "Adults"			
	Age Groups		Ratio of Age Groups	Median Age of the Population
	15-29 Male/Female (000)	30-64 Male/Female (000)	15-29/30-64 Male/Female	
1861	368/358	333/292	1.11/1.23	17.8
1881	667/674	612/558	1.10/1.21	20.1
1901	754/731	899/830	.84/.88	22.7
1921	1102/1098	1649/1450	.67/.76	23.9
1941	1543/1515	2347/2135	.66/.71	27.0
1961	1945/1911	3433/3365	.57/.57	26.5
1981	3441/3396	4806/4859	.72/.70	29.6
1991	3126/3080	6081/6147	.51/.50	33.5
2001	2970/2937	7143/7342	.42/.40	41.3

Adapted from: Estimates for 1861 to 1991 are from Allahar & Côté, 1998; for 2001 estimates are from 2001 Census of Canada. Catalogue number 95F0300XCB01004, Age (122) and Sex (3) for Population, for Canada, Provinces, Territories, Census Metropolitan Areas and Census Agglomerations, 2001 Census–100% Data, Ottawa: Statistics Canada, July 16, 2002. 2001 Census of Canada. Catalogue number 95F0300XCB01004.

Statistics Canada projects that the median age will be 43.7 in 2011. Based on their figures, we project that the overall competition ratio will be .38.

2002), increasing by more than one year per decade between 1861 and 2001. The 1990s recorded the biggest Census-to-Census increase in the median age—2.3 years—in a century (Statistics Canada, 2002).

The purpose of pointing out these demographic changes is to draw attention to the possibility that "population aging" has influenced intergenerational competition for scarce resources, particularly those found in the workplace. To facilitate discussion of this point, the term "competition ratio" is used to refer to the competition between younger and older cohorts in statistical terms (Allahar & Côté, 1998; cf. Esterlin, 1978; Betcherman & Morissette, 1994). When the Canadian Census data from 1861 (the first available Census records) is analyzed, as in Table 3.1, it appears that those in the age range of 15 to 29 years actually outnumbered those in the larger range of 30 to 64 years. This observation is even more striking when we consider that the first age range spans only 15 years of life while the second spans over twice as many years of the life course. In this sense, at one time, young people could then have been considered a "majority group" in Canadian society in terms of age-status.

When changes in this ratio are examined over the twentieth century, the ratio drops steadily, with the exception of the 1981 figures, reflecting the bulge of Baby Boomers. By 1991, there was a competition ratio of about one to two, or .50. The 2001 Census showed that it continued to drop to about .40, and this drop is expected to continue at least for the next decade (Statistics Canada, 2002). In other words, there are now more than twice as many older people (aged 30 to 65) than younger people (aged 15 to 29), and this is part of a long-term trend, not a cycle that is expected to reverse itself.

In support of the competition-ratio thesis, most of these older Canadians are now potential competitors in the postindustrial workplace, affecting the relative utility of young workers, especially young males. For example, in the 1800s, many in the older population would not have been as able as the young to work in the physically demanding primary (resource exploitation) or secondary (manufacturing) sectors that provided most of the paid labour then. Nowadays, older workers are more physically suited to the modern work-place than they once were, which is dominated by the tertiary (or service) sector, where strength is not an issue. Further, few women were active in the formal workplace then, especially after marriage. By 2001, women made up 46% of Canada's labour force, up from 34% in 1971 (Cooke-Reynolds & Zukewich, 2004). Consequently, from the per-spective of the young male, the competition ratio is now more like 1:6 ($\approx$.17), because he has to compete with not only twice as many older males ($\approx$.34), but also twice as many older females ($\approx$.34), and an equal number of same-age females ($\approx$.17). This decline in their marginal utility has adversely affected the identity formation of many young Canadian men, especially those who have been brought up to believe that they should ful-fill the "good provider" role in adulthood and who cannot find a workable alternative model of manhood (cf. Bernard, 1981; Goode, 1980).

One consequence of this demographic trend is that the majority status of the younger age group has changed into more of a minority status. Another consequence is that the integral role, and bargaining power, of the young person as worker has decreased dramat-ically. There are simply more people in the older age groups available to engage in paid labour. In the 1990s, the impact of this development has become more intense as a num-ber of older workers affected by corporate restructuring were forced to take entry-level jobs normally performed by younger workers (Foot, 1996). This was in part because cor-porations have in the past been largely pyramid—or triangle-shaped. However, the chang-ing demographic pattern has meant that, as the larger youth cohorts of the late twentieth century tried to pass through this triangular corporate structure, many found themselves blocked. As Foot argues,

> we have been trying to promote a rectangle up a triangle, and it can't be done . . . . This system only works when there are more younger than older employees, which was exactly the case over most of the 20th century as the modern corporation took shape. (1996, p. 58)

With many of the jobs taken up and down the career hierarchies, an increasing number of young people looking to get a hold in the labour market (a) were unsuccessful and became "discouraged workers,"[1] or (b) took a chance in attempting to obtain (more) higher-educational credentials (below), or (c) were forced into part-time, low-paying posi-tions which provide little opportunity for advancement—what Coupland (1991) dubbed "McJobs" (Schlosser, 2001; Tannock, 2001).

This demographic shift of the twentieth century also represents a change in the life course of the average Canadian. In particular, the very nature of the transition to adulthood changed as the period of pre-adult dependency grew. This process began at mid-century with adolescence (the teen years) becoming a prolongation of childhood dependency; by late-century, the period of "youth" or "emerging adulthood" (the twenties) had taken on many of the characteristics of adolescent dependency. In fact, by the mid-1990s, the Canadian Youth Foundation (CYF) called upon the Canadian government to officially recognize that the period of youth be defined as extending to age 29, because the "definition of youth used by the government . . . is not an accurate refection of the ages [at which] young people are leaving school and beginning careers" (1995, pp. 2-3). The CYF called for this measure so that employment policy initiatives would be directed *beyond* the 15-to-24 age group. Their reasoning was as follows: "unemployed young people who are in the age cohort between 25 to 29 are . . . not fundamentally different from unemployed youth in their early 20s except that they have more experience with chronic unemployment."

CHANGES IN THE EDUCATIONAL AND WORKPLACE OPPORTUNITIES INVOLVED IN THE TRANSITION TO ADULTHOOD

In the earliest colonial days, there was very little paid labour and the vast majority of men and women worked the land and produced most of their own necessities of life. Paid labour grew slowly, and it was largely males who performed it.[2] Even at the turn of the twentieth century, about 65% of the population still lived in rural areas and some 40% of the population was engaged in agricultural labour (Denton, 1970; O'Neill, 1991). Overall, at that time, about 45% of the labour force was still employed in the primary sector, about 27% was in the secondary sector, and only 28% was in the tertiary sector (McDonald & Chen, 1993). By the 1990s, though, the percentage employed in the primary sector had dropped precipitously to only 6%, the secondary sector remained relatively stable at 23%, and a full 71% were employed in the tertiary sector (McDonald & Chen, 1993). As of 2003, the shift continued toward a larger service sector (75% of jobs), and gradual declines in primary (4%) and secondary (21%) sectors.[3]

Few would dispute the fact that these changes have taken place. What is in dispute is how Canadian society adjusted to these changes in terms of how wealth and the opportunity to accumulate it has been shared among all of those entitled to the rights of Canadian citizenship. To begin our examination of this, we will consider the history of the educational system as the primary route to wealth accumulation. Here is one way in which the young have increasingly become second-class citizens, relegated to adult-controlled institutions for an increasing portion of their lives. We will see how the "opportunities" that many people associate with higher education are not only far more complex than most think but also more unequally distributed than is commonly believed. Hence, in many cases it is difficult to see the "opportunities" of education as more significant than the "challenges" it now poses.

Educational Opportunities and Challenges

The educational system now provides the basic structure for many aspects of the prolonged transition to adulthood in Canada and other developed countries. Table 3.2 shows the historical trends in Canada regarding school attendance among those in their late teens and early twenties. In the 1920s, only about 25% of those aged 15 to 19 attended school, but by the 1990s three quarters did so. Of those aged 20 to 24, only about 3% attended in the 1920s, but by 2001, about 40% did. In fact, this latter age group increased its participation about threefold in the 1980s and eightfold by the early 2000s.

Currently, Canada has one of the highest participation rates and most expensive publicly funded systems in the world: Of those aged 25 to 34, 28% have university-level

TABLE 3.2	Percentage of Young Men and Women Attending School Full-Time, 1921–2001			
	15- to 19-year-olds		20- to 24-year-olds	
	Men	Women	Men	Women
1921	23	27	3	2
1931	32	35	4	2
1941	34	37	5	3
1951	41	40	7	3
1961	62	56	12	5
1971	74	56	12	5
1981	66	66	21	16
1991	73	74	32	33
2001	72	75	37	43

Adapted from: Estimates for 1921-1981 are from Normand, 1995; Estimates for 15- to 19-year-olds for 1991 and 2001 are from Almey and Normand, 2002 (the 2001 estimate is based on figures for 1998–99); estimates for 20- to 24-year-olds for 1991 and 2001 are from Statistics Canada, 2003a.

qualifications, and an additional 21% have a community college diploma (Statistics Canada, 2003a). On the face of it, this looks like an enviable achievement and something that less developed countries should emulate. Indeed, modern democracies are much more vibrant when they have a greater proportion of citizens who are educated about the world and willing to participate in the political process. Indeed, the benefits of education can extend far beyond what is learned in school (e.g., Schuller et al., 2004). However, not only are there questions about how well the Canadian educational system produces citizens who fit the democratic ideal (as examined later in this book), but there is more to this issue than simple enrolment figures.

In the contemporary workplace—euphemistically called "the new economy" (e.g., Statistics Canada, 2003b)—if one does not have higher educational credentials, one's economic prospects are severely limited. Indeed, the unemployment rate of young people without postsecondary credentials is about two to three times higher than those with these credentials (e.g., Allen, Harris, & Butlin, 2001). In addition, those without a postsecondary degree are at a great disadvantage in terms of employability in most sectors of the economy (e.g., Betcherman & Morissette, 1994; Halperin, 1998; Morris & Western, 1999; Tannock, 2001). Moreover, whatever the current advantages of higher credentials, we should not forget that many workers in previous generations could make good career progress without them, especially in business and government jobs. Moreover, many of these business and government jobs involve essentially the same skills as they did before the advent of "credentialism."

Clearly, a university education is now a good investment in terms of one's salary level and future earning power.[4] When looking at the accumulated experiences of past cohorts for the population as a whole, university graduates made substantially more than those with high school. In 2000, salary comparisons for the Canadian workforce were as follows: Full-year, full-time workers with university degrees made on average $62 000, while those with only high school made just $36 000; if part-time, part-year workers are included, these figures drop to $49 000 for those with university versus $25 000 for those with high school (Statistics Canada, 2003b).

We can use the above figures to estimate the lifetime payback for a university education by taking the difference between the respective averages and multiplying by 40 to represent the average number of years people will spend in the workforce after earning their degrees. When we do this, the lifetime benefit of acquiring a university degree beyond a high school diploma is on average over one million dollars (62 000 – 36 000 = 26 000 × 40 = 1 020 000). For all workers (including those employed less than full-time), this can still translate to just under one million dollars (49 000 – 25 000 = 23 000 × 40 = 960 000).

Evidently, not only is completing a higher-educational degree on average a wise investment, but the knowledge, skills, and personality development acquired during the college years may have "sleeper," or long-term indirect, effects that are difficult to calculate (e.g., Montgomery & Côté, 2003; Schuller et al., 2004).[5] Thus, long-term occupational and personal-fulfillment outcomes may be enhanced in ways that are very difficult for researchers to study, given the time spans involved (cf. Lockhart, 1975). Those with higher educations should also make "better citizens" who vote more, even when young (e.g., Gidengil et al., 2003), but who also stay apprised of world events and more engaged in society's institutions (Putnam, 2000).

On the other hand, as we see below, academic credentials are often arbitrary in terms of workplace preparation, in the sense that many highly educated workers perform tasks that have little directly to do with their formal education, especially those with nontechnical degrees. This can be referred to as the "credentialism paradox," namely, that credentialed skills often have little to do with the work that is eventually preformed; but without the credentials, one's employability and earning power are seriously jeopardized (Allahar & Côté, 1998). To understand this paradox, we need to have a sense of the history of the educational system through all three levels, from the primary through tertiary levels.

Historical analyses of the growth of primary and secondary educational systems reveal that they emerged in part to provide daily structure to those children and teens displaced by the increasing technologization of agriculture and manufacturing (Lapsley, Enright, & Serlin, 1985). Primary-school enrolment in the nineteenth century was low and sporadic. For various reasons, many parents were not supportive of compulsory education and it was difficult to get children to attend regularly (Phillips, 1957). Even by 1901, although efforts to implement compulsory education had been underway for two decades in many provinces, the average daily attendance in primary schools was only about 60%. Moreover, the typical Canadian received only about six years of lifetime schooling. As for secondary schools, the history is even more chequered. According to Phillips,

> in 1841 secondary schools were class institutions attended by very few. Between then and 1871 these class institutions gave way to high schools, superimposed upon the elementary schools. By 1901 the high schools were attended by many preparing to be teachers, by a smaller number intending to enter university, and by some others. (p. 183)

It was not until several decades into the twentieth century that enrolments increased to the point where the educational system began to take its current form as the major institution governing the lives of young Canadians. In Ontario, for example, although the entire population only doubled between 1900 and 1950, enrolments in secondary schools increased sixfold (Phillips, 1957). Table 3.2 can be consulted to review these trends.

Again, we do not wish to be misunderstood here. It is commendable that Canada has attempted to educate its citizens to this extent. Given the choice, most societies would surely prefer more formally educated citizens than non- or undereducated ones. Clearly, there are benefits to having an educated population and it is a laudable democratic ideal that everyone be educated to his or her full potential (e.g., Schuller et al. 2004). However, clear differences between principle and practice are evident in the realities of the Canadian educational system (and others, like the American system). In particular, the problem of credentialism has emerged as an unintended consequence of mass-educational systems, which place many of their graduates in a labour market that does not need the skill-repertoire that they took so many years acquiring (Allen, Harris, & Butlin, 2001; Collins, 1979; Hunter & McKenzie Leiper, 1993; Livingstone, 1998).

At the same time, the increase in the number of higher credentials heightens the competition in the youth segment for low-level jobs. This can especially put at a disadvantage those with lower levels of education, and dishearten those in high school who do not feel they could ever compete at these higher levels, leading them to drop out from a sense of resignation. It is essential that this insight be shared, especially with those who will lose in this educational competition for jobs. And not only will they lose big, but they will be told to blame themselves for it (cf. Furlong & Cartmel, 1997). As we will see, however, in view of the limitations of the current job market, we are "overpromising" young Canadians as a group about the benefits they can expect from pursuing higher education credentials to the extent now in evidence, and in the process may be adversely affecting their well-being (cf. Bibby & Posterski, 1992).

The current credentialism problem for university graduates originated in the 1960s when the higher educational system was expanded dramatically with the building of many new colleges and universities. This expansion led to a ninefold increase in postsecondary enrolment between 1950 and 1990 alone (Gregor & Jasmin, 1992). The assumption was that the skills transmitted through higher education in the form of "human capital" (i.e., skills that translate into income) would meet the needs of an advanced industrial economy and generate economic wealth for the individual graduate and for the society as a whole (Allahar & Côté, 1998). This human capital assumption has been borne out to some extent, but is faulty as a full explanation of educational outcomes (Hunter & McKenzie Leiper, 1993). In particular, most higher-educational skills are "passive" in the sense that they need an existing occupational context in which to be used—they do not on their own create new jobs or economic activity. This faulty logic of human capital theory has been called a "field of dreams" logic ("build it and they will come"; Lowe, 2001; Teixeira & Mishel, 1995). While writing skills and critical thinking may be useful in certain occupational contexts, outside those contexts, they do not generate income on their own.

This flaw in human capital theory became evident in the mid-1970s when graduate underemployment was becoming visible as a widespread problem. For instance, stories about graduates with PhDs driving taxis abounded in the media. By that time, the public sector had reached its capacity to absorb university graduates, yet the numbers of people with higher degrees continued to grow (Lockhart, 1975, 1978). Without the continued expansion of the public sector (education, health, and the public service), graduates increasingly turned to the private sector. Although "good jobs" were still available in business and professional services, an increasing number of graduates found only "bad jobs" in consumer services (Picot, Myles, & Wannell, 1990). As the supply of graduates grew, a buyer's market in favour of employers resulted in most sectors. In this situation, employers could take those with the highest credentials, even for lower-skilled jobs, so many of those with higher degrees increasingly found themselves taking jobs that did not require any or all of their skills. Consequently, there was a downward cascading effect whereby those without higher degrees faced increasingly stiffer competition for jobs, leaving them with fewer and poorer-paying jobs (Davies, Mosher, & O'Grady, 1994).

Studies by research branches of the Canadian government have found that, throughout the 1980s and 1990s, up to one half of Canadian university (under) graduates found themselves in jobs two years after graduation not requiring a university degree (Frenette, 2000), a proportion that declined to about one third after five postgraduation years (Nobert, McDowell, & Goulet, 1992). In 1994, 37% of those aged 20 to 29 with bachelor's degrees felt they were overqualified for their jobs (compared with 22% for all Canadian workers with college or university degrees; Kelly, Howatson-Leo, & Clark, 1997).

The most recent studies indicate that the feelings of overqualification are increasing, especially among young, educated workers. A 2000 Statistics Canada survey of 25 000 Canadians found that, among all workers aged 20 to 29, 33% felt they were overqualified, up from 30% in 1994 (Crompton, 2002, p. 25). Among those aged 20 to 64 with postsecondary educations, 25% responded "yes" to the following question: "Considering your experience, education, and training, do you feel that you are overqualified for your job?" (Crompton, 2002, p. 24). Within this subsample of overqualified workers, only 16% felt that there was a close relationship between their current job and past education (30% said the two were somewhat related, while 45% thought they were unrelated).

As these statistics show, there are a number of ways to assess the level of underemployment. Another way, one that calls into question the often proclaimed notion that the labour force requires, and by implication fully employs, workers with increasingly higher education credentials, is to compare the growth in the number of jobs requiring university degrees (which Statistics Canada defines as "highly skilled") with the number of degrees that have come onto the labour market. As shown in Table 3.3, between 1991 and 2001, some 600 000 highly skilled jobs were created in the Canadian workforce (Statistics Canada, 2003e, p. 25). While this is good news to the people who secured those jobs, some 1.2 million university degrees also came onto the labour market over the same time period (Statistics Canada, 2003a, p. 29; it is predicted that another 1.6 million BAs will be produced by 2011, Association of Universities and Colleges in Canada, 2002). This means that there were two new university degrees for every one job created requiring them. Hence, using an objective supply-demand estimate, the underemployment rate for university graduates of 50% initially estimated in the 1980s based on subjective appraisals of credential fit (above) appears to have prevailed in the 1990s. The situation was even worse for community college graduates, with only about 200 000 new jobs for them, but 900 000 diplomas produced between 1991 and 2001 (cf. Statistics Canada, 2003e, p. 25 with Statistics Canada, 2003a, p. 29).

Table 3.3 also shows that there were about a half million fewer workers with high school or less in the 1990s, yet the workplace demand for them grew by over 5%. University and community college graduates who could not find employment commensurate with their credentials apparently took many of these lower-level jobs. Given that it appears to take half of university graduates at least 15 months to secure a full-time job

TABLE 3.3	Educational Attainment and Workplace Opportunities 1991–2001: Do the Math				
Numbers in Job-Skills and Credential Categories	1991	2001	New Jobs Created Between 1991 and 2001	New Credentials Obtained Between 1991 and 2001	New Jobs Minus New Credentials
Highly skilled jobs (normally requiring university credentials)	1 904 445	2 530 896	626 450 (+32%)		
Workers with university credentials	2 443 330	3 676 620		1 233 290 (+50.5%)	
					-606 840
Skilled jobs (normally requiring community college)	3 172 000	3 369 510	197 510 (+6.2%)		
Workers with community college credentials	2 007 485	2 917 890		910 405 (+45.4%)	
					-712 895
Unskilled jobs (normally requiring high school or less)	6 417 200	6 762 640	345 440 (+5.4%)		
Workers with high school or less	8 168 485	7 596 645		-571 840 (-7.0%)	
					+917 280

Adapted from: "Occupational skill groups by sex, Canada, 1991, 1996 and 2001," from the Statistics Canada publication, *The changing profile of Canada's labour force, 2001 Census*, Catalogue 96F0030, February 11, 2003, p. 25; and from "Levels of education attainment in the working-age population, by sex, Canada, 1991 and 2001," from the Statistics Canada publication, *Education in Canada: Raising the standard, 2001 Census*, Catalogue 96F0030, March 11, 2003, p. 29.

(Betts, Ferrall, and Finnie, 2000), it is understandable that they eventually would take unskilled jobs, even those requiring only high school diplomas (Frenette, 2000).

However, many of those faced with such disappointments in securing a job to match their credentials chose to seek further credentials in an attempt to get ahead of the pack. Thus, since the late 1980s, many people have been scrambling for credentials, trying to gain some advantage to enhance their career possibilities. By the early 1990s, as many as 50% of community colleges and university graduates were re-enrolling in subsequent educational programmes (Clark, 1999; Nobert, McDowell, & Goulet, 1992), and this has continued, with 7% of those with BAs obtaining community college diplomas within five years of gaining their BAs (Clark, 1999). In economic language, with an oversupply of higher degrees, workplace demand for many of them decreased, so higher-education graduates had less to bargain with—their credentials lost market value (Davies, Mosher, & O'Grady, 1994).

In fact, the market value of many credentials has dropped in historically relative terms since the *mid-70s*, as an increasing number of people obtained higher degrees. This was further fuelled in the *1980s* when higher-educational enrolments in Canada increased by some 40% (most of which constituted women going on to higher education). Moreover, as Table 3.3 shows, during the period 1991 through 2001, the number of university graduates in the workforce increased some 50%, from about 2.5 million to over 3.5 million (out of a total workforce of 14.5 million), while community college graduates increased by almost the same percentage (Statistics Canada, 2003c, p. 30). Further increases are predicted in the magnitude of 30% by 2011 (Association of Universities and Colleges in Canada, 2002). However, the recent rate of increase has been much steeper than anticipated, by about 10 times for 18- to 21-year-olds (Charbonneau, 2004).

Now, at the beginning of the twenty-first century, the educational system has become perhaps the most important institution regulating what has become a prolonged period of adolescence and emerging adulthood. Its role has become even more apparent over the past 20 years, as an increasing number of graduates have encountered diminished job opportunities, and returned to it, only to find themselves caught up in a scramble for educational credentials in many cases. Consequently, the stakes are now higher for everyone, making it necessary to undergo many years of expensive education in the hope of even being in the running for a rewarding career and a decent salary. As Davies, Mosher, and O'Grady conclude,

> the transition from school to work is increasingly imposing an "involuntary moratorium" on many young adults, whose commitment to education offers them some competitive advantages, but also condemns them to periods of underemployment in the expectation of longer-term payoffs. (1994, p. 366)

This notion of the involuntary moratorium is addressed again in the next chapter, and its various drawbacks noted. One obvious problem is that, while this longer preparation for work roles is fine for those with parents who can afford to pay for a postsecondary education, the bulk of the population cannot afford it and therefore face a continuing struggle in terms of their standard of living. Hence, credentialism is implicated in social class reproduction, whereby parental wealth and status (social and cultural capital) can still affect life chances more than merit, in spite of government efforts to make higher-educational accessibility entirely merit based.[6] It appears that few people are aware of this, or if they are, accept it without question. As noted in Chapter 2, functionalists see this sort of parental investment of wealth into their offspring as a normal aspect of healthy social functioning, but this sanguine interpretation of these trends is only possible if one ignores the social class discrimination involved.

In sum, over the past several decades, young Canadians have increasingly found traditional career paths blocked or nonexistent, and many have repeatedly turned to the educational system in what can turn out to be a gamble to increase their odds of improving their career chances, but in the process have not only accumulated more personal debt but have inadvertently raised the stakes for those with fewer qualifications. With higher stakes, many from less privileged backgrounds are now more economically stymied than they were before the rise of the "meritocratic" educational system. In a sense, then, the "democratic" mass-educational system has reinforced the class barrier it was intended to remove; moreover, it has promised the young something that many of them cannot obtain through that system.

WORKPLACE OPPORTUNITIES AND CHALLENGES

The Changing Means of Production, Technological Displacement, and the Redistribution of Wealth

The decreasing demand for younger workers and the competition faced by them in the workforce have been exacerbated by changes in the technologies affecting the industrial production of goods and services. At the same time, owners and managers of capital have refined the techniques of mass production to increase their profits (Rifkin, 1995). The increase in profit has been possible largely by replacing workers with machines: In the secondary sector, robots and other forms of automation continue to replace factory workers; in the tertiary sector, the computer continues to replace both lower and middle managers, clerical workers, and various service workers. In reference to this problem, Foot (1996) notes that, while as late as the 1980s workers were "cheaper" than machines, "by the 1990s, the cost of labour in Canada was twice the cost of machines" (p. 68). Consequently, businesses look to use machines whenever they can instead of human labour. While this improves profits, it also increases unemployment and underemployment. Foot goes on to draw the conclusion that "technology continues, at a relentless pace, to destroy far more jobs than it creates" (p. 69).

These technological trends have had the overall effect of carving the middle out of the labour force, and workers have been in greatest demand at either pole. Picot and Myles (1996, p. 17) argue that this "increased polarization of earnings has been among the most significant economic developments of the past two decades." They go on to conclude that the "drop in earnings of young workers is part of a larger story regarding the widening gap between low- and high-wage earners" (p. 17).

Referring to the situation in the United States (which is directly comparable to the situation in Canada, as we see below),[7] Rifkin (1995) predicted a decade ago that this polarization would reshape the class structure into what is in effect a "new bourgeoisie" and "new proletariat." Similarly, Lasch (1995) made the case that 20% of the American adult population constitutes a self-interested élite whose control of the wealth has increased to the point where it represents one half of the entire wealth of the United States. Meanwhile, the size of the middle class (middle earners) has declined in the face of corporate downsizing and government cutbacks. Lasch argues that this new upper middle class élite among the adult population no longer shares a sense of common life and purpose with the "masses," whose economic prospects have dimmed as their share of the wealth has declined over the past several decades. Instead, this adult élite selfishly protects itself—with its wealth—against the new risks of late-modernity (e.g., against poor public education, rising health costs, and crime), and no longer supports public initiatives to minimize these risks (e.g., using their taxes or corporate taxes to finance the social infrastructure of the nation).

Lasch further argues that the loyalties of this group are more global than local, so it is unwilling to support tax dollars going to the common nation-building enterprises that characterized the middle twentieth century. At the same time, this élite 20% of the adult population accumulates wealth from the masses, either through high professional and managerial salaries in delivering services to the masses or through high profit extraction made possible by a lowering of the income of the workers from the "non-élite" 80% mass of the population. When *Critical Youth Studies* speaks of adult interests, it refers primarily to this wealthy 20% of adults—the group in charge of the corporate and political sectors. As we see, many have built their wealth on the backs of the young either through the low pay they give them or through the consumer items they sell them.

An implication of this redistribution of wealth and decline of the middle earner is that successive youth cohorts are going to be sorted accordingly. Consequently, many children of middle-class Baby Boomers face the prospect that not only will they not do as well financially or occupationally as their parents, but that the middle-class lifestyle that emerged during the second half of the twentieth century will be beyond their reach.[8] Indeed, Rifkin argues that most new workers (i.e., young people) will be needed only at the lower end, particularly in the types of service work that are not worth the cost of mechanization, given the available pools of cheap labour. Nightingale and Fix (2004) note this in reference to recent studies conducted by the U.S. Bureau of Labor Statistics:

> Recognizing that there is an increasing demand for high-tech skills . . . it is important to acknowledge that . . . about two-thirds of all jobs today do not require any formal education or experience. . . . The Bureau also projects that two-thirds of all new jobs over the next 10 years will require limited skills and education. (p. 51)

Of the top 20 occupations with the largest projected increase in number of jobs during the first decade of 2000, the U.S. Bureau of Labor Statistics lists "food preparation and serving workers" first. Most of these 20 high-growth occupations are low skilled, with "computer software engineers" listed as ninth, and "postsecondary teachers" as fifteenth (Nightingale & Fix, 2004, p. 51).

As the economy changes and the workforce is reshaped, fewer than 20% of new workers will be needed at the upper end, where considerable expertise is needed to design and maintain the technology, and to manage complex managerial and professional systems. Recruitment into this new élite will be mostly through the higher educational system, which clearly favours the most economically advantaged. Those who cannot afford a university degree (or, more appropriately, degrees) will be effectively locked out. In those cases where university graduates are hired for certain service jobs in spite of being overqualified, the economically disadvantaged young person who might have performed this job in past generations faces a new form of job discrimination ("downward cascading credentialism," Montgomery & Côté, 2003).

These shifts can be seen as part of the age-based redistribution of wealth that has taken place in Canada over the time period during which the transition to adulthood has lengthened (the past half century). For example, Morissette, Zhang, and Drolet (2002) report findings from Statistics Canada's studies of Canadian families showing that, between 1984 and 1999, it was almost entirely among those already in the top 10% of Canada's wealthy families—the adult élite in Canada—who actually increased their wealth (defined as assets minus debts). Most other Canadian families lost wealth over this period, with the most important factor determining this loss being age and education. Those families whose major income earner was 24 or younger experienced a 95% decrease in median wealth (from $3100 in 1984 to almost nothing—$200—in 1999). Those in the 25-to-34 age category lost 36% overall in median wealth, but they lost 48% if the major income earner was "not a university graduate" (p. 18).

The picture becomes clearer when we look at the actual distribution of wealth among all Canadian families. Most people think of the class structure in terms of a bell-shaped "normal curve," which rises from a lower and upper "tail" on either side. With this image, the "middle class" comprises those at the height of the curve, and therefore represents most of the country's wealth. In fact, this is not the case at all. Most of the country's wealth is held by 10% of Canadians in the highest wealth category. Families in this category own 53% of the wealth, and their average wealth is over $1 000 000 per family. If we include the next 10% of Canada's wealthiest with the top 10%, 70% of Canada's wealth is owned by this 20% of the population. In contrast, if we look at the "middle" categories, the third through the eighth deciles (60% of Canadian families), we find only about 30% of Canada's wealth (Kerstetter, 2002).

This information on wealth distribution is presented to open readers' eyes about where to look for the power in this country—especially that influencing government policy. The point is that, when we want to understand major differences among young people in how the transition to adulthood is traversed in terms of financial support and the ability to withstand losses in age-status and requirements for prolonged education, we need to start by looking at the wealth of the family from which the young person comes. In this respect, capital can be seen as a primary structural determinant in Canadian (and American) society.

One final point regarding the (re)distribution of wealth in Canada is with salary adjustments during the 1990s, following the assault on people's wages in the 1980s. The latest Census reports show us what happened (Statistics Canada, 2003b). While "average" Canadian workers gained only about 7% in their inflation-adjusted earnings during the 1990s, the percentage of low earners actually increased by 5%—to just over 40% of Canada's labour force (low-wage earners made $20 000 per year in 2000, which translates to about $10 per hour even when working full-time, full-year). Moreover, 16% of these low earners had university degrees.

At the same time, according to Statistics Canada (2003b, p. 5), "the number of earners in higher income brackets—those earning $80 000 or more a year, and especially those earning $100 000 or more—soared during the 1990s." Later this book will return to the fact that the highest-growth occupations for high earners were "sales, marketing, and advertising managers" (Statistics Canada, 2003b, p. 25). This meant that there was a 70% increase in the number of high earners in Canada at the same time that there was a 5% increase in low earners (as above). Put another way, the 2.4% of Canadians who are "high earners" make $100 000 per year or more, but 41% of Canadians who are "low earners" make $20 000 a year or less (all figures from Statistics Canada, 2003b).

Whatever the future might hold for the economy as a whole, it appears that the competition ratio and technological displacement have dovetailed in the present era and, within the context of corporate restructurings in the quest for high profit margins through cheap labour, have helped to strip the bargaining power of the young worker. As we see next, in spite of being the most educated generation in Canadian history (Davies, Moser, & O'Grady, 1994; Fournier, Butlin, & Giles, 1994; Saunders, 1996), many young workers experience considerable difficulties in even getting a foothold in the workforce, let alone pursuing the types of careers that their educators and parents told them constitute the basis of happiness and success (cf. Bibby & Posterski, 1992, p. 230). As Foot (1996, p. 69) notes, those "unskilled entry-level jobs leading to middle-class security no longer exist. That is why the labour force participation rate for people between 15 and 24 fell to a 19-year low in 1995." In another time and place this would constitute a potentially volatile situation. In Chapters 5 and 6, we will see how governments and their erstwhile allies in the media have endeavoured to diffuse it.

Wages, Participation, and Placement

As noted, it is difficult to find many new "opportunities" for young people as a group when it comes to changes in their role in the workplace. Instead, "challenges" in the transition to adulthood have been mounting for several decades. The new challenges are most readily apparent with respect to declining wages, reduced participation, and job ghettoization.

Wages When the changes in wages over the past several decades are examined, we find a steady and significant redistribution of income by age in Canada. For example, in the late 1960s, males aged 16 to 24 earned incomes that were much closer to those of males over 24 years of age than they are now, depending on the job (cf., Howe & Strauss, 1993, for U.S. figures; see Schuller, 2004, for comparable figures for the United Kingdom).[9] Picot and Myles (1996, p. 17) show that there was less variation in wage levels among the various age groups in Canada in 1969, but since then there has been a steady and linear differentiation among them. By 1993, the 17-to-24 age group was only making about 5% more than it did in 1969, while the oldest age groups were making about 30% more. However, adjusting for inflation, the annual earnings of those in the 17-to-24 age group declined about 19%, while those of the 25-to-34 group fell 10%.

As of 2000, the age-based redistribution of income in Canada has continued, and is highlighted in the 2001 Census reports produced by Statistics Canada (see Table 3.4 for some summary statistics). For example, according to Statistics Canada (2003b, p. 11), a "generational divide in the labour market" emerged during the 1980s and 1990s, which for men splits at the height of the baby boom, "with those younger than 40 experiencing earnings losses, and those over 40, particularly over 50, experiencing gains." This divide can be tracked with figures provided in that Census report (Statistics Canada, 2003b, Table on p. 33, partially reproduced here in Table 3.4). Men aged 25 to 29[10] during the 1980s (who would have been mid- to late-Baby Boomers, born between 1950 and 1965) experienced decreases in earnings ranging from -11.9% for those with less than a high school education to -5.7% for those with a university degree. At the same time, women in this age group also suffered losses, but not to the same extent that men did. During the 1990s, only those Baby Boomers with college or university degrees made earnings gains, while those with high school or less experienced more earnings losses.

This Census report also shows that during the 1990s those aged 25 to 29 (who would have been mainly Baby Busters, or "Gen-Xers," born between 1960 and 1975) experienced decreases in earnings in all educational categories except university degree, ranging from -14.7% for those with less than a high school education to -4.7% for those with a college diploma (Statistics Canada, 2003b, p. 33). Women in this age group suffered losses during the 1990s in all educational categories. This Census report also identifies a "generational divide" for women at age 30, but the modest gains of women over 30 (7-8% over 20 years versus a 10-12% loss for younger women) did not do much to help them catch up with men: Those with university educations still made only 81% of what men made in 2000, while women with high school educations made 77% (Statistics Canada, 2003b, p. 10). Thus, adult women continue to be a source of cheaper labour (profit extraction) for employers and hence can be seen as competitors for the cheaper labour of younger workers. Given the employment equity movement for women (but not youth), women's continuing

TABLE 3.4	Percentage Changes in the Average Earnings of Workers 25–29 Years of Age in the 1980s and 1990s, by Sex and Highest Level of Educational Attainment (inflation adjusted)

Highest level of education	Men			Women		
	1980–1990	1990–2000	Total 2-decade change	1980–1990	1990–2000	Total 2-decade change
Less than high school	-11.9	-6.5	-17.4	-7.0	-5.5	-12.5
High school	-1.6	-14.7	-16.3	-6.3	-4.6	-10.9
Trade school	-10.6	-3.2	-13.8	-7.4	-3.6	-11.0
Community College	-6.9	-4.7	-11.6	-5.0	-7.0	-12.0
University	-5.7	+5.5	-.02	-2.4	-0.6	-3.0

Adapted from: "Change in average earnings of those working full-year, full-time, by highest level of educational attainment, sex, and selected age groups, Canada, 1980-1990 and 1990-2000," from the Statistics Canada publication, *Earnings of Canadians: Making a living in the new economy, 2001 Census*, Catalogue 96F0030, March 11, 2003, p. 33.

lower salaries help to explain why adult women have made the greatest gains in the labour force in terms of participation.

What these, and other analyses show (e.g., Ross, Shillington, & Lochead, 1994; Morissette, Zhang, and Drolet, 2002) is that, contrary to media claims, what has taken place is *not* a simple competition for resources between the so-called "greedy" Baby Boomers and the Generation-Xers who followed them as a cohort. Rather, the redistribution follows different age lines, with economic benefits accruing to the cohorts preceding the Baby Boomers (and to some extent the earliest Baby Boomers, who led the pack and derived the first benefits of the affluence that produced their generation). Contrary to public perception, the early Baby Boom cohort (aged 35 to 44 in 1991) actually suffered losses in the 1980s (Ross & Shillington, 1994; although they recovered some of that in the 1990s, Statistics Canada, 2003b). Moreover, the later Baby Boom cohort (aged 25 to 34 in 1991) suffered even more losses (that were not recovered in the 1990s, Statistics Canada, 2003b). However, both cohorts were not hit as hard as the so-called Gen-X cohort (aged 25 and younger in 1991).

Finally, it is telling that the groups making the bulk of the decisions about wages, benefits, etc. (those 45 and over—the cohorts before Baby Boomers) were the only ones who made gains during this period (Ross & Shillington, 1994). On this issue, Morissette, Myles, and Picot (1993, pp. 12-13) offered the following account, based on internal labour markets theory:

> In the face of downward wage pressures from globalization, older workers are better able to immunize themselves from growing wage competition as a result of seniority rules, firm-specific training and other "institutional" barriers that favour job incumbents over new labour market entrants.

This seemingly endless marshalling of statistics serves to emphasize that there is now little question about whether there was a "real" trend regarding declining youth wages, and making this point requires the use of statistics because mere assertions can be easily dismissed as rhetorical. In reference to the reality of this trend, Morissette, Myles, and Picot (1993, p. 9) noted a decade ago that "the declining earnings of younger workers is the most robust finding in the literature." Moreover, Betcherman and Morissette (1994) showed that youth wages (male and female) dropped "within all educational levels . . . within all major industrial groups . . . and all occupational categories" (p. 8). Accordingly, they concluded that the drop in earnings cannot be attributed simply to the increase in service work taken up by young workers, or to fluctuations in business cycles.

Participation rates Not only are the youngest workers being hardest hit in earnings, but they now participate less in the labour force. According to Lowe (2001), the labour force in Canada grew by about 7% overall between 1990 and 1997, but the youth segment shrunk by some 11%. More striking is the fact that *full-time* employment among 15- to 24-year-olds declined by 27% during that period (Lowe, 2001). More generally, and encompassing the entire 1990s, the participation rate of 15- to 24-year-olds dropped from 70% to 64%, compared with a stable labour force participation rate of about 85% for 25- to 54-year-olds (Human Resources Development Canada, 2000a). In the early 1990s, some 300 000 young Canadians apparently gave up trying to find work—became discouraged workers—so were no longer counted as unemployed (Little, 1995). The group that primarily benefited from labour force changes in the 1990s were adult women who, during the decade, obtained one half of new jobs, even though they constituted just over one third of the labour force (Sunter, 1994). Interestingly, Betcherman and Morissette (1994) argue that the drop in youth participation might have been greater if it were not for the lower wages younger people now make. In other words, their low wages have enhanced their employability in some sectors.

Some argue that the declining participation rate is because young people *choose* to invest in more education rather than taking a job. For example, the authors of a Human Resources Development Canada (2000a) report claimed the following:

> The fall in the overall participation rate of youth can be attributed in large part to the decision of youth to postpone their entry into the labour market and stay in school longer. Thus the main concern is not whether the difficult labour market of the 1990s has damaged the job prospects of this generation of youth. Indeed, given that more educated youth tend to perform better in the labour market than less educated youth do, the prospects for youth are likely to improve if they invest in human capital rather than struggle to make a living in a weak labour market. (p. 17)

This statement is from a government publication and is therefore likely to be influential in shaping government policy. However, it is uninformed on a number of levels, not least of which is the fact (discussed above) that the "college premium" has been at the expense of lower levels of education (Lowe, 2001, refers to this as the "educational premium"). In other words, young people now need a postsecondary education just to "tread water" to hold wage levels from 20 years ago; these higher levels of education have not actually catapulted the graduate beyond those with lower levels of education; instead, those with lower levels have "sunk" in the labour pools.

At another level, the issue of choice is a tricky one because it is unlikely that such choices are unconstrained for most people. Certainly, a number from any generation choose to seek higher education for the sake of it. However, lessons from history suggest that generational-level "choices" are not unconstrained, but rather follow economic trends. For example, Lapsley, Enright, and Serlin (1985) found that, in the first part of the twentieth century, high school enrolments were inversely proportionate to the access that young people had to jobs. When more jobs were available to them, fewer enrolled in high schools.

We can also give this issue some common-sense tests. A quick examination of the figures in Table 3.1 shows that the current generation faces circumstances far different from those faced by previous generations, including their parents' generation. Apparently, many are now "choosing" to pursue higher education, while previous generations did not. Why?

First, consider the conditions experienced by those in the early Baby Boom cohort when they were coming of age in the 1961-to-1971 period (these are the parents of many in the current 15-to-19 age cohort and most of those in the 20-to-24 age cohort). Only two thirds of 15- to 19-year-olds were in school (mainly high school), and only a handful of those in their early twenties were in school full-time (about 1 in 10 males and 1 in 20 females), in spite of the generous financial incentives available at that time to attend university. The most important point to be emphasized here is that those who were not interested in staying in school generally simply left (voluntarily, or were expelled). And, in contrast to the current generation, those who left could generally find employment paying a wage that would at the least have kept them out of poverty and at the most have allowed them to achieve financial independence from their parents. In addition, this employment was more likely to be the bottom rung of a career ladder. Today, as noted above, starting at the bottom is far less likely to lead up a job ladder; increasingly, education credentials (including multiple postsecondary degrees and certificates) determine career progress.

This last point is crucial to current arguments that more young people are now going to university because they "choose" to. While this is undoubtedly true for a good number of students, many more students would prefer to take secure, well-paying jobs if they were available. Given the choice between having a good job now and getting on with their lives versus postponing their adulthood to go to school year after year accumulating debts, with no guarantee of a secure future, most would make the sensible decision of taking the good job at hand. These were the choices available to Baby Boomers, and only a small minority chose to postpone things for the sake of a higher education. For those who believe that pursuing a higher education is a "pure choice" option, their challenge is to explain why this "choice" was not as common in previous generations.

The authors regularly ask their classes how many would rather be working at a decent job than going to school (with the hopes of a decent job in the future). Among those who have considered this point, many say that they would take a job now without hesitation and that they resent having to jump educational hoops year after year, accumulating high debt loads or balancing work and school, knowing that they will only qualify for entry-level jobs with a BA. A surprising number of their students have unreflectively continued their educations because of the pressures to do so; consequently when the question is posed, it is the first time they have considered the issue of what they would do if they had an unconstrained choice.

One trend that *is* alarming policy-makers is the growing number of young people who are neither in school nor registered in the labour force—some 10% of those aged 15 to 19 (Human Resources Development Canada, 2000a). One explanation for this is the decreasing utility of lower levels of education. This is a direct consequence of the credentialism paradox discussed above. In this case, those with higher levels of education are taking lower-skilled jobs that used to be performed by those with lower skills. This leaves those with lower skills with fewer job opportunities. While this "downward cascading effect" (Montgomery & Côté, 2003) is indeed a concern, the common functionalist interpretation of the overall youth employment situation is overly sanguine when the entire education-to-work situation is taken into account (as above), especially the credentialism paradox.

To return to the quote from Human Resources Development Canada, 2000a, there are further problems with such statements, which are commonly repeated by journalists, academics, and policy-makers who seem to prefer conservative interpretations of societal trends. Not only is it clear that they are not aware of the nature of "choice," as previously discussed, and the credentialism paradox, but the logic of the "if they could only get more education" recommendation is flawed. We have only to consider the following to see this: (a) Not everyone has the mental ability to earn higher degrees; (b) there is not enough room in our colleges and universities to process all young people, even if they had the ability; and, (c) there are not enough highly skilled jobs for those who would successfully complete higher educations. Further to this last point, given that only 16% of jobs currently require university degrees (Statistics Canada, 2003e, p. 7) and more degrees will not create a proportionate number of jobs (Livingstone, 1998), as the underemployment statistics reviewed above show, we are simply telling young people to keep spending great amounts of time, effort, and money in pursuit of something with dubious economic benefits. This is a clear example of how a functionalist interpretation of economic trends is limited, and how blanket "macro" recommendations based on a limited consideration of a complex set of factors are ill-advised.

Another trend that goes against the idea that young people would rather "stay in school" than "get a job" is the steep rise in involuntary part-time employment over the last 30 years. The ratio of part-time to full-time employment rose from just over 20% in the mid-1970s to about 45% in the late 1990s. Of course, many of those going to school full-time might want or need a part-time job (although 6% of full-time university students also now have a full-time job, up from 4% twenty years ago; CAUT, 2004, p. 36), but it appears that it was among those not in school that the ratio of part-time to full-time increased, almost doubling in the 1990s. And, among those not attending school full-time, "more than half are working part-time involuntarily" (Human Resources Development Canada, 2000a, p. 19). This gives us an estimate of underemployment among the general youth labour force of around 50%, slightly higher than that of college and university graduates.

One other factor to be considered here is youth unemployment, which generally runs about two to three times that of the adult workforce. During the 1990s, for example, the unemployment rate for 15- to 24-year-olds ran at about 15%, while the rate for those between 25 and 54 ranged between 6% and 10% (Human Resources Development Canada, 2000a); during the 2000–2003 period, the youth rate lowered slightly, while the adult rate hovered consistently around 6.0% (Statistics Canada, 2004b). Moreover, the youth labour market is vulnerable to changes in the economy, mainly because of the nature of the jobs held by young people (i.e., low-level service jobs with little job security that are sensitive to consumer spending ability). What is telling, though, is that the shrinkage of the youth labour pool (with young people either going into higher levels of education or dropping out entirely as discouraged workers) should have restricted the supply of young workers and lowered the unemployment rate. However, unemployment actually rose, "suggesting that the decline in demand for youth during the 1990s exceeded the decline in supply that accompanied lower participation" (Human Resources Development Canada, 2000a, p. 20). This goes directly against the idea that young people return or continue their education independent of their opportunities in the labour market. In fact, it suggests that the increased proportion of those seeking higher education *plus* the involuntary part-time worker *plus* the unemployed provides us with an estimate of the decreased demand for youth labour, at the same time showing how young people have responded to that decreased demand.[11]

Job Ghettoization Studies show that on average young workers are not only paid less, and participate in the workforce less, but they are becoming less well-represented in all job categories, except consumer services. Indeed, it is in the subordinate service occupations that their cheap labour is most in demand. During the 1980s, the proportion of jobs held by young workers (16 to 24) that were in the service sector rose from 69.7% to 75.8%, while in the goods sector it dropped from 30.3% to 24.2% (Betcherman & Morissette, 1994). The two most common service sector jobs held in 1989 were retail trade (22.7%), and accommodation and food (13.7%). These authors note "the substantial absolute decline of youth employment in the goods sector and in public administration, health, social services, and education" and they conclude that for "earlier generations of young people, these industries typically offered good entry-level opportunities" (1994, p. 3). When broken down by gender, over 84% of females aged 15 to 19 worked in the service sector, compared with about 60% of their male counterparts (Statistics Canada, 1994, p. 21). These trends did not reverse in the 1990s.

From a critical perspective, this reorganization of the labour force, and the redistribution of wealth that has followed, was not merely the result of certain isolated individuals feathering their own nests, or the nests of their age-mates. Indeed, many of the policy adjustments undertaken by the Canadian government have made it a key mediator between the interests of adult-controlled Capital and youth wage-labour. One key policy pertains to the setting of minimum wage levels. In the mid-1970s, minimum wage would have put one about 40% *above* the official poverty line; it now puts one 30% *below* that line (see Schlosser, 2001, for comparable figures from the United States). Moreover, two thirds of minimum wage earners are under 24 years of age (Hess, 1991). In this example, government policies endorsed by the Canadian electorate have clearly contributed to age-based discrimination, with the interests of the adult élite of professionals, managers, and owners, as previously discussed, clearly getting preference over youth wage-labour interests. Few people seem to be aware of the role that the State has played in mediating the interests of this élite in this regard, and many of those who are aware seem to see nothing wrong with it. Had young people taken part in this decision-making process, it is doubtful that things would have worked out this way for young workers.

CONCLUSION: THE DISENFRANCHISEMENT OF YOUTH

When the statistical evidence presented above is evaluated with the theoretical perspectives discussed in Chapter 2, it becomes apparent that the political-economy perspective most completely accounts for recent changes in the circumstances confronting young people. Clearly, each social scientific theory examined in Chapter 2 is useful for understanding some aspect of the youth experience, but the political-economy approach provides the most comprehensive explanation of the changing prospects of the young, particularly their declining fortunes against the increasing fortunes of older age groups, especially those in the élite 10-20% of adults who own most of the wealth and who control business and government. Indeed, the data examined above pertaining to wages, wealth, unemployment, and underemployment consistently point to an increasingly prolonged sequestering in the education system as well as an increasing segregation of young people in exploited sectors of the workplace. With the young thus positioned, a redistribution of wealth has taken place, with age serving as a primary axis. Thus, there is strong support for the political-economy position that, in advanced industrial societies like Canada, the young have been increasingly used as a surplus army of cheap labour, a role justified by their lost status and independence. With this source of cheap labour, prices in certain sectors of the economy have been driven down, and corporate profits have risen, as have the salaries of the élite of adults at the highest end of the salary scale, especially in sales, advertising, and marketing.

This redistribution of wealth can be seen as part of a behind-the-scenes power shift, of which many people are unaware. This power shift has been possible because the younger age groups have been unrepresented, while those in the oldest age groups have made most of the decisions affecting how corporations are structured, how many jobs to export to sweatshops in developing countries, where to set the minimum wage rate, and what to pay workers from different "identity groups" (young vs. adult, male vs. female, White vs. non-White, etc.). Many of the decisions have heavily favoured the personal fortunes of those of older age groups, even those not directly involved in making the decisions. The cumulative weight of these decisions, encouraged by prejudices regarding the nature of youth (discussed above), has created a legitimacy regarding the exploitation of the young, so that few question its prevalence. Consequently, those running businesses and corporations have found an increasingly cheap supply of labour, and they have taken full advantage of it.

As is often the case, the least desirable jobs go to those with the least power in a society, in part because there is less protest regarding this practice. While the dimensions of power have long been thought of along the lines of race, gender, and class, the evidence, as previously reviewed, indicates that *age* is an increasingly important indicator of power and therefore economic and social franchise.

It is also the case that, once a job category becomes predominantly associated with low status people, the pay drops along with associated benefits and security. Businesses and corporations have both played a role in, and capitalized on, the diminishing social status of young people by restructuring jobs and reducing salaries. The best example of this is with fast-food chain restaurants (Schlosser, 2000; Tannock, 2001). Now, when looking for work, young people often have no choice but to take such jobs, which are usually at or below minimum wage, part-time, with few benefits, and with little opportunity for career advancement. It is part of discrimination against the young that these practices are seen to be "normal" and "just," even by many of those who say they speak for equal opportunities for all groups in society. When ethnic groups or women are the targets of occupational ghettoization, the unfairness of the practice is much more likely to gain public and academic attention.

Finally, many people balk at the critical perspectives like the political-economy view, finding them too "conspiratorial." In fact, it is now common to dismiss social criticism as "conspiracy theory" because the actual agents making decisions that create social and economic changes are not identified. After the publication of *Generation on Hold*, journalists suggested that it evoked the image of a cabal of evil men who were meeting regularly to conspire against the young. Of course, no such claim was made, nor was any such image intended. Instead, the object was to show readers how the countless decisions made every day in contemporary societies around the world *tend* to be motivated by self-interest (see Bailey & Gayle, 2003, for distinctions among structural theory, self-interest theory, and conspiracy theory). When applied to the boardrooms of corporations, the caucuses of ruling political parties, the meetings of trade organizations, and so forth, it is easier to understand how the changes that increasingly affected the young could have taken place over the span of the past several decades.

The explanation for why it is implausible, indeed unnecessary, to theorize that youth disenfranchisement was orchestrated by a cabal of consciously conspiring adults is simple, and the logic follows from the evidence presented in this chapter as well as a basic knowledge of how capitalism works. Simply stated, in laissez-faire capitalist societies, there is an overall tendency for those with wealth and power to try to keep and increase them, while those without them try to get them, and there are few formal or moral constraints on these practices (cf. Bakan, 2004). This is not absolute and there are many exceptions, but there are enough people who are so motivated to have an effect on the changes that take place in the economy, and therefore in the society and culture. Moreover, those with wealth and power often have conflicting interests (e.g., those whose wealth depends on imports versus those whose wealth depends on exports), and in many instances, their self-interests cancel each other out. However, on certain matters, they have similar interests, especially in extracting profit from the labour of their employees. And the lower the wages of their workers, the more profit they can extract.

This status quo of unregulated economic wrangling means that certain people or groups in a society will inevitably receive lower wages, just as others will accrue great profits. This is exactly what was noted previously in the redistribution of wealth that has taken place in Canada. Just who receives these low wages depends on the bargaining power of specific people and groups, and those with the lowest status in a society will be more pressured to accept them. Historically, minorities and women have been the groups whose lower wages reflect their lower status. However, this has become less acceptable and anti-discrimination laws and affirmative action practices have reduced, but not eliminated, wage discrimination against them. As the youth segment of Canadian society progressively lost status since that time, it emerged as a group that potentially could be offered lower wages. And, as their status declined over the last few decades, more and more young people had no choice but to accept low wages, which contributes to a greater lowering of their status, in a cycle of progressive iterations.

Thus, corporations and their CEOs have not really conspired against young people (although their consistent efforts to keep them as a source of cheap labour are well documented by Schlosser, 2001, as discussed in Chapter 5) so much as they have taken advantage of their diminished status to use them as a reserve army of cheap labour to be hired and fired at will. They do not likely do this out of maliciousness, but rather because it is an essential characteristic of the modern corporation to do what it takes to maximize profits (Bakan, 2004). In fact, the survival of corporate entities is contingent on their ability to give the highest possible dividend to their stockholders, to keep their profits high and expenses low so that people will invest in them, and to make sure the value of their stocks is as high as possible.

Given the necessity of profit maximization in a climate of low government controls or no expectations for social responsibility (i.e., neo-liberalism), it should come as no surprise that corporations would lobby governments to keep the minimum wage low, as well as to reduce corporate taxes, the latter of which have dropped substantially over the past few decades in both Canada and the United States (Klein, 2000). Is this the result of conspiracy or business as usual? In a neo-liberal economic climate, what is the difference?

Moreover, it is perfectly rational for businesses, in this economic climate, to hire the cheapest labour possible by looking to those with least power in the society for their lower-level employees (in spite of the rhetoric about our skilled labour-force demands, most jobs still only require basic literacy and a few weeks of on-the-job training; Berg, 1970; Nightingale & Fix, 2004). As noted, corporations previously depended on women and minorities for their cheapest labour. But to the extent that governments have defended the rights of women and minorities, the youth segment stands as a logical alternative because there are few regulations prohibiting their exploitation, and it is still politically correct to hold negative stereotypes about them (dating back to the storm-and-stress myth). As a result of several decades of this treatment and declining status, the youth segment of the workforce now constitutes one of the most economically disadvantaged groups of the entire population. The remainder of this book is about the consequences of this disenfranchisement and what we might do about it.

ENDNOTES

1. Discouraged workers are those who stop looking for work altogether and therefore do not show up in the official statistics (e.g., Akyeampong, 1992). When the number of discouraged workers is added to the number of officially unemployed, the resulting unemployment rate can be about 50% to 100% higher than the official one, depending on how it is calculated (Côté & Allahar, 1994). Because many young people find their work opportunities so limited, they have gone into higher educational institutions hoping to increase their chances for better-paying and higher-level jobs. Accordingly, the estimation of the number of discouraged young workers would be much higher if they were included. However, most models assume that people go into educational systems voluntarily; as we argue below, this is now a dubious assumption for a significant proportion of young people.

2. In the early 1900s, about 15% of the paid labour force was made up of women (Denton, 1970), who were largely young and unmarried (Synge, 1979).

3. Statistics Canada, CANSIM, Employment by industry, table 282-0008 and Catalogue no. 71F0004XCB, last modified 2004-03-11, retrieved 2004-04-03.

4. In 1994, Statistics Canada predicted that "almost two-thirds of new jobs between 1991 and 2000 will require at least 13 years of education or training and 45% will require more than 16 years" (1994, p. 22). This appears to have been somewhat of an overestimation (Statistics Canada, 2003e), but it is more telling to look at the way jobs are currently distributed: Only 16% of jobs currently require a university degree, up from only 13% in 1991, and only 30% require community college or apprenticeship, down from 33% in 1991. Accordingly, only about 46% of jobs in the Canadian labour force require higher education, and a full 43% require just high school or less, down from only 45% in 1991 (Statistics Canada, 2003e).

5. Evidence of a sleeper effect for humanities and social science graduates was reported by Giles and Drewes (2001) who concluded that "in comparison with applied-program graduates, those graduating from programs in the humanities and social sciences had considerably more difficulty with the school-to-work transition. . . . But once that transition was made, the generic nature of the skills they acquired appeared to stand them in good stead—because of these skills they have a greater longevity and . . . [aptitude for] continued lifelong learning in the face of labour market changes." (p. 33)

6. According to Halperin (1998), in the United States, children from families among the top 25% (quartile) of earners are 10 times more likely to earn a college degree than are those from the bottom 25% of families. Figures from Canada indicate that income is not such a deterrent for participating in higher education. According to Zhao and de Broucker (2001), children from high income families are only 2.5 times as likely to participate in university (not necessarily getting a degree, though) than those from low income families. This gap apparently narrowed by the late 1990s, with the participation rate of those in the lowest income quartile rising to 19% (vs. 40% for those in the highest quartile), up from 10% in the early 1980s (Corak & Zhao, 2003). In terms of parents' education, young Canadians are more than twice as likely to go to university if their parents did so, than if they simply completed high school, and three to four times as likely than if their parents did not complete high school (Finnie, Lascelles, & Sweetman, 2005; this is controlling for other factors like parental and student attitudes toward education, urban/rural residence, etc.).

7. Echoing Rifkin in reference to Canada, Picot and Myles (1996, p. 17) argue that this "increased polarization of earnings has been among the most significant economic developments of the past two decades." See also Morissette, Myles, and Picot (1993) and Myles, Picot, and Wannell (1988).

8. According to Schoeni and Ross (2005), parents in the United States contribute on average $2200 per year to their children between the ages of 17 and 34, a significant increase over the past few decades. The total support for this period ranges from about $23 000 for young people from the lowest parental income quartile to over $70 000 for those from the highest quartile.

9. Using figures from *The Statistical Abstract of the United States*, which is an annual digest of population and economic statistics, in 1970, young male workers (16 to 24) made 70% of the median weekly income of older male workers (25 and over). Over the next 30 years, this gap increased steadily. By 2000, the ratio was 53%, meaning that young male workers now make about one half that of older male workers (cf. U.S. Census Bureau, 1981, p. 407, with U.S. Census Bureau, 2001, p. 403). At the same time, young females went from making 92% of the earnings of older females in 1970 to 66% in 2000. The net result of this was a "gender convergence" in wages among young workers, with young women making 91% that of young males in 2000, up from 78% in 1970. However, some of this convergence is due to the fact that the earnings of young males were the slowest to grow over those three decades (by 330%, in current dollars, not adjusted for inflation), while those of young females grew by 440%. Women over 25 made the greatest relative gain over this period, with earnings increasing by 540% in current dollars (i.e., not adjusted for inflation), but they still made only 74% of what men over 25 made, up from 60% in 1970.

10. The age range 25 to 29 is used to reflect the fact that it is only in this age period that there is a sufficient percentage of young people out of school and in stable employment.

11. Worldwide, young people make up 47% of the unemployed, but only 25% of workers. Depending on the country, the youth unemployment rate runs from about twice to six times that of the adult labour market. Around the world, the youth unemployment rate increased on average by 23% from 1993 to 2003, while in some regions it almost doubled (International Labour Office, 2004).

chapter four

The Conquest of Youth: Survival of the Fittest in a Corporate Culture

INTRODUCTION

When viewed historically and across the range of human cultures, the way in which the transition to adulthood is structured often depends on the needs and affluence of the culture in question. For example, if a culture needs the labour contribution of all its members, people will tend to be recruited directly from childhood to adulthood, so there will be little or no period akin to what we call adolescence in modern Western societies (Brown, Larson, & Saraswathi, 2002). Such cultures generally use the labour of children, and simply increase the labour requirement after puberty, in part because puberty is associated with increasing physical capacity. To hasten this process, cultures in need of the productive contributions of their young members typically use puberty rites or other rites of passage to quickly confer adult statuses. Moreover, because of the clear definition of roles in these cultures, the transition to adult roles can be relatively unproblematic, and the stresses that can accompany modern, Western adolescence and youth are usually absent (e.g., Mead, 1928, 1970; Condon, 1987).

The way in which the transition to adulthood is structured also depends on the stability and coherence of a given culture (Mead, 1970). If a culture is going through rapid changes that create social instabilities, ambivalences toward the young can develop. This can be especially the case if the identities of adult members are themselves ambiguous; when confused about themselves, adults are less able to help their young learn to know themselves. In other words, if what it means to be an adult in a culture is uncertain, adults are less able to help their young develop adult identities. Consequently, adults are more likely to feel threatened by the young, and to be less welcoming of the young into adult society. In turn, young people will more likely see the adult world in disarray and be less likely to value it or see reasons to move toward it (this was referred to as the "generation gap" by Margaret Mead, 1970). Thus, when a culture lacks coherence in values, it will likely have fewer mechanisms to guide the young, and may precipitate widespread crises among the young who find themselves in a limbo between the immaturity of childhood and the maturity ostensibly found in adulthood.

Similarly, the transition to adulthood is influenced by the cultural definition of what it means to "come of age," and this definition can depend on the ethos of the culture along a collectivist-individualist dimension. On one hand, if the cultural ethos is predominantly one of an individualist "survival of the fittest," the young will tend to be judged in terms of having to "stand alone" (cf. Arnett, 2002). In societies informed by such cultural values, adults who are self-interested will tend to be more rejecting of the young, and less sympathetic to their plight. On the other hand, collectivist societies will tend to be more supportive of the needs of the young in exchange for their agreement to participate in the society in ways defined by adults. In turn, adults will tend to be more welcoming of the young into the central spheres of production and power, and more willing to address the hardships in getting there. In more collectivist cultures, values like caring and sharing will be broadly applied to all types of youth.

At the same time, some societies may be in a continual state of "crisis," in the sense of being unstable, the result of a culmination of factors. As previously noted, contemporary Western societies are commonly referred to as "late modern" by sociologists who examine the ways in which the institutions of traditional Western culture have become destructured and fragmented. In late-modern societies, many people may have little guidance from their families of origin or an organized religion when dealing with fragmented transitions between institutional contexts like educational institutions and the workplace (Côté, 2000). Correspondingly, in comparison with traditional societies, it is more common for those who live in late-modern societies to be confronted with conflicting or inadequate life-transition options in the context of the requirement to individualize their life plans. Characterized in this way, it is often argued that there is a crisis of meaning in the West that afflicts the young and old alike. However, among Western societies, there are notable differences in the societal responses to this crisis, especially in terms of the survival-of-the-fittest mentality that can govern the political response to the difficulties that the young face in making the transition to adulthood.

In short, cultures vary in their general dispositions toward those making the transition from childhood to adulthood. As we will see later in this book, these dispositions can vary within a culture according to certain ascribed social identities of the young associated with social class, race, gender, sexuality, and the like. Cultures can establish practices that are welcoming, guiding, and accepting, or they can treat segments of the youth population in ways that are hostile, rejecting, and stigmatizing—imprisoning a significant proportion of the young or leaving them to fend for themselves. This can even happen within institutions like schools, where great variation can be found in how students are treated. Schools that are welcoming and guiding help new members learn how and where they might fit in by developing their sense of competence and social participation; in so doing they also help the young develop a sense of purpose, direction, and meaning in life. In this sense, the transition to adulthood can be seen as a "pulse" of a society—how the young are treated tells us much about a society. Societies in crisis themselves, or in which leading adult members are highly self-interested, are more likely to produce young people who are confused about themselves and how they should plan their life courses.

The final chapter examines national differences in this survival-of-the-fittest mentality taken toward the young, especially in comparing Canada, the United States, and the United Kingdom with Sweden in terms of how specific segments of adult society have become predatorial toward, rather than protective of, the young. This chapter illustrates some of the ways in which the self-interested corporate sector of adult society in North America has become aggressively manipulative of the young, especially in terms of taking advantage of unmet needs for secure identities.

THE INDIVIDUALIZATION OF IDENTITIES: FREEDOM OR OBSTACLE?

Individualism is currently highly valued in Western societies. However, the collectivism of earlier Western societies that predate the modern era of capitalism is often forgotten, with many people now assuming that Westerners were always as individualistic as is now the case (e.g., Mumford, 1944). Moreover, the nature of individualism itself is not well understood by many people, and individualism carries with it certain liabilities that are often obscured by ideologies that promote unrestrained self-interested behaviours.

Take for example the "posttraditional" requirement to engage in self-socialization discussed in Chapter 2. This requirement to individualize their identities clearly presents potential benefits to young people, but it also presents them with potential pitfalls. While it provides more freedom from traditional normative constraints (like restrictive norms concerning sexual orientation), it does little to help people overcome the economic obstacles associated with the "new economy" and "old" social class, which were described in detail in the previous chapter. So that this approach to Critical Youth Studies is not misunderstood, it must be stressed that individualization involves *freedoms from* normative constraints, not *freedoms to* pursue activities independent of systemic barriers like racial and gender discrimination and social class disadvantage. Moreover, the freedom to individualize has emerged because of *a lack of structure*, which can create serious challenges for some people, whereas persisting social stratification along class, race, and gender lines presents *too much unwanted structure* for those placed at a disadvantage because of those structures.

Moreover, not all opportunities are the same, and not all choices made in the context of new freedoms are good ones or in one's best interest over the long term. As noted in Chapter 2, in the context of freedom without guidance (the absence of normative structure), people can exercise the choice to pursue a lifestyle totally devoid of traditional social markers, with or without exerting much mental effort. This can be done by simply selecting a number of "default options" now available in popular culture, as in the imitation of the latest fashion and music trends. This involves following the paths of least resistance and effort. Alternatively, people can now pursue life courses based on extensive and agentic deliberations of the alternatives and opportunities now available in pursuit of stimulating and liberating possibilities (cf. Anisef & Axelrod, 2001; Evans, 2002).

On the surface, then, this new-found freedom of choice can be taken as a positive development, with late-modern societies ostensibly giving young people greater amounts of freedom and self-determination. However, as discussed in Chapter 2, when we examine the ideology of free choice, we often find an absence of guiding structures and norms—a situation of relative anomie that can present serious challenges to some people. Without guiding structures to give meaning to the choices people face, continual decision-making becomes burdensome for many people, young and old alike. This may be especially critical for those who may not have the personal wherewithal to chart their own life course, especially those from disadvantaged backgrounds, those with mental challenges, and so forth.

The mistaken belief in unbridled freedom can also be a problem of double jeopardy for those facing systemic barriers, because the ideology of free choice concerning things like education and consumption can obscure many of the old barriers that keep people of lower economic origins and minority groups from actually making certain choices (Furlong & Cartmel, 1997, refer to this as the "epistemological fallacy"). Similarly, Schwartz (2000, 2004a, 2004b) argues that Western societies now present people with a tyranny of "freedom and choice" that actually decreases their quality of life and, to some extent, diminishes their life chances. Even choices that are attainable in principle can be so complex and uncertain that they can create problems for some people. This is the case because the information and training needed to make many realistic and correct choices can be extensive, so the probability of making a wrong or regrettable choice is greater in these instances.

For example, to pick up on the educational theme developed in the previous chapter, many young Canadians seek higher educations in the hopes that these credentials will eventually lead to rewarding careers, yet most apparently have little idea what that career will be or even whether they will be suited for it. Research shows that about 90% of students in the first year of secondary school expect to go on to a postsecondary education, while only 0.1% expects not to finish secondary school. The apparent reality is that 10-20% will drop out of secondary school at some point, and fewer than half will complete some form of higher education (Bowlby & McMullen, 2002). Something is dreadfully wrong therefore in the relationship between the beliefs students adopt as a basis for future choice-making and the realities they face. As a result of this mismatch of choice-making and reality, over half of young people drift into the labour market largely unskilled and without having made realistic choices about where they are going. Among the more fortunate half who go on to higher education, as we saw in Chapter 3, more than half either drop out or take up jobs that do not require higher credentials. As we also saw, the reality is that only 16% of jobs in the Canadian economy require university credentials (Statistics Canada, 2003e, p. 7). If students in the early years of secondary school knew this, they might make different, and more meaningful, decisions about how to invest their time in education and learning (cf. Schuller, Hammond, & Preston, 2004, concerning a similar situation in the United Kingdom).

The consequences of this poor guidance in relation to decision-making is evident when we consider the situation regarding the acquisition of skills related to the trades. Driven by a middle-class bias that only white-collar jobs are the mark of success, skilled blue-collar occupations can find it difficult to recruit new members from young people, and the ratio of younger to older trades workers is declining in Canada. Astonishingly, the average age of entering an apprenticeship program in Canada is 27 (Human Resources Development Canada, 2000b), whereas in countries like Germany apprenticeships are integrated with secondary education. The unfortunate consequences of this misplaced obsession with middle-class symbols of success range from long periods of marginal employment and unemployment for many young people to skills shortages for the society. What some people who advocate the middle-class model of career success do not realize is that many of the skilled trades jobs pay much more than lower- and middle-level white-collar jobs, so the young people who have been misdirected away from the skilled trades are also being directed away from more direct and earlier trajectories to financial independence.[1]

When viewed in these more critical terms, it would appear urgent that the potential risks and liabilities associated with the current transition to adulthood be better understood in terms of recent societal changes. For example, most of the Canadian youth population now undertakes a transition that is far more prolonged than even 50 years ago, with about eight times as many now using the higher educational route during their early twenties (see Table 3.1). This means that those who went to university and college 50 years ago were more likely to have chosen to do so from a variety of alternatives. In making the choice to undertake a higher education, they would have been "pulled" into a prolonged transition to adulthood because of the intrinsic gratifications associated with higher learning.

Now, the reasons for undertaking a prolonged route to adulthood via the higher educational route are much less varied because it has become the "bottleneck route" to most non-manual jobs, especially lower-level white-collar jobs that were performed by high-school graduates a generation ago. Consequently, far more people are being "pushed" into higher educational programs for extrinsic reasons—to qualify for white-collar jobs. For many in the middle class, university attendance has now become a sort of rite of passage, with most parents simply assuming that their children will attend, even if the parents did not do so themselves. The difference from a generation ago is that many with university credentials now only qualify for lower-level white-collar positions whose job titles have been changed to add prestige to the jobs, but there has been little actual change in the skill level required for them, except perhaps a computer literacy that is now commonplace regardless of education. For example, many sales staff are now called "customer service representatives" or "associates," and secretaries called "administrative officers." In turn, among the working class, there are fewer alternatives to community college as a means of moving directly into the workforce, and although some may initially try to avoid college, several years of minimum-wage jobs appear to be an incentive for eventually attending college or undertaking an apprenticeship (cf. Human Resources Development Canada, 2000b).

In other words, previous generations were more likely *pulled* into higher education and responded to its intrinsic qualities more as a matter of free choice; now, young people are more likely to be *pushed* into this prolonged transition, because the alternative choices are not desirable. If one is forced into an undesirable choice, this is not an example of "free choice." When viewed in this way, it seems that young people are now *less free* and *less self-determining*, when it comes to educational options, than the generations that came of age in the twentieth century. As a consequence of these trends, contemporary university students tend to be more extrinsically motivated: more grade-oriented in school and more financially concerned in terms of career choices (Cooperative Institutional Research Program [CIRP], 2004). This, in turn, can create problems in gaining a sense of intrinsic meaning in their life courses as a result of their educational experiences (e.g., see Levine & Cureton, 1998, for evidence that the values "being well off financially" and "developing a meaningful life philosophy" have traded places as top priorities since the 1960s).

In light of the above, the supposedly high degree of freedom and choice now granted the young of late-modern societies should have rather predictable positive and negative consequences. The benefits of a loosely structured, prolonged choice-oriented transition should include accelerated cognitive, emotional, and identity development if an individual makes propitious choices in relation to the opportunities available. However, the liabilities of loosely structured transitions can also include living with the consequences of poor educational guidance, as in the case where young people are encouraged to earn devalued or even useless educational credentials that can lead to dead-end jobs or no jobs at all (cf. EGRIS, 2001).

But even these misdirected young people may be better off than many in the "forgotten half" who are falling further and further behind those with postsecondary educations in terms of jobs and earning prospects (Halperin, 1998). The liabilities can also include having to make choices among what appear to be opportunities for growth and development, but for which the person is ill-equipped to make. The lack of preparation may be because of inadequate information or emotional immaturity—both of which can be paradoxically associated with the lack of experience produced by the delay in assuming adult responsibilities (i.e., some maturational tasks may now be simply postponed from adolescence to emerging adulthood).

At the same time, those with intellectual and psychiatric challenges face increasing difficulties in individualizing or self-socialization because of their greater need for benign and caring settings, without which even day-to-day functioning can be burdensome. Last, but not least, liabilities can include the squandering of prospects if the prolonged transition is devoted mainly to hedonistic activities and immediate gratifications not associated with occupational identity development or other forms of self-improvement (Côté, 2000).

YOUTH AS A MORATORIUM PERIOD

It is a popular notion in the social sciences to view adolescence, and more recently emerging adulthood, as constituting a "moratorium" of identity, or permissible delay of adulthood, during which young people can take the time to explore and "find" themselves (Arnett, 2000). This notion stems from the work of Erik Erikson (1963, 1968), the first social scientist to write in the area of "youth and identity." This "time-out" is a result of a societal permission for people to explore their vocational and personal potentials. If used in this way, the identity moratorium can provide tremendous opportunities for the exercise of agency through self-discovery and the development of special competencies. In theory, opportunities are provided to experiment with roles, ideas, beliefs, and lifestyles; this experimentation can set the individual on a life course that is rich and rewarding; and individuals can undo old psychological problems and start life afresh (e.g., Côté & Levine, 1987).

While these things can and do happen among the more fortunate and/or privileged, in reality many people get lost, sidetracked, and confused in their identity moratorium. Consequently, for some young people, this can be the most destructive or "wasted" period of their lives. This is the case particularly for those who cannot use the moratorium for identity exploration, because of the limited economic and social prospects in their lives. Clearly, many young people from racial and ethnic minorities and the "lower classes" often cannot afford the "luxury" of elaborate forms of self-exploration, such as world travel or trying different schools and academic majors. Instead, their identity moratorium can provide neither opportunity nor guidance, especially if it takes place in the same neighbourhood or community in which the person was raised as a child and will live as an adult.

Still, some people are able to "make" their own moratorium and to benefit from it, in spite of economic or social disadvantage. For example, backpacking has been a time-honoured moratorium (e.g., Erikson himself did it in the 1920s). Travel experiences can range from completely unstructured *Wanderschaft* to well-planned trips. Either way, the places visited and the way the travelling is done can reflect the individual's need to explore him- or herself, to test and develop capacities, and to put him- or herself through an initiation lacking in mainstream society. Moreover, removing oneself from all familiar social supports and stressors can give one a much better sense of how one really feels about things deep inside. This can be a valuable antidote for a life that has become dictated by superficial pushes and pulls and in which the person has lost a sense of meaning and purpose.

Other people have a very difficult time with this moratorium, particularly when they are unsupported in their need to explore themselves, or when they actually do not realize there may be a need to explore and develop themselves. Such people often drift and/or remain stagnant, regressing or developing mechanisms that shut the world out, along with any chance for personal growth. Some of these people fit well into those pockets of adult society filled with adults who did the same thing. Those who cannot make their own moratorium or fit into these enclaves will have a difficult time, and may turn to the more extreme forms of youth subculture. Indeed, for many, these subcultures constitute a form of moratorium, if only based on a negation of their parents' values. At the same time, it appears that the experiences in these subcultures can foster identity development and some people may eventually "grow" out of it.[2] For others, these subcultures become a permanent lifestyle or even a death trap, as in the case of heavy drug use or hazardous street gang involvements.

Despite the lack of research into the problems facing young people who opt out or who are pushed out of the educational system—the forgotten half—it appears that their life chances are seriously reduced during this period. For example, in the United States, the deteriorated economic situation for this segment of young people is associated with the doubling of the incarceration rate of emerging adult males from the 1980s to the 1990s. Currently, 10% of American males in their twenties are involved in the criminal justice system, on probation, in jail, or on parole (Halperin, 1998), a figure that rises to 40% for African-American males of this age (Howe & Strauss, 1993). In fact, African-American men have a greater chance of going to prison than to college.

As noted in Chapter 3, because of the credentialism dictating entry into most jobs of even moderate prestige and remuneration, those without the required credentials are essentially locked out of career tracks. There is still some room for mobility in certain businesses that hire by the old code of rising from the shop floor, but such opportunities are rare today. Dropping out of school and then trying to do well do not mix, unless one comes from a wealthy family, or can work in the family business or farm. By describing this situation, our intention is not to legitimate it. As should be obvious now, those locked out of the educational and occupational systems may be in that predicament not because of lack of ability—university students as a group have only slightly above average IQs—but rather for reasons of social class background, or a refusal to conform to a system that they feel is oppressive (cf. Bowles & Gintis, 1976).

From an Eriksonian perspective, the identity moratorium potentially provides a tremendous opportunity for self-discovery and the development of special competencies. The exploration and experimentation that is undertaken during this time can set the individual on a life course that is rich and rewarding. The individual can undo old psychological problems and start life afresh. On the other hand, the individual can get lost and confused, and this can be the most destructive period of the life cycle. Whether this period is a benefit or a liability for the individual has much to do with the type of environment (structure and guidance) that is provided. For Erikson, the central question was this: Does that environment nurture the person's capacities and encourage role exploration and self-discovery, or does it stifle these things, causing the individual to withdraw from others and to forgo potential self-development? Accordingly, when studying the circumstances facing young people, it is pertinent to examine whether a moratorium setting nurtures self-discovery, personal development, and intellectual growth—developmental individualization—or whether the social setting stifles these things, particularly by exploiting or ignoring vulnerabilities associated with an underdeveloped sense of identity—default individualization.

When we do examine the social settings in which young people in Canadian (and American) society must now undertake the transition to adulthood, it is evident that the social environments to which they are exposed can be the source of much of identity confusion and emotional turmoil. Identity problems appear to be commonplace in late-modern societies (e.g., Berman, Montgomery, & Kurtines, 2004; Côté, 2005). Moreover, as suggested by the political-economy perspective, and as shown later in this chapter, corporations have exacerbated the situation by further exploiting young people on a variety of fronts. In short, there is strong evidence that, as a group, young people have become socially and psychologically vulnerable as a result of the declining normative structure governing the transition to adulthood, and that vulnerability has been manipulated out of profit and power motives (e.g., Nader & Coco, 1999).

YOUTH AS A PERIOD OF PROLONGED SOCIETAL MARGINALIZATION

While the concept of the moratorium is useful, it potentially carries with it the conservative, functionalist implication that a prolonged delay of adulthood, as found in late-modern societies, is a natural and inevitable phase of the life course. While the idea of the moratorium applied to adolescence may be reasonable, it is less palatable to argue that a moratorium extended to age 25 or 30 is necessary. As we saw in the last section, however, it is rather easy to upset this Pollyannaish view by pointing out ways in which it does not apply. This section will reconsider the youth period in more critical terms, without the assumption that young people are necessarily being granted something positive by their society in having their adulthood delayed.

For example, the long-term consequences of the late-modern trends of low social support for self-socialization can only be speculated upon at this time, but a case can be made for our seeing a transmutation of the life course beyond the phases of adolescence and emerging adulthood to include an optional period that has been referred to as "youthhood" (Côté, 2000; cf. Mørch, 1997). This new period of life may be a prolonged extension of these earlier phases, or even a permanent lifestyle, that an increasing number of people seem to be undertaking.

The term "youthhood" was coined to parallel the established English words "childhood" and "adulthood," where the suffix "hood" designates "a group sharing a specified state or quality" as in the word "sisterhood," or "a condition, state, or quality" of the person as in the term "womanhood." Accordingly, youthhood designates both a quality of the individual's state of mind, and the nature of a group within which the individual can establish some sort of personal and social identity. Youthhood thus can have both a social structural quality that is related to a delay of adulthood imposed on certain people by circumstance or design, and an individual quality undertaken based on individual disposition and choice to take a delay. In either case, youthhood constitutes a variant of the identity moratorium, in the sense that it is socially permissible in late-modern societies to remain "young" for an indefinite period. This stands in contrast to earlier societies where social sanctions would have pushed the person to accept adult roles and adult self-definitions during what are now called late adolescence and early emerging adulthood. However, if permanent, this period would not perform the preparatory function of a moratorium, but rather would signal some sort of mutation of it associated with arrested development. In recognition of this, Erikson (1970, p. 157) wrote, "a true moratorium . . . must end." Erikson would identify those who act as if they are in a perpetual moratorium from adult responsibilities as experiencing an aggravated and prolonged identity crisis characterized by profound and fundamental identity confusion (e.g., Erikson, 1968, p. 212). However, in the case of youthhood, the destination may never have been "adulthood," so little or no preparation for it may be intended or undertaken.

As a phenomenon experienced on a mass scale, the primary structural root of youthhood most likely lies with the exclusion from the labour force and/or the extended education necessary to enter the labour force now. Extended education not only keeps more young people in school, but also keeps many of those who are not in school waiting longer for a later age-appropriate entry into permanent employment. In either case, once a person is "in" this period, there are differences in how it is handled. Some may heavily invest their individualization of identity in popular youth culture, others in higher educational systems, and yet others in the now disjunctive education-work cycles that often do not culminate in financial independence (Tannock, 2001). For some, youthhood can be an extended period of relative playfulness, with little preparation for an adulthood that might follow, while others may mix work and "play." In the latter case, the work experience may constitute a preparation for eventual self-sufficiency, while the play experience is simply making the best of an imposed set of life circumstances (the delay in self-sufficiency).

Whatever the initial causes of the delay, those who delay occupational preparations for an economically independent adulthood too long may find such a passage more difficult. Not only might they find it difficult to relinquish some of their playful youth-culture activities, but they might not have a viable skill-set that would give them access to economic self-sufficiency. In these cases, youthhood more likely becomes a permanent state; indeed, in the individualized societies of the contemporary West, pressures to relinquish youth are relatively weak compared with more traditional-collectivist societies where normative pressure to adopt adult roles and responsibilities override desires to carry on in a carefree, noncommittal fashion (see Mead, 1928, for early observations of this difference).

Having a large proportion of the population remain in a state of semi- or full dependency—which amounts to social marginalization—may seem like an entirely unintended consequence of social change. Indeed, this social marginalization might not have been planned, but it certainly seems to serve (or complement, as discussed in Chapter 6) dominant interests, including bureaucracies, by giving them a continual source of dependent clients, and corporations, by giving them mass markets of consumers who are looking for means to individualize their identities in the absence of meaningful alternatives. When viewed from a political-economy perspective, this marginalization amounts to a disenfranchisement of full citizenship, or the "conquest of youth," that has created a politically powerless social group, with few public defenders. As noted, unlike women and racial minorities, it is still legitimate to speak of the young as biologically inferior, with inherent mental problems (ostensibly caused by raging hormones), and to have their biological inferiority used to justify their unequal treatment in society and in the economy. This social and economic exclusion was outlined in Chapters 2 and 3.

The idea of "youth as proletariat" is by no means new, having been used by political economists over the past few decades. But in the present neo-liberal era of corporate capitalism, it is given a renewed vigour in North America. Left on their own without official spokespersons and personal lobbyists, the young emerge as more vulnerable than traditional working-class and minority labour. However, because this exploitation can produce a sense of alienation and discontent among the young, corporate and governmental élites must be careful to diffuse feelings of disaffection so that they do not stimulate widespread rejection of, or refusal to take part in, the production-consumption cycle that drives the economy. This is not only in terms of preventing open violence like we have seen in antiglobalization protests, but also because the youth segment constitutes one of the largest consumer segments of the population, not to mention a chief source of cheap labour. According to Palladino (1996), in 1990s America, teenagers constituted "a red-hot consumer market worth $89 billion," not counting the $200 billion their parents spend on them. This was a tenfold increase over the previous 40 years, and the youth market continues to expand each year. Quart (2003) put the discretionary income of American teens at $155 billion in 2000 (not counting what they get from their parents). The most commonly cited estimate of total expenditures in the total youth market (teens and twenties) is about $300 billion (e.g., Rushkoff, 2001), a figure equivalent to the entire U.S. defence budget before the latest Gulf war.

From both a late-modern and a political-economy perspective, then, the paramount problem for the young citizens of many advanced industrial societies is how to formulate a viable and stable identity under ambiguous and even hostile circumstances. As we saw in Chapters 2 and 3, young people, and teenagers in particular, have limited legal rights and economic resources available, are not considered to be fully responsible for their actions, and are generally treated as incomplete human beings. However, even common sense tells us that people grow and mature by acting in the social world in a meaningful and validated manner. Many young people, however, are denied this as part of their social marginalization. Thus, the paradox facing many young people is how to develop an individualized identity that will lead them to adulthood in the absence of the resources for doing so.

The essential problem is that, in order to develop a sense of self as an active agent in the world, people must be capable of visualizing themselves in the future, particularly in meaningful adult roles. The more that people are capable of conceiving of themselves as having a viable future as a full member of society, the more they can function in an agentic manner. To the extent that people have trouble doing this, the more they can experience a confusion of identity. The longer they experience this identity confusion, the more difficult it is to develop the maturity necessary to enact roles that may serve as a basis for a coherent identity—adult or otherwise (Côté, 2005). And so goes a spiral toward passivity, incapacitation, or arrested development. Thus, while one might look for examples of youth agency, and support the view that young people are capable of personal agency (depending on how this is defined), it must also be admitted that from a macro perspective the more autonomous forms of agency appear to be quite limited in many circumstances, because much such "agency" merely involves choosing among a limited number of credential and consumer choices. "Multiple-choice agency" is not the same as autonomous self-determination, and is not what most social scientists have in mind when they speak of personal agency as a means of overcoming structural obstacles (e.g., Emirbayer & Mische, 1998; Evans, 2002; Rudd & Evans, 1999).

In other words, to say that people are "agentic" because they choose among a series of options put in front of them is not the same as claiming that people are autonomous and self-determining (recall the distinction made between default and developmental individualization, or what Evans and Heinz, 1994, call passive versus active individualization). It is merely to state the obvious—that people will make choices when they have the opportunity to do so. Evans (2002) finds it useful to describe this issue with the terms "structured individualization" or "bounded agency," which includes the desire to act proactively and the belief in personal control with the reality of limited options under many circumstances.

Anisef and Axelrod (2001) summarize active-passive variations in agentic processes based on their longitudinal study of the "Class of '73," in which a large number of people were tracked for two decades from the time of their high-school graduation to the mid-1990s. With respect to the role of agency (involving more than simply passively choosing easy options), they note a key divide in the people they studied and how their lives unfolded:

> A close examination of personal biographies among members of the Class of '73 revealed important personal differences. Some articulated a clear vision of the future in their adolescent years, while others drifted through adolescence and early adulthood, giving little thought to the conscious pursuit of goals. Those who drifted were more likely to succumb to the constraining aspects of social structures which operated around them, while those who articulated a clear vision and sought to enact their dreams were able to take creative advantage of the enabling aspects of these social structures. (pp. 485-486)

THE CORPORATE MANIPULATION OF YOUTH IDENTITY FORMATION

In addition to being marginalized producers in the economy, the young are targeted by various marketing strategies that seek to promote a high level of consumerism that is essential for contemporary corporations. A steady stream of books has been documenting this in the past few years (e.g., Frank, 1997a, 1997b; Klein, 2000; Quart, 2003), confirming our analysis of the situation a decade ago in *Generation on Hold*. Our argument remains the same: Many of these marketing strategies are designed to sell young people sources of identity that are missing from their lives or which they have been encouraged to crave (e.g., Jhally, 1997). This identity-based consumerism seems to have been made possible to the extent that young people do not have the material means to form adult identities suitable for functioning in mainstream society. At the same time, youth culture (or popular culture) has been hijacked by this corporate marketing. As young people turn to youth culture because of their marginalization from adult culture, the various anti-adult attitudes and activities of youth culture push adulthood further beyond their emotional grasp. A number of books have also been published over the past few years on this issue (e.g., Calcutt, 1998; Danesi, 2003; Heath & Potter, 2004).

The separation of young people from mainstream society has taken place slowly over time, beginning over a century ago (as noted in Chapters 1 and 2). It began with a series of laws concerning employment practices and compulsory education that set the basis of new customs and institutional practices that rigidly separated adolescence and adulthood. From this de jure exclusion from mainstream society, and in conjunction with a series of economic and political arrangements that developed over the twentieth century (previously noted), corporations like Nike, Reebok, and Calvin Klein learned through careful research and marketing experiments that they could sell "identity packages" (e.g., "cool" co-ordinated fashion accessories) and "packaged identities" (e.g., skateboarder or Goth; prep or jock) to young people as commodities that they could use depending on their identity needs. Young people could make statements of "individuality" (by mixing and matching), group solidarity (by adopting a "uniform" as with Goths and skateboarders, or by simply wearing jeans or certain running shoes), or "rebellion" (through body piercing or other forms of dress and behaviour objectionable to adults). Corporations also included music, movies, and various technological gadgets for the mix, providing a sense of unlimited freedom and individuality for many unsuspecting young people.

Of course, to buy these things, young people need money, so in spite of limited job opportunities, young people have taken low-paying jobs to buy these things—hence the army of cheap labour. As early as 1990, Fine, Mortimer, and Roberts reported that among working secondary school students in the United States, when asked about their motivations for employment, most cited the desire for discretionary income. Most of this income went to buy clothing (among 70% of those studied), while a substantial portion went to music recordings, sports equipment, stereos, TVs, and movies. Only about one in five were saving any of this money and only 7% gave any of it to their families. There is no evidence that this pattern has changed since that study was conducted.

Certainly there has been evidence of individual resistance to consumerism among some young people (the antiglobalization movement, "culture jamming," "subvertizing," and so forth; Quart, 2003), and many young people do not buy into the corporate-consumer model of identity formation, preferring instead to establish their own developmental, individualized route through the moratorium. However, some young people take on resistance to consumerism as part of their identity, and it is not clear that this actually does anything to change the system, as opposed to providing a "rebel identity" among those involved (Heath & Potter, 2004). In fact, a case has been made that youth resistance of this sort not only has not been a threat to the corporate-capitalist system, but has been a source of its renewal. This argument is based on the charge that mass marketers not only learned how to feed off young people's attempts at agentic resistance by appropriating them at each turn through the marketing of products as "hip" or "cool," but that marketers actually count on resistance to consumerism to increase youth consumption. Their logic is that resistance is the source of new ideas and at the same time it makes old fashions "uncool" and therefore in need of replacement.

Thomas Frank (1997a) documents these marketing tricks in *The Conquest of Cool: Business Culture, Counterculture, and the Rise of Hip Consumerism*. Heath and Potter (2004) extend Frank's ideas in *The Rebel Sell: Why the Culture Can't Be Jammed*, noting that even the rebels themselves are caught up in their own form of competitive consumption and need the capitalist system for their own identities. Frank notes that marketers discovered some time ago that the concepts of "cool" and "hip" can be used to trick the mass consumer into believing that he or she could be set apart from the masses and meaningfully react against a standardizing and exploitative establishment. The chief marketing strategy in rebellion consumerism documented by Frank (1997b) is "liberation marketing," which tacitly admits that business now rules the world, but a corporation's products or services can liberate consumers from this oppression, if only momentarily.

As a consequence of the above trends, the industries producing music, fashion, and cosmetics now have age-differentiated masses of consumers awaiting the next season's fashions, or fashion fad. In these respects, youth cultures, whether predicated on "resistance" to the mainstream or celebrating it, are increasingly indistinguishable from the fabrications of corporate research, development, and marketing. Cool hunting, trend spotting, viral marketing, peer-to-peer marketing, and the like have seen to this. Corporations now have the benefit of several cohorts of highly educated business and social science graduates,[3] whom they hire to monitor, imitate, and commodify expressions of youth dissent among their age-mates and immediate juniors. In addition to those who will readily devote their careers to exploiting young people's need for self-affirmation, numerous marketing firms proudly advertise their army of "youth culture spies" who will provide immediate marketing feedback for corporations (e.g., look-look.com, where the website address is the corporate name, and Teen Research Unlimited, which can be visited at www.teenresearch.com). Hence, whenever signs of protest or innovation emerge, they are skilfully manipulated to have cachet in youth culture by being defined as "cool." In turn, those young people who are looking for validation adopt these mass-produced "identity kits" and maintain the paradoxical illusion that these mass-produced items are a mark of "individuality," which for many is their only source of an individualized identity. This process of commodifying dissent and distracting young people with trivial "identity pursuits" keeps their sense of agency focussed on making choices about minor day-to-day concerns such as how to act and what to wear and, in so doing, diverts them from exercising "political agency" against the many social, economic, and political injustices that affect their current lives and future prospects, not to mention developing their inner character, moral fibre, and self-actualizing talents.

As an example, consider the 1990s commodification of feminism and female political identity under the term "girl power," popularized by the British pop-music group known as the Spice Girls. Capitalizing on the popularity of feminist politics and the increasing desire of females to assert their agency in matters of personal freedom of choice and independence of actions, the Spice Girls spoke to a whole generation of girls during their formative years of becoming young women. However, they did so in a superficial and politically irresponsible way, seeking to convince them that they control their own lives and destinies, when most of them do not. The "control" portrayed is mainly over boyfriends who are the object of competition among these supposedly empowered girls.

This is simply one of the more blatant examples of the manipulation of the notion of free choice and its redefinition to mean "freedom of consumer choice." In essence, however, the choice these young girls were given was really quite empty. The choice was either to buy or not buy a set of glitzy, prepackaged images of the Spice Girls, who were themselves packaged—recruited, trained, and marketed—along with expensive dolls, clothes, posters and compact discs that represent a multimillion-dollar industry to the creators and owners of the Spice Girls—yes, the creators and owners. The Spice Girls were a product of a long-term marketing strategy, in which a large number of young women auditioned, and a few were selected for their looks. Those who were sexy enough were trained to sing and perform on stage in a bold and sexual manner. Clearly, the Spice Girls were a marketing vehicle, and their "girl power" was not a means to achieve social justice for women.

Although it applies mainly to a group that is younger than the focus of this book, the Spice Girl phenomenon is but one example of the successful conquest of cool. Consumer compliance was achieved among a market segment (now known as tweens) by appropriating their desire for personal control in the sound bite "girl power." But girl power simply amounted to making their own decisions around purchasing and consuming "identity commodities." The corporations that profited from the Spice Girls did not create the marginality of these young girls, but their marginality made them vulnerable to manipulations to the extent that corporations have access to their innermost thoughts and feelings in their day-to-day lives. With the widespread embracing of electronic gadgets that bring the mass media into every aspect of young people's lives, conditions are right for the introduction of influences that will shape and fundamentally change behaviour patterns, belief systems, and lifestyles. As we have seen, these influences are not always benign; as shown in Chapter 6, these shallow consumerist influences continue through the teen years and beyond.

The social-psychological or micro side of the identity manipulation equation has just been described. Applying a macro sociological perspective to these formulations, we can gain a sense of some of the causes of the difficulties many young people face in trying to make it through the moratorium imposed upon them. For example, if we change the language we have been using, we gain an insight into the implications of the "objective conditions" (material or economic reality) facing many young people. When we speak of a "moratorium" or a "delay," we are also speaking of the possibility of a disenfranchisement, because something has been taken away to produce the postponement of adulthood and the denial of full citizenship rights. The result of this over an unduly long period is that young people become second-class citizens when in the past they would have been more integrated into mainstream society. When we speak of "personal development" or "experimentation," we can also speak of the possibility of emotional vulnerability and economic exploitation. Hence, sociologically speaking, we can examine adolescence and youth in terms of possible forms of identity manipulation.

In sum, when a population is controlled educationally and economically, it is then possible to control them emotionally—to define their sense of self and to manipulate their identities. Indeed, much of "mainstream" youth culture appears to constitute a special type of consumer culture: an organization of individuals hungry to have their emotions, identity, and tastes defined and redefined for them by the youth-oriented "leisure industries" that market fashion, music, art, and other consumer items. Even the rebels of this system appear to be either caught up in it as a function of their own identity needs (the need to be defined as a trendsetters, nonconformists, avant garde, etc.) or their own competitive consumption habits by which they distinguish themselves from what they see as lesser beings (Milner, 2004).

As noted in Chapter 2, youth culture commodities produced by corporations all have in common an identity-conferring quality that helps people produce a "statement" about themselves. In order to be "cool," one has to possess or consume certain items. The youth consumer group is the perfect market segment for such manipulation because its members are kept "identity hungry" by their marginalization from adult society and by their sequestering into mass age-graded groups (defined by year level in school during the teens and early twenties) with roles that often provide them with little meaning. For those who buy into this, these industries can make their products obsolete or in constant change year after year, requiring consumers to follow the trends they have arbitrarily set and announced through the various media. The entire system works in unison and is an arrangement virtually perfected by corporations that have as their sole objective profit maximization, regardless of the social costs.

THE UNDERMINED SENSE OF WELL-BEING IN THE TRANSITION TO ADULTHOOD

Declining opportunities, diminishing status, and identity manipulation are not without their consequences. Decreases in the well-being among a significant proportion of young people are evident over the decades during which the transition to adulthood lengthened and became more precarious. Among the cohorts that came of age during the 1960s through 1990s, suicide, depression, crime, and violence increased dramatically. Among the current cohort attempting to come of age, the deteriorated conditions for their transition to adulthood are a "new normal" and they have little reason to expect otherwise, because from their point of view "things have always been this way." However, as Call et al. (2002, p. 77) note, "despite the prosperity in the West, increases in the prevalence of some mental health problems among adolescents, such as depression, suicide, and eating disorders, were seen during the last half of the 20th century."

Two factors are at play here. First, as documented in the previous chapter, the material conditions for coming of age have been undermined by the diminished status and economic role of the young. Second, as already discussed in this chapter, there has been a loss of meaning and direction in the lives of the young that are traceable to long-term trends in Western societies where community bonds have been undermined by progressively intrusive forms of capitalism, creating the widespread anomie now identified as a characteristic of late-modern society. These longer-term changes in community structure have in turn undermined the social markers that once provided the guideposts for the transition to adulthood. Combined, the loss of economic independence (factor 1) and the loss of a meaningful passage to adulthood (factor 2) have created a period in life that many people experience as stressful and hazardous.

It should be emphasized that, although some of these consequences may have plateaued or declined slightly, this is no reason for complacency; any "new normal" is unacceptable when the lives and well-being of people are at stake. Previous generations of adults would have been shocked at the prevalence of some of these problems. Why are current adults so complacent? If it is simply because they have grown accustomed to these problems, this is no reason to mindlessly let the young suffer through them.

This section draws freely on both Canadian and American studies, in part because some things have been more thoroughly studied in the United States. However, many problems are far more severe in the United States, where the survival-of-the-fittest, individualistic ideology prevails. Young Americans are apparently more vulnerable because of the greater economic inequalities associated with less market regulation by, and fewer safety-net policies from, the American government. These contrasts are especially important to the extent that some people would like Canada to become more like the United States in terms of these "freedoms," and therefore stand as warning of what we could expect if we followed what are some of the United States' "worst practices."

Suicide

Suicide is both a "key indicator of youth alienation and disengagement . . . [and] one of the leading causes of death among adolescents in many nations" (Call et al., 2002, p. 74). The suicide rate for young Canadians increased almost fivefold from the early 1960s to the early 1990s (Galambos & Kolaric, 1994; Korenblum, 1986), as it did in many countries around the world (World Health Organization, 2003). Although it seems to have plateaued in Canada[4] "the high rate of suicide among young persons in their late teens and early twenties" remains a "major concern among parents and health professionals" (Langlois & Morrison, 2002, p. 22). Currently, suicide is the second leading cause of death for this age group in Canada (Almey & Normand, 2002) and the third in the United States (McWhirter et al., 1998). Suicide has been displaced in the United States as the second leading cause of youth death only because of increases in the rate of homicide, where firearm murders among the young are five times higher than in Canada (Arnett, 2002).

Young men have been particularly affected by this trend. In many countries, (young) women are three times more likely to attempt suicide, whereas (young) men are about three to four times more likely to succeed (e.g., Almey & Normand, 2002; Langlois & Morrison, 2002). While the suicide rate for the population as a whole increased in Canada over the past 40 years, the greatest increase was among younger men; by the mid-1980s, the rate for Canadian men in their early twenties had risen to the point where it was the highest for any group except men over 70 years of age (Beneteau, 1988).

From a critical perspective, one would predict that suicide rates are higher in stigmatized minority groups, whether racial, cultural, or age minority (cf. Stockard & O'Brien, 2002). The available statistics support this prediction. For example, the rate for Native Canadian men aged 15 to 29 exceeds 100 per 100 000 (Beneteau, 1988), one of the highest rates in the world. Similarly, the suicide rate for young African-American males tripled between the 1960s and 1990s, breaking the historic trend for Black suicides in the United States to be lower than White suicides (Willis et al., 2002), while the rate for Native American youths increased tenfold (Nielsen, 1991). As in Canada, the overall suicide rate for Natives is the highest of the major racial/ethnic groups, and it peaks during young adulthood (Cole, 1991), with the rate of Aboriginal youth suicide five to six times higher than non-Aboriginal youth (Almey & Normand, 2002). Importantly, the exception to the high rate among Native American youths is with those who have not been as culturally disenfranchised: those who observe traditional customs or who live in areas "where the opportunities for employment and education exist within the tribal community itself" (Nielsen, 1991, p. 521). It appears that marginalized groups can preserve some internal integrity by socially and economically organizing themselves.

This protective factor has been studied by Chandler (2001) among Native Canadian youth, who found very clear links between the emotional well-being associated with a sense of ego identity (self-continuity) and the extent to which their tribal community evidences its own well-being and coherent structure. Chandler concludes that suicide among First Nations youth is a direct function of factors that represent community-based efforts to reconstitute a form of cultural continuity and integrity. His research links six protective factors with reduced youth suicide. In every Native community in which all six of these protective factors were in place, no youth suicides were reported during the five years in which he studied them. In contrast, communities that lacked these protective factors showed suicide rates between 5 and 100 times the national average. The protective factors he identified concern whether communities have (a) secured aboriginal title to traditional lands, (b) achieved a measure of self-government, (c) control their educational facilities, (d) control their health services, (e) run their own police and fire protection services, and (f) set up facilities to preserve and enrich their indigenous culture.

While official suicide statistics are alarming, many experts feel that the actual rate is higher than the official rate (Galambos & Kolaric, 1994, suggest it is 50 percent higher, while Nielsen, 1991, argues that it is three times higher). Experts believe that many sui-cides are "covered up" or mislabelled for various reasons. For example, car "accidents" are the leading cause of death for this age group in both Canada and the United States, but many such "accidents" have direct or indirect suicidal characteristics. The statistics get even worse as we delve further into this issue. Surveys have revealed that between 10% and 15% of people in their teens and twenties attempt suicide at some time, while between 35% and 55% will admit to having recently thought about committing suicide (Strang & Orlofsky, 1990). Some experts estimate that there are as many as "200 suicide attempts for every adolescent death by suicide" (Cole, 1991, p. 1113; cf. Galambos & Kolaric, 1994).

In short, suicide, attempted suicide, or thoughts about suicide are part of the reality that many young people face today, directly or indirectly, and the situation appears to have worsened over the time span examined in this book. These statistics can hardly be said to reflect the idea that these people are going through their "best years." Indeed, if young people were going through their "best years," one would think they would not be taking their lives at such an alarming rate.

Psychological Well-Being

Estimates from the mid-1980s indicated that some 20% of "normal" teenagers (i.e., not psychiatric patients or convicted delinquents) would admit on a questionnaire to "gross psychiatric symptoms" like "feeling empty emotionally" or "being confused most of the time" (Offer & Sabshin, 1984, p. 101). With so many admitting to such symptoms on an impersonal questionnaire, one wonders how many more would admit to similar problems under conditions where a clinical rapport is established. In fact, mental health disorders are "the leading single cause of disability among adolescents" (Ozer et al., 2002, p. 133).

While an immediate reaction might be that these figures constitute evidence that young people are prone to these symptoms because of a storm and stress of biological origin as Hall claimed (Chapter 2), an examination of the psychological world of young people over the past four decades reveals an increase in problems that cannot be attrib-uted to such a biological "affliction." Instead, a more plausible explanation is related to disenfranchisement.

Data are available from the United States for each of the decades of 1960s, 1970s, and 1980s, providing three reference points to gauge how societal changes associated with cul-tural disenfranchisement have affected the manner in which coming of age is experienced in Western cultures (Offer & Sabshin, 1984). Referring to these changes, Offer and Sabshin note that, in comparison with adolescents from the early 1960s, those of the late 1970s and early 1980s were "less secure about their body image and self esteem." Moreover, they had "more overt behavioural problems . . . [were] more worried about their future and less hopeful about their ability to function as adults" (p. 92). Offer and Sabshin's research also indicates that in the early 1960s, the young people they studied "were less lonely and valued friendships somewhat more than do current adolescents" (p. 93). Finally, by the early 1980s, many teenagers believed "they should be more sexually active" and felt "insecure or inferior" as a result (p. 94).

From another longitudinal study, Seligman argued in the 1980s that "today's young [American] people [are] about 10 times as likely to be depressed as were their parents and grandparents" (1988, pp. 50-52; cf. Birmaher et al., 1996; Fombonne, 1994; Robins & Regier, 1991). Seligman attributed this "epidemic of depression" (among Baby Boomers as they made the transition to adulthood) to the tremendous expectations placed on the "self" to be both the source and the "architect" of most forms of gratification—to "decide, prefer, plan, and choose [its] own course of action" (p. 52). However, he added that this self-centredness "need not lead to depression as long as we can fall back on large institutions" (p. 55). Seligman argued that the "rampant individualism" of American society, along with a decline in commitment to common social institutions, led to this epidemic. With the institutions that are supposedly guiding the young into adulthood themselves in disarray, it is little wonder that some young people lose faith and become depressed. These psychological conclusions were drawn independently of the sociological position outlined previously concerning late-modernity, self-socialization, and compulsory individualization.

Further support for this trend comes from Galambos and Kolaric (1994), who argue that depression has become a serious problem among Canadian teens, citing research that suggests that up to one third are mildly to clinically depressed at any point in time. Among those in their late teens, about 40% of females and 20% of males report these levels of depression.

Recent research in the United Kingdom suggests that these trends toward an increasing prevalence of mental health problems researched in the 1980s have continued to the present. This research finds increasing levels of depression and anxiety problems among British youth, along with a continuous rise in conduct problems over a 25-year period (especially on such indicators as lying, stealing, and disobedience, Hagell, 2004). Checks on the longitudinal design undertaken by researchers eliminate the possibility that these results are simply attributable to possible changes in what is considered a problem or an increasing tendency for people to see teenage behaviour as problematic (see also the report by Kelleher et al., 2000, of an increase in psychiatric symptomatology in children during the 1980s, using the same controls to eliminate the possibility of an increased tendency to see the same behaviours as more problematic over time).

Risk and Crime

The leading cause of death of the 15- to 24-year-old group is the automobile accident (48 per 100 000 in Canada and 52 per 100 000 in the United States; Statistics Canada, 1989). This rate dropped in Canada in the 1990s, but young people still have the highest rates of any age group (Almey & Normand, 2002). Young people are more likely to drive faster, not to wear seat belts, and to drive more closely to vehicles in front of them; those aged 12 to 25 are five times more likely to use street drugs than those over 25; and the 15- to 25-year-old group are arrested for a disproportionate number of crimes, especially property crimes and violent crimes (Arnett, 1992; Lerner & Galambos, 1998).

Again, some would say that these statistics merely confirm the belief that these people are "naturally" or biologically immature and therefore incapable of handling their impulses or managing responsibilities. Perhaps this is true as far as some forms of risk-taking go, but this line of reasoning can assume some sort of developmental deficiency in young people (associated with a hormonal imbalance and/or biological immaturity). Such an assumption cannot account for the same statistics showing that over the past four decades most forms of risk behaviours have become much more common among the young. A biological line of reasoning to explain increases in risk-taking would have to be based on the implausible assumption that our genetic make-up changed in just four decades. Furthermore, such a "developmental deficiency" argument does not explain dramatic increases in crime rates in countries like the United States. For example, Arnett (1992) reported a tenfold increase in the arrest rate for persons aged 14 to 24 between 1950 and 1985 (from 10 per 1000 to 100 per 1000), while Halperin (1998) found that this youth criminalization trend continued with the incarceration rate for men under 25 doubling between 1985 and 1995. As a result, as previously noted, by the 1990s, it was routine for 10% of all 20- to 29-year-old American males to be in prison, on probation, or on parole. Halperin (1998) also reports a continuing rise (60%) in the arrest rate for violent crimes among teens between 1985 and 1995. A similar increase in the arrest rate for violent crimes occurred in Canada (Frank, 1992; Stevenson et al., 1999) and in almost all countries examined in a 14-country study (Hoffman & Summers, 2001).

In defence of young Americans, who appear to be the most violent in the world, they have inherited a culture of violence, rather than having created it. Today, American adolescents are twice as likely to be victims of violent crimes than are adults. Homicide is now the leading cause of death among African-American adolescent males, accounting for half the mortality rate of this group (Ozer et al., 2002). Homicide, mainly from handguns, has risen to the second leading cause of death for all American adolescents (18% of mortalities), taking over suicide for that place in the 1990s (McWhirter et al., 1998), which now accounts for 12% of adolescent mortality (Ozer et al., 2002). Thirty years ago, street gangs used switchblades and iron pipes. Now automatic weapons are not uncommon. Young Americans do not manufacture these weapons—they buy them from adults who are licensed by the State to sell them. The firearm homicide rate in the United States is five times higher than in Canada, and more than 50 times higher than in the United Kingdom (Arnett, 2002). These weapons are partly responsible for the fact that 5% of African-American males will be murdered. In one year alone in the 1980s, more young African-American males were murdered than were killed in almost ten years of fighting in Vietnam (Nielsen, 1991). In reference to the growing gang phenomenon in the United States, Flannery et al. (2003) review evidence that suggests that some 30 000 youth gangs are now in about 5000 American cities. Flannery et al. conclude from this review that

> one thing is certain—gangs affect more cities and jurisdictions than ever before . . . with dramatic increases since the 1990s in reported gang activity in rural and suburban areas. . . . Just over half of suburbs now report having gangs, as do 35 percent of small cities and one in four rural communities. Gangs are no longer a uniquely urban phenomenon. (p. 511)

The general public tends to believe that the aforementioned problems are "normal" for young people. However, they are accepted because of a common-sense belief in an inherent emotional instability caused by "hormones" or incomplete development. This age group is often not taken seriously or treated with due respect because of the widespread belief that they are not "mature" enough to look after themselves properly or to make responsible decisions. This is especially the case for those who are still in their teen years. The problem with this line of reasoning, however, is that most young people are no longer given opportunities to assume roles that would help them to learn how to act maturely and responsibly. Instead, they are increasingly dependent on adults, mainly on their parents, or on surrogate parents such as teachers, to whom the State has given control over key aspects of their lives. This situation of forced financial and emotional dependency, and a concomitant erosion of rights and social status, directly contributes to the diminished sense of well-being among the youth population and can lead to all kinds of socially and individually dysfunctional behaviour.

CONCLUSION: THE INDIVIDUALIZATION CONTRADICTION

Apparently, "freedom" does not come without a price. Young people today are told they are freer and appear to have a wide array of options available to them, but upon closer examination, much of this choice does not involve self-determination in overcoming social and economic obstacles, but rather a serious of multiple-choice options among a limited number of educational paths and consumer options. At the same time, people are told that their destinies are in their own hands. However, the nature of this freedom of self-determination is much more complex than it seems at first blush. Some freedom has come as a result of a destructuring of society, with a decline in the normative structure and social markers associated with adulthood and the transition to it. This freedom is not without costs, though, for those who cannot capitalize on it. At the same time, some freedoms are simple illusions, related to mere multiple choices in consumption behaviour in the materialist culture that has replaced the destructured traditional cultures. Some young people think "outside the box" of consumerism, but this does not appear to be the most common response to it.

While those at all socioeconomic levels may be mystified by "multiple-choice freedom," at least those with greater economic means can ride out the various educational delays that are commonly encountered because they have fewer financial obstacles to doing so, and they can draw on their parents' networks for eventually finding a place in the workforce. Even so, many of these more privileged young people will encounter a series of disappointments and misdirected trajectories in a world that they were told is limitless, whether out a lack of ability on their part or because of structural constraints in the system (e.g., there are only so many places in medical, law, and business schools). Herein lies the individualization contradiction: People are expected to be the architects of their own destinies, but for many the avenues do not exist to turn this expectation into a reality. Instead, they are fed false promises, given cheap trinkets, and told that their futures are bright if they only co-operate. Sound familiar? Well, this is how the "West was won," but it is also how corporate interests have conquered the youth segment.

ENDNOTES

1. Similar laments are being expressed in other countries as the lure of high-level careers entices more and more people to shun more mundane occupations. For example, in England, new apprenticeship schemes are having trouble attracting recruits because more parents are pushing their children to go to university in spite of the fact that these schemes can get young people into well-paying jobs in their early twenties. Cassidy (2004) reports that officials in charge of these schemes are appealing to parents to "drop their prejudices" about the trades.

2. Compare Levine (1984) in which he discusses the therapeutic value of cult membership for those who are unable to make a break from their family.

3. It should be noted that the Canadian government pays most of the cost of the education for those hired by corporations. Because public revenues are raised primary through public taxation, in effect average Canadians subsidize the costs of educating future corporate employees even if that education is beyond their own means as taxpayers.

4. Almey and Normand (2002) report that during the 1990s the suicide rate declined somewhat for males in their late teens, but rose for females in this age group.

chapter five

Ideology and Conformity: The Political Economy of Youth

INTRODUCTION

In the previous chapter, arguments and evidence were presented that the transition to adulthood now involves an individualized and often marginalized passage during which young people must formulate some sense of coherence and place in the world—identities that both differentiate them from others and integrate them into some form of social organization. It is apparent that this transition is replete with hazards. Not only can young people find a lack of meaningful social support from the adult community, but they now face predatorial strategies on the part of corporations to manipulate their identities as consumers (primarily) and producers (secondarily). One serious consequence is an undermining of many young people's sense of well-being.

This alarming trend is often overlooked in analyses of youth transition, especially among those who only want to see the positive aspects of social organization and/or young people's behaviour. One typical response we get from colleagues when trying to discuss this concern is that we are looking at things in terms of the "glass being half empty" while they see the "glass as half full" (cf. Arnett, 2004). While the glass may appear to be "half full" for affluent youth or those with exceptional native abilities, unfortunately, such a stance merely preempts serious consideration of those issues facing a significant proportion of young people, as laid out in Chapter 3. Our response to the glass analogy is to take an objective, practical stance that examines the entire glass in terms of both its structure and contents. When this is done we then ask colleagues whether they, or their children, would like to have the portion of the glass that is half empty; in this case, poor job prospects, educational failure, poverty, discrimination, prolonged dependency on others, and heightened risk of violence and mental distress.

This chapter examines the ways in which the "half empty" situation facing many young people is disguised, through design, opportunism, or the simple fact that many people's view of the world is slanted by their need to see things in an unrealistically positive, "half full" manner that ignores the entire situation in terms of both structure and content.

THE POLITICS OF SOCIAL CONTROL: DISGUISING CORPORATE MANIPULATIONS

As noted in Chapter 2, political economists argue that the roots of structures in society lie in "objective conditions" produced by the distribution of power, particularly economic and political power (e.g., Bailey & Gayle, 2003; Levitt, 1984; Marcuse, 1964, 1969, 1972; Rowntree & Rowntree, 1968). In contemporary capitalist societies, young people are viewed as a disenfranchised "class" without significant economic, political, or social power in the larger society. Political economists look to ways in which young people are lulled into a state of "false consciousness" to mask this, so that they accept practices and beliefs that work directly against their own interests. Often associated with false consciousness is the belief that if something bad happens to someone (even oneself), he or she is at fault, not the system (cf. Dittmar & Dickinson, 1993). In other words, false consciousness involves an acceptance that one's alienation is the normal state of affairs.

Further, when people are financially vulnerable, or fearful of their economic security, it is easier to control them emotionally, by influencing how they define their sense of identity and by shaping their tastes and attitudes. Thus, it is argued by political economists that much of youth culture has come to constitute a special type of consumer culture, as marginalized and disenfranchised young people have been left hungry to have their emotions, identity, and tastes defined and redefined for them by the corporations that market clothing, music, sports, and other consumer items. These goods are made appealing to young people because they are marketed to have an identity-conferring quality built into their "brand." To be "someone," to be "in," one has to have, wear, or consume that item. Corporations can make their products obsolete or in constant change year after year, requiring consumers to follow the trends they arbitrarily set and announce through the media. From this political-economy perspective, the entire system works in unison and is the perfect arrangement for capitalist enterprises that have as their primary objective profit maximization. However, in order to perpetuate this system, it is necessary to maintain a consensus that this system is not only good, but the best, and that all alternatives are bad. To accomplish this, it is necessary that certain efforts be devoted to the "manufacture of consent."

THE MANUFACTURE OF CONSENT

The term "manufacturing consent" was coined by the journalist Walter Lippmann in the early twentieth century and has subsequently been popularized by Herman and Chomsky (1988), and Caldicott (1992). Herman and Chomsky use the concept to show how the mass media filter information so that the interests of political, military, and economic élites are not challenged. Caldicott employs the concept in her description of how American business interests spread anti-unionism and a fear of "communism" using public relations techniques, while at the same time establishing an equation of "free enterprise" with "democracy" and God. Caldicott argues that it became necessary to manufacture public consensus in the United States (and other liberal democracies) after the right to vote was extended to all citizens above the age of 21. By the 1920s, women in Canada and the United States had finally won the voting franchise. Prior to this, only (White) men who owned property had the right to vote. With this development, women, men, and all ethnic groups of all social class backgrounds had a potential say in government policies, making them a force to be reckoned with in the formal political realm.

Before the spread of the voting franchise, the economic and political élites were essentially one and the same, and simply voted their own members into positions of power, who in turn developed policies to promote their collective interests. When every citizen over 21 years of age finally had the right to vote on who would represent their interests (and therefore indirectly determining political and economic policies), élites had to take measures to assure that the public voted in favour of policies that were in the élite's interests. One important tool they relied on was public relations campaigns designed to establish the dominance of certain beliefs among the general public.

In political matters, those responsible for manufacturing consent are referred to as "spin doctors," whose job is to take information that is either neutral or opposed to those they represent, and twist it to suit their ends. For example, since the advent of televised election debates, official "spin rooms" are set up, and reporters now generally refuse to declare a winner of a given debate before the "spin" is complete. The idea is that the actual exchanges between the candidates are insufficient for the public to make a decision, so everyone has to wait two or three days for the process to be completed. One implication of this is that, because the public is not expected to think for itself, people are encouraged to let others tell them what is best for them. And as we shall see, this appears to be equally true for the adult segment as it is for the youth segment.

Using a concept similar to the manufacture of consent, Bernays coined a comparable expression reflected in the title of his book *The Engineering of Consent* (1955). Although not politically sensitive to the implications of "engineering consent," Bernays's book is a revealing description of "persuasion" techniques developed by mainstream public relations firms. Indeed, he pioneered many of the public relations techniques that are still in use, and his book was a standard text in the public relations industry for years. When one reads his book, it becomes clear how mass consent could be engineered through the "adjustment" of public opinion. His insensitivity to the implications of doing so is illustrated with his pride in having "taught" women how to smoke cigarettes by equating smoking with women's liberation, with cigarettes representing "torches of liberty" for their "emancipation." He launched this campaign by hiring a group of New York debutantes to march, smoking cigarettes, in the 1929 Easter parade. Prior to this, the only women who publicly smoked were prostitutes; photos of these "liberated women" were subsequently circulated in newspapers worldwide by his PR firm (De Graaf, Wann, & Naylor, 2001). The rest of the story is well known: decades of aggressive marketing campaigns to women and countless deaths from smoking-related illnesses. Today, more Canadian teen females smoke than do teen males (Media Awareness Network, 2004).

In all of its usages, the manufacture of consent or the creation of what is also known as hegemony refers to the process by which the political acceptance of forms of rule and government is literally moulded or engineered. In other words, while the so-called "consent of the masses" is not coerced in an overtly physical manner, the mass media and other similar socializing institutions that are charged with "informing" the public are said to be engaged in campaigns of "persuasion." Political ads at election time are a case in point. There is, however, an ideological dimension to this point. For if we were talking about North Korea or the former Soviet Union, for example, we would more readily be expected to refer to these practices as propaganda campaigns because they supposedly involve misinformation and manipulation. But whether it is called persuasion or propaganda, the result can be the same: What passes as a freely-arrived-at consensus that ostensibly informs free political action is often a set of fictions that have been fabricated by paid image-makers in the employ of powerful interest groups. Thus, writers such as Chomsky and Caldicott paint the social and economic order —the shared agreement and the peace that are said to characterize advanced industrial societies—as quite superficial and inherently unstable in the absence of continual efforts to maintain a fabricated consensus that feeds a false consciousness.[1]

However, when that superficiality and instability are broken, consent can give way to dissent. When the illusions of order give way to the reality of control, and when the disgruntlement and alienation that were hitherto kept beneath the surface begin to erupt above the surface, a chaotic social situation can result. Thus, in the very process of attempting to manufacture or engineer consensus, there can be much frustration and anger that is repressed. In the specific case of youth in contemporary Western societies, a certain amount of "dissent" has built over time, some of which is now taken for granted and used as evidence against the youth population for the apparent need to vigilantly monitor them. Although many observers associate youth culture with dissent, the previous chapter revealed that most of youth culture "dissent" is not only *not* a threat to the economic system of capitalism, but is now an integral part of it (Heath & Potter, 2004). Instead, this dissent increasingly takes the form of youth-on-youth violence (which began rising in the 1980s, especially among young women), the use of weapons detectors and armed guards in some high schools, and youth gangs, which are all now taken-for-granted realities in many areas of the United States and, increasingly, Canada. In fact, they are so taken for granted that it is now common for people to believe that things have always been this way, but that society is now just harder on young people (no evidence is ever presented for this belief, but it still prevails). Stated differently, attempts to manufacture consent among alienated and disenfranchised groups can backfire and manufacture a climate of dissent.

In spite of the impossibility of producing absolute conformity, the manufacture of consent remains politically expedient for those in authority. This is because, in order to preserve their positions of privilege, they must convince the nonprivileged that their positions at the bottom of the social hierarchy were freely and fairly arrived at; once accomplished, the latter are led to believe that they have only themselves to blame if their glass is "half empty." To the extent that the belief is nurtured that, in these "open" and democratic societies, both failure and success are totally under individual control, system-level problems go unrecognized (cf. Furlong & Cartmel, 1997). Without this belief, the potential for social disruption emerges because the disenfranchised come to understand their problems in systemic rather than in individual terms. The manufacturing of consent must therefore be an ongoing concern for the élites commanding the heights of the leading economic, political, and social institutions.

Moreover, this all becomes quite crucial in an era when the forces of globalization are increasingly encompassing remote areas of the globe and bringing their inhabitants under the sway of multi-national Capital. The sweatshops of Indonesia, Taiwan, Singapore, Bangladesh, Mexico, and similarly situated countries target both women and children as workers who produce electronics, high-tech gadgets, designer clothing, jeans, running shoes, and other such commodities under often-horrendous working conditions. The commodities in question, which are usually beyond the financial reach of the direct producers, are destined principally for the North American and Western European markets where more-affluent consumers buy them, including young people. In the case of the North American Free Trade Agreement (NAFTA), for example, cheap labour in.Mexico eliminates jobs in the United States and Canada. Consequently, the youth labour market in the latter countries is heavily concentrated in low-paying service sector jobs, whereas in previous generations young people would have been employed in the industrial sector as the beginning of a ladder they could climb to economic self-sufficiency. This is where it becomes necessary to ensure that the youth in question do not develop the political consciousness to disrupt the "new economy" wrought by globalization forces that erode tax bases (which would have provided them with good educations and other social services while growing up) and eliminate local jobs (which would have given them a good financial start in adulthood).

Powerful evidence for the manufacture of consent around materialistic values as opposed to the more personally empowering sense of purpose in life is available from the largest and longest continuing study of American young people entering institutions of higher education (CIRP, 2004). Each year since 1967 over 500 schools and some 300 000 students have participated. Among other things, this survey finds that since the mid-1960s the values "developing a meaningful philosophy of life" and "being financially very well-off " have almost traded places in terms of being rated as primary for these students. During the 1970s, out of a list of seventeen other personal values, "being financially very well-off" rose to the top of the list while "developing a meaningful philosophy of life" dropped precipitously (CIRP, 2004).

That study suggests just how effective the consent-manufacturing mechanisms have been in transforming the way young people think so that their priorities are more complementary to dominant interests. That is, young people have been increasingly encouraged to think within the narrow confines of personal materialism and consumerism, from which big business is the principal beneficiary. It would also appear that the development of a meaningful philosophy of life and the social conscience that might go along with that philosophy are given lower priority by a majority of recent cohorts.

Not only does consumption by young people divert attention from larger concerns, but it is a major engine in the advanced capitalist economy. As discussed in the previous chapter, entrepreneurs know exactly how much discretionary income the youth market has and they target it by appropriating the indigenous symbols of youth rebellion and revolt, and turning them into consumer goods like black leather jackets and blue jeans, baseball caps and designer running shoes. Indeed, so effective is this advertising machine that the most radical and revolutionary anti-capitalist icon of the past 60 years, Ché Guevara, is now successfully packaged and marketed as a hot sale item aimed at today's mainstream (nonradical and nonrevolutionary) youth population. Moreover, according to Fine, Mortimer, and Roberts, the music industry "has been largely underwritten by teenagers' cash" and one of its appeals is that, like sports, music holds the promise for a meteoric rise to fame about which young people can dream (1990, p. 232).

The moral-ethical concern is that among young people there has been an increasing emphasis placed on a "feel-good" existence, with little or no regard for long-term objectives or costs. As a result, young people are encouraged to escape into technological "trivial pursuits" that entertain them while leaving the power structure intact. But the point is that this is no accident and the young are not to blame. Indifference is complementary to the dominant economic and political interests, so it is cultivated in everyday life and educational systems; a critical consciousness and political awareness are not complementary to this system, so they are not cultivated, especially in school, but certainly not among the mass media. The way in which youth experience is now structured is remarkably like the society portrayed in Aldous Huxley's classic *Brave New World* (1932), a world where every organization and activity is designed to either produce something or consume something. Sanctioned activities that did neither had long been eradicated in Huxley's dystopia, and "deviants" who did not conform were swiftly dealt with.

We can get a glimpse into just how calculating business interests are in manipulating young people to devote their time and income to consumerism if we look at their marketing publications. One of the early marketing books in this area was *Youthtrends: Capturing the $200 Billion Youth Market* (Graham & Hamdan, 1989), which laid out for entrepreneurs how to finagle this discretionary income from young Americans. Around the same time, marketing researcher Jo Marney (1991) reported in *Marketing* that this "spending skews heavily toward style and recreation. Clothing, sporting goods (especially shoes), beauty products, electronics equipment and fast foods top the list of teen spending preferences" (p. 14).

Since the early 1990s, the youth marketing literature has steadily grown, showing not only that tremendous attention is now directed at understanding the changing transition to adulthood, but there are extensive efforts directed at affecting these changes. This should not surprise anyone, however, given the vested interests of marketers: They need to be able not only to chart out current consumption patterns, but to affect them, because their careers are based on predicting and affecting future consumption patterns. The most accessible marketing magazine is *American Demographics: Consumer Trends for Business Leaders*. It is published monthly with short, informative articles using the most recent statistical analyses. Articles appearing in the 1990s included such titles: "Marketing to Generation X" (Ritchie, 1995); "Talking to Teens" (Zollo, 1995); "Getting Inside Kids' Heads" (McGee, 1997); "Marketing Street Culture: Bringing Hip-hop Style to the Mainstream" (Spiegler, 1996); and "College Come-ons" (Speer, 1998).

By the late 1990s, marketers began to cast their eye to the even younger youth populations: "tweens" and "pre-tweens" (aka children). This is a demographic previously off-limits to predatorial marketing (Nader & Coco, 1999), but no longer, at least in most countries (as we will see in Chapter 7, some countries like Sweden still attempt to protect their most vulnerable members). Although this line of inquiry strays somewhat from this book's focus on youth and adolescence, the branding of today's children affects tomorrow's youth, so those interested in youth studies await with interest the long-term impact of kiddie-marketing.[2]

The Ideology of Youth

Any researcher investigating how coming of age is experienced and structured in advanced industrial societies has encountered a number of beliefs regarding what is taking place (as discussed in Chapters 1 and 2). Those beliefs appear to be sustained by what is called the "common-sense stock of knowledge" of contemporary Western culture. When these common-sense views that negatively characterize young people are examined—the views that ordinary citizens in "mainstream" Western societies take on the matter—the following beliefs, among other things, are found: The period called "adolescence" is a natural and necessary period of development; this period of development is the best time of one's life when one has no worries—just freedom from responsibility—and; an advantage is being granted to young people because they are not required to assume many responsibilities.

Along with these, there is often the assumption that the way the young are regulated is in their best interests and should therefore be eagerly accepted by them. This regulation is thought to be necessary because young people are seen to be biologically immature and functioning in a "reduced capacity," and therefore in need of time and protection to help them mature into "adults." At the base of many of these views is the assumption that "adulthood" in contemporary Western societies requires a prolonged period of preparation because of the complexities associated with life in modern industrial societies.

These beliefs are "normal" and widespread. It can be argued, however, that they actually make life more difficult for many young people because they are based on stereotypes that deny them basic respect as citizens in their own right, especially when applied to "emerging adults" in their late teens and early twenties (as in recent research on brain structure discussed in Chapter 2). Stereotypical beliefs function in this way by establishing the following "logic loop" that makes it difficult for young people to escape the prejudices directed at them: Since young people appear to be acting immaturely, they must be inherently this way; since they do not seem to be able to handle responsibility, there must be something about them that makes them irresponsible; thus, these immature and irresponsible people must be closely watched and regulated by adult authorities.

What makes life difficult for many young people is that they do not, or cannot, accept such narrow conceptions of what they should be like, particularly when the stereotypes deny essential parts of their character and abilities. Moreover, when young people openly reject the conditions imposed by this new stage of life, others believe that there must be something wrong with them—something within them that makes them unable to control themselves. The common-sense view does not appreciate the self-fulfilling nature of a situation like this, whereby people are denied experiences involving mature and responsible roles, but where this denial produces people who are immature and irresponsible. To understand this paradoxical situation in which many young people are put, one must adopt a sociological explanation that begins where common sense leaves off.

Based on this sociological understanding of the situation facing young people, it is unreasonable to expect people to learn the requirements of maturity and responsibility without allowing them to perform roles in which maturity and responsibility are exercised. Maturity and responsibility are attributes of character that must be learned through experience. These attributes cannot be adequately learned from textbooks or through classroom instruction alone; they must also be learned through practice. Until society understands this and acknowledges its impact on young people, many of the problems associated with them, and blamed on them, will continue. Thus, for many young people there is a bitter irony in being *free from* many things but being *free to* do very little that they find meaningful (cf. Fromm, 1955).

Where did this negative view of youth come from? As explained in Chapter 2, adolescence was "discovered" by social scientists early in the twentieth century when young people appeared to pose a problem for industrial society. This discovery eventually gave rise to an "ideology of youth" that has contributed to a consensus about the "true nature" of the transition to adulthood. Interestingly, this scientific ideology also serves corporate interests in Western societies, so it is exploited by those interests. To this end, the latter are able to capitalize on pre-existing modes of thought about youth to further their own ends (e.g., cheap labour and compliant consumers), fully supported by these social scientific theories. At the very least, dominant interests simply have had to heed the words of Aldous Huxley, who wrote in *Brave New World* that, in order for the status quo to be maintained and for the established system to run smoothly, the disenfranchised must be made to love their servitude, or at least not to recognize it as servitude.

The analysis in Chapters 3 and 4 suggests that, contrary to the ideology that the period of youth is the best time of one's life, "young people" now constitute one of the most disadvantaged and "at risk" groups in the entire population. Of course, as noted, there are internal divisions within this group that create variations in their fortunes, especially along class lines (also along gender, race, and sexuality lines), but the main concern is with the implications of their common age-status excluding them from a full participation in adult society. Furthermore, there are clear indications from statistics describing their life chances and quality of life that the circumstances facing young people have worsened dramatically in the past several decades. In order to justify this advantage given to adults (as a group) and business interests (as a force), it would appear that it has been necessary to perpetuate this ideology by manufacturing the consent of the young in order to convince them to accept a set of circumstances that are not always in their best interests.

To understand the perpetuation of the ideology of youth we must begin with the fundamental question of politics, which, in the present context, speaks directly to the distribution of power in society. Young people lack power, rights, and legitimacy—they are disenfranchised. At the same time, however, they are crucial to the reproduction of the economic system because they constitute a ready and pliable source of cheap labour, as well as a massive consumer market with disposable incomes earned from a wide variety of part-time jobs and given them by their parents. This is understandably very attractive to certain business interests. Politically and economically speaking, then, those in control have no interest in the majority of young people realizing the extent to which they are crucial to the profitability of corporations; accordingly, they have no interest in young people developing a political consciousness that would lead them to organize against that system. Clearly, to the extent that the young do not perceive the full extent of their manipulation, potential problems with resentment and rebellion are minimized. This is where the use of ideology and subtle ideological control are crucial to maintaining dominant interests in the societies under discussion.

As a point of departure for understanding how ideologies are implicated in the manufacture of dissent, an ideology may be said to comprise a body of systematic beliefs that function simultaneously to magnify certain aspects of social reality while masking other aspects. However, the strength with which an ideology can be embraced, particularly its persistence in light of contradictory evidence, leads us to distinguish it from a related phenomenon: a body of ideas. Ideologies are largely belief systems and thus cannot be proven false: For the true believer, no amount of proof (evidence) is necessary; for the nonbeliever, no amount of proof (evidence) is sufficient. The distinction between beliefs and ideas is more than just semantic, though, for while ideas are generally open to scientific testing, validation, and verification, beliefs are not so open (Rejai, 1971). Hence, as systems of beliefs, ideologies are difficult and sometimes impossible to examine on empirical grounds.

While capable of exerting a tremendous influence on peoples' perceptions and behaviour, then, ideologies are not strictly subject to verification, and this raises an additional consideration: the relationship between ideology and science, or ideology and truth. Ideologies are like dogmas. Their adherents make claims of truth but do not propose a method to substantiate such claims or to put them to a test where they might be shown to be false. Science, on the other hand, provides for a pursuit of certain forms of knowledge and truth in a fashion that is demonstrable and falsifiable. For the most part, scientific principles and evidence can be questioned, tested, refuted, or upheld. The scientist agrees to debate publicly his or her theories and to let others play a role in determining whether there is any relationship between ideas and "facticity." As Bergmann suggests, an ideological statement is "a value judgement disguised as, or mistaken for, a statement of fact" (1951, p. 210). Or, following McCain and Segal, who equate ideology with dogma, "one way of contrasting science and dogma is to say that a scientist accepts facts as given and belief systems as tentative, whereas a dogmatist accepts the belief systems as given; facts are irrelevant" (1969, pp. 31–32).

In sum, an ideology is a system of mobilized beliefs that claims to represent the truth and reality, but is not open to empirical verification. To make itself accessible to the majority of the population, ideology simplifies its depiction of truth and reality by using symbols, images, appeals to emotion, socially accepted values, and high-sounding moral principles. In all of this, the role of language is of paramount importance.

Ideology and the Politics of Language Language is essential in structuring the perception of reality. Without language, the ability to think in complex terms beyond the immediate situation is undermined. Language provides us with complex sets of names or symbols, and it is with these symbols that we can communicate meanings with each other about how we perceive reality. Even thinking about concrete, immediate objects and events is compromised unless one first has a name for such things. As noted earlier, a particular language was developed that disparages "adolescents," but these same words also served to delegitimize them, and depict them as marginal to what is positively valued in the society. Adolescence has been framed as a problem period in life when raging hormones take hold of young people and turn hitherto well-behaved children into demanding, unstable, and unmanageable tyrants. As shown in Chapter 2, this view is especially prevalent among those who subscribe to the medical/psychiatric model of development, which now has its own technical language to disparage young people.

Accordingly, in this analysis it is necessary to examine the ideological aspects of language and its use for explicitly political ends in the social control of youth. In this light, it is argued that language plays a key role in ordering, controlling, and manipulating young people today to serve the interests of specific groups. Where this kind of control is most telling is in its ability simultaneously to manipulate people in an open fashion, while having those same people and the rest of the population see such control as a good thing—as beneficial to the society at large.

From the perspective of a capitalist economy that claims the political legitimacy of liberal democracy where citizens are endowed with many freedoms and rights, and where any type of overt economic or political coercion is out of place, the language of order and control are indispensable. In this case, language is charged with defining coercion in acceptable ways—with portraying exploitation in benign terms. This is the power of ideology: It confers the ability to define a specific situation or phenomenon in a given way, to have others willingly and unquestioningly accept that definition, and therefore to gain and maintain political power. Hence, if exploitation is portrayed in benevolent terms as "giving one an economic break," and if that portrayal of the situation is accepted by workers, then the latter are far less likely to rise up against the "benevolent" employer and demand such things as higher wages, better labour agreements, more benefits, healthier working conditions, and so on.

Youth and Ideological Control   Whether one deals with the West as a whole, or with a discrete country in the West, one thing is certain—neither is a homogeneous entity. Within each country, economic, political, and social interest groups and élites abound, and each of these groups attempts to influence citizens' perceptions and actions in some ways and to varying extents. It is in this context that one must examine the categories of youth and adolescence with a view to assessing the degrees to which various public and private institutions, groups, and agencies in the "free" world control, cajole, and manipulate fellow citizens without their knowledge. Even in those cases where there appear to be manipulations for the public good one has to separate the immediate from the long-term consequences of such control and manipulation. For example, when governments create temporary youth employment initiatives and use public funds to finance such things as summer job training programs, the immediate beneficiary may be the young person looking for a job; but the major benefit often accrues to the private employer who will get a person trained at public expense, and who is able to work efficiently and thus be exploited more (Allahar, 1995; Schlosser, 2001).

Speaking of the callous manipulation of young people is admittedly a radical way of posing the problem and identifying the processes by which control is effected. However, it is necessary because Westerners are all too quick to point to other countries for examples of controlled populations, while refusing to entertain the possibility that even they are also subject to even some control. After all, this is why Westerners see themselves as "free"! They equate freedom with the absence of control, particularly physical control; it is on this basis that Iranian, North Korean, and Cuban citizens, for example, are traditionally depicted as "unfree." But even a cursory look at the so-called "War on Terror" will reveal that the overwhelming majority of dead and wounded American soldiers are under the age of 24. How informed were/are these young soldiers about the cause they were/are fighting for? Most were likely more informed by blind patriotism than a working knowledge of the world and its politics (National Geographic Education Foundation, 2002).

Ideology and Illusion   Politically, it has always been convenient for those who occupy the commanding heights of Western economic and political institutions to be able to distract the disenfranchised citizenry from the reality of their own exploitation by pointing to the sad fate of the hapless prisoners of Third World underdevelopment. Hence by comparison, the lowest-paid workers, the unemployed, the underemployed, and all other manner of disenfranchised groups in the West are made to feel better about their otherwise unflattering positions in their own societies. Though they may not be able to boast the material trappings of success, they are convinced (a) that theirs is a free society, (b) that they as individuals are really free, and (c) that they could acquire the material trappings if they really tried hard enough. For those who accept these manufactured ideologies, the meaning of their own poverty and low status can escape them, as can the realities of systemic racism and sexism affecting young people living on reserves and in ghettos, the largely uncounted homeless citizens, and the millions of poor, especially poor youth. To the extent that these things are present in a "free" society, both the victims and the more fortunate are conditioned to believe that the victims must be individually responsible for their plights. For along with the individual freedoms afforded by the society, there also come individual responsibilities. In socialist and other noncapitalist countries, on the other hand, any social malaise that can be identified is automatically attributed by Westerners to shortcomings of their entire social system itself. The ideological implication is that, while people may fall through the cracks in the capitalist, liberal-democratic system, problems in rival social and political systems indicate that the latter's entire systems and philosophies are flawed.

This is not meant as an apology for communist and other countries where large amounts of social control are evident. Rather, it is intended to alert those who live in the West to the fact that they are not immune from similar (albeit more subtle) types of manipulation. Further, in most of the nonsocialist, totalitarian countries where social control is not so subtle, and where human rights are denied daily to millions of people, it must be acknowledged that the West often puts the tyrants in power and maintains them there (over the years, in countries like Chile, Panama, and Guatemala). And once more it is the poor and the young of these societies who pay the highest price as they are sent to fight the wars against these tyrants. Thus, among the countries that constitute the "coalition of the willing" in the war against terrorism, plans for nation-building and democracy in Afghanistan and Iraq are merely the most recent examples of this historically patterned phenomenon.

Within the Western countries themselves, however, the situation faced by the young is not an isolated case in point. Quite apart from youths and adolescents, who make up a very substantial portion of any population, it is equally possible to trace the means by which women, racial and ethnic minorities, workers, and many other groups are the target of manipulation efforts, often without their even realizing it. Again, this can be traced to the power of language and the power of the mass media to define reality in ways that are consistent with certain interests; and simultaneously to distract target populations from a realization of what may be in their own best interests.

The use of language is ideological in that it conceals more than it reveals. It masks key aspects of social reality that, if subjected to critical scrutiny, would seriously challenge the basis on which certain voices in the West claim to speak and act from the moral high ground, and could also serve to disrupt the social order that is built on their supposedly superior morals. In other words, critical studies of the present type call into question the very legitimacy on which the system is founded and threaten to expose manipulation by entrenched interests.

The Politics of Social Control

It is understandable, therefore, why those who stand to benefit from the exploitation of the young are not politically interested in enlightening them, as would happen if they were well educated and privy to a full set of facts about what is behind many political and economic decisions. The key concern is with control at both the physical and the ideological levels. The agents of physical control are well known: police, courts, prisons, asylums, armies, and so on. What is not so well known, though, and what needs clearer analysis and explanation, are the indirect and subtle techniques of ideological control that are employed very effectively to manipulate people without their even being aware of this manipulation.

Social control can have one of two consequences. It can either deny group and individual liberty, or enhance it. But far from being an all-or-nothing phenomenon, control and freedom are multi-dimensional and matters of degree. Further, they are not mutually exclusive and contradictory phenomena, for clearly some degree of control is indispensable to freedom, both individual and collective (cf. Heath & Potter's, 2004, appeal to young activists to realize this). The central questions, therefore, are: control by whom? And freedom for whom?

These are questions of power and social class, for the dominant class, or fraction thereof, in any society is advantageously placed to exact obedience or compliance from the subordinate classes. The observation by Marx and Engels (1969) that "the ideas of the ruling class are in every epoch the ruling ideas" is usually taken as those authors' summary statement on ideology. Among other things, it implies a relationship not simply between class and ideology, but also between power and ideology—the organized and structured power of a given class:

> the class which is the ruling material force of society is at the same time its ruling intellectual force. The class which has the means of material production at its disposal, has control at the same time over the means of mental production. (1969, p. 39)

It is clear, then, that any discussion of ideology will also involve considerations of social control. As a mechanism of control it is far more efficient and less costly than physical coercion, although it cannot totally replace the use of force, as was evidenced in the invasions of Afghanistan and Iraq. Not only does ideological control obviate the need for rigid and all-pervasive supervision, it also makes for more social and political stability. If a given population, or more narrowly, a concrete social class or category (e.g., youth), can be made by another to pursue actions that run counter to its own interests (whether immediate or long-term), without perceiving those actions as harmful to itself, then there is no need to embark upon an elaborate program of interventive control aimed at that population or class. This is the sense in which some political economists speak about "false consciousness" in a subordinate population as one of the surest means by which a dominant class or group can guarantee its continued dominance over the former (Allahar, 2004).

A WINDOW INTO CORPORATION MANIPULATION OF YOUNG WORKERS: THE FAST FOOD INDUSTRY

Some find the political-economy perspective to be too "conspiratorial," especially as applied to the young. While many activities involved in the manufacture of youth consent have been difficult to document in the past (Côté & Allahar, 1994), over the past decade several studies have done just this. Most notably, Schlosser has done so in his book *Fast Food Nation: The Dark Side of the All-American Meal* (2001); see also Bakan's, 2004, *The Corporation: The Pathological Pursuit of Profit and Power*. Interested readers may learn from Schlosser's book the details of the fast food industry's manipulation of the lives of young Americans, and increasingly young people around the world. Here is a focused summary of his observations and conclusions.

Although Schlosser is a journalist, he tells a story of the changing political economy of American society (and societies affected by it) over the past several decades. In his words,

> the extraordinary growth of this industry. . . did not take place in a political vacuum. It took place. . . when the inflation-adjusted value of the minimum wage declined by about 40 percent,

when sophisticated mass marketing techniques were for the first time directed at small children, and when federal agencies created to protect workers and consumers . . . behaved like branch offices of the companies that were supposed to be regulated. . . . Far from being inevitable, America's fast food industry in its present form is the logical outcome of certain political and economic choices. (p. 8)

Schlosser carefully documents these claims, showing how the fast food industry has lobbied Washington politicians since the early 1970s to oppose minimum wage and workers' rights laws. He provides specific details regarding the actions of Ray Kroc, one of the founders of McDonalds and the mastermind of its long-term success. Kroc's influence on the American political economy includes lobbying the government in 1972 to allow employers to pay young workers (under 18) 20% less than the minimum wage (the so-called "McDonalds Bill"). After openly giving a quarter million dollars donation to then President Nixon's re-election campaign, a stir was created, teaching Kroc to be more subtle in his techniques.

In its relentless search for cheap labour, the American fast food industry has also been given hundreds of millions of dollars in federal government subsidies (up to $2400 per worker) to "train" low-income workers. This continues despite the fact that jobs in the industry are designed to require little training and have little opportunity for advancement. In fact, the high turnover is part of the plan to maintain high profits because new employees do not have to be paid certain benefits. The U.S. Department of Labor also knows that over 90% of subsidized workers would have been hired anyway (Schlosser, 2001, p. 72). Apparently, few Americans know that their tax dollars are subsidizing this industry that exploits their children.

Does the fast food industry need subsidies? Apparently not, because the annual bonuses given to the average corporate executives continue to rise (the average annual bonus was well over $100 000 in the mid-1990s). At the same time, if the minimum wage were raised by even one dollar, the cost of the average hamburger would increase by only about two cents (Schlosser, 2001, p. 73). Surely, customers would be willing to pay a few more cents for a hamburger. But this is not the point. Keeping their workers economically insecure is part of the corporate plan. If workers got too comfortable financially, they might ask for more benefits and security and better treatment.

Periodically, fast-food workers have asked for more and have attempted to unionize to achieve it. However, no unionization attempts have succeeded on any long-term basis. If they do, or it appears that they will succeed, the particular restaurant is simply closed and the building destroyed. This is the advantage of a franchise system—employees are local to each restaurant. In cases where serious attempts to unionize have been made at particular McDonalds restaurants, the Corporate headquarters has sent an army of attorneys to file legal motions and intimidate the union organizers (in one case they sent one lawyer for every four workers at the restaurant; Schlosser, 2001, p. 77).

As everyone knows, fast food restaurants are spreading around the globe based on this model of profit maximization and minimal care for employees. Schlosser has a number of recommendations for protecting young people, as both consumers of the products and workers in the restaurants, including banning advertising to children and stopping the subsidies. However, he is also aware that in the current neo-liberal political economy of the United States, this is unlikely to happen because the political clout of this industry leaves Washington politicians in a no-win situation. Given the millions spent on lobbying federal politicians to support their interests and the billions spent on elaborate marketing campaigns to win public favour, the wealth and influence of the fast food industry make it unlikely that any politicians will speak out against it (Schlosser, 2001, p. 267).

Is this a conspiracy, or business as usual in a corporate-capitalistic economy? Decide for yourself, but be sure to be fully informed before doing so.

THE MANUFACTURE OF DISSENT

The strategies of distraction and the ideological manipulation of language do not always work to manufacture consent in the intended manner. Indeed, when attempts to manufacture consent backfire, dissent can be inadvertently manufactured in the form of opposition to mainstream society, rebellion from authority, immature acting out, the adoption of potentially harmful attitudes and behaviours, and various forms of destructive behaviour. This is especially the case when those targeted are insufficiently rewarded for their conformity, as Huxley also wrote in *Brave New World*. The more serious and threatening forms of youth dissent that have emerged in acts of both individual and gang violence bear testimony to this. For example, rates of violent youth crime have risen steadily since the mid-1980s, at twice the rate of rise of violent adult crime (Frank, 1992; with the rate of the rise in female crime three times that of the male rate). Since the 1980s, American-style youth gang violence has been spreading through Canadian cities, especially Toronto.

The past decade, therefore, has seen unintended consequences of the "discovery and conquest of youth" in their dissent and resistance. This dissent is increasingly externalized in violence, various forms of acting out, appearance displays intended to evoke reactions from adults, and the like. But, inadvertently manufactured dissent is probably more often internalized in the problems of well-being outlined in the previous chapter, like depression and suicide. However, both of these can hamper and impede the transition to adulthood, with extreme forms effectively locking the person out of the labour force, creating a self-fulfilling prophecy of marginalization.

In addition to not providing sufficient rewards for conformity, the attempt to manufacture consent may not be fully effective, owing to the human capacity for agency: as noted previously, the ability for people to think purposively and deliberately, and to act in a self-determining manner. People have demonstrated this potential throughout history, in their personal lives and through political movements. However, the ability to fully exercise agency in the sense discussed here is sometimes a precarious matter because it is easily subverted by social pressures from peers, parents, teachers, or advertisers. More recently, corporate interests have developed extremely effective techniques for subverting this form of agency and replacing it with conformist thoughts and behaviours that only appear purposive and deliberate (as outlined in Chapter 4). The high-technology society of the twenty-first century provides the perfected tools necessary for those with power and money to systematically undermine people's potential for exercising agency by permeating their consciousness (especially with TVs, cell phones, and computers, and the gadgets associated with them) and providing the content for social patterns of daily life (e.g., both in the time taken up using high-tech equipment—a displacement effect—and the messages transmitted through them—a cultivation effect).

In the past, these efforts to manufacture consent were less obvious because of their insidiousness; now they are so commonplace there is little attempt to disguise them. As suggested above and as recommended by Huxley in *Brave New World*, the trick is to keep people focused on immediate short-term concerns, like their appearance and how much fun they are having. This gives people a (false) sense of personal agency, but there is little chance that they will have any impact on the political economy. Meanwhile, those who manipulate the political economy manufacture the options people have to address their immediate short-term concerns, like their appearance and entertainment choices. From a political-economy perspective, then, one can see how people can experience mass conformity as a freedom of choice. It is simply a "multiple-choice" freedom, however, with the answers determined in advance. This example points to a key difference between macro and micro levels of analysis referred to in Chapter 4. At the micro level, people make decisions all the time, and they do so regardless of the society in which they live (i.e., whether it is a "free" liberal democracy or a totalitarian regime). However, at a macro level, the patterns of this decision-making become clearer, and apparent individual variations become observable as group variations.

Dissent Among Young Women   The previous chapter discussed the 1990s singing group Spice Girls as an example of the conquest of cool. One can further understand this phenomenon as part of the larger manufacture of consent in steering young girls to equate "freedom" with "girl power," but which really involves making choices that leads them to formulate a sense of identity around possessions that define their status relative to their peers. Thus conceived, the net result is that these girls are simply asserting their rights to make their own decisions around purchasing and consuming "identity commodities," but this can also be manifested in fights with each other over who has the coolest or hottest boyfriend. This assertiveness, when not accompanied by an appropriate impulse control, can result in spending behaviour that greatly *complements* the interests of those who own and manage the associated industries. Thus, whether or not the creators of the Spice Girls deliberately set out to change the mass consciousness of teenage girls and young women is not important. At the same time, no one can disagree that they set out to make money by influencing the behaviour of this gender and age group. What is important, however, from the perspective of the manufacture of consent, is that the Spice Girls influenced the economic behaviour, spending habits, and sense of identity among a large proportion of a whole generation of young females. Since the 1990s, there has been a succession of female pop singers who have eagerly taken up this extremely lucrative position of "role models" for the young (e.g., Britney Spears, Christina Aguilera, and the like).

However, there was one particularly disturbing trend that may have been associated with "girl power": the rise in violence among young females as they fight with each other over their (unstable) images, possessions, and even boyfriends (Cox, 1997; Artz, 1998). Fights among girls and young women are no longer simply verbal, but have escalated to the types of fistfights and brawls that used to be found mainly among young males who were fighting over girlfriends. While media reports of such incidents have become more frequent, the problem of violence among teenage girls has been getting more social scientific attention. For example, Artz (1998, pp. 14–15) reports that "while the population of adolescents in British Columbia increased at a rate of 6% [between 1986 and 1993], the number of male youths charged with assault increased 118% . . . and the number of female youth charged increased by 250%." Artz goes on to note that, by 1993, females accounted for 42% of all assault charges laid against youths, compared with 26% in 1986. Similar statistics apply for the rest of Canada (a 190% increase for females versus 117% for males) and the United States. In her own survey of students, 20.9% of females (and 51.9% of males) admitted to beating up a peer once or twice in the last year (Artz, 1998). While ratios reported during the 1980s of male/female violence of this sort were 4:1, Artz reports the ratio in 1994 was under 2.5:1, reflecting an increase in the level of violent "dissent" among young females in relation to males.

Obviously, one cannot blame the Spice Girls for increases in female violence, but, wittingly or unwittingly, they may have played a part in the new climate of sex and violence that is increasingly influencing young females today. According to Cox (1997), teenage girls are under pressure to look sexy in whatever they do, and they look to the various media for images and role models as examples. Since sex and looking sexy are the primary messages from sources like the Spice Girls and Britney Spears, those who are unsuccessful at achieving the level of attractiveness and power portrayed by these sources can experience anger and frustration. This frustration can brew and find outlets mainly with peers who are seen as competitors, or who are used as scapegoats. Sometimes the violence is one-to-one and sometimes it involves a group of girls ganging up on one targeted girl. In schools, many young women now find themselves literally and figuratively "running the gauntlet" among their in-group and out-group peers.

In the case of the manufacture of consent among young women, then, what society has been witnessing over the past two decades is *not* the nurturing of solid feminist concerns over responsible self-determination and impulse control coupled with empathic social responsibility, but a side-effect distortion of these into pathological social and behavioural patterns, where self-restraint and empathy are mocked. The Spice Girls are but one part of a larger picture in which teenage girls have been influenced by consumer-corporate interests: Consent has been manufactured among many girls as they buy corporate products, but dissent has also been manufactured as many of the same girls strike out at each other in frustration when they cannot experience the ideals of popularity and pleasure promised by these products.

What Is Sex? Another, perhaps more obvious, example of the inadvertent manufacture of dissent comes from the potentially unintended consequent of attempts to spread messages about "safe sex" in public health campaigns directed at young people over the past couple of decades. In an attempt to encourage the use of condoms during sex, these campaigns may have altered the definition of "sex" among recent cohorts to include only vaginal or anal penetration (Randall & Byers, 2003). For example, in a sample of Canadian university students, only 25% defined oral sex as "having sex." This helps explain the many media reports of rampant oral sex among even young teens (e.g., reports of the notorious "rainbow" parties where young girls wear different shades of lipstick and young boys see how many shades of lipstick they can get on their penis by the end of the party). The contradiction in their attitudes is revealed by the fact that most of the same students in the survey would consider that someone had been a sexual partner had that someone given or received oral sex, and 97% would see a romantic partner as having been unfaithful had they given or received oral sex from someone else (Randall & Byers, 2003). Something has apparently happened to the definition of "sex" in the recent past, so those who are attempting to manufacture a consensus about safe sexual activities should be careful how they phrase and present things, otherwise they may be inadvertently manufacturing a form of "dissent" from the sexual mores that parents and schools are attempting to establish.

High School Shootings In the late 1990s there was a rise of high school shootings (mainly in the United States). The most notorious of these was the incident that took place in 1999 when two young men walked into their high school in Littleton, Colorado, heavily armed with pistols, rifles, and dozens of homemade bombs. By the time they finished their rampage, twelve of their fellow students were murdered, as was a popular teacher. Twenty-three other students were wounded, some critically. The two young men also killed themselves. Following this carnage, a similar act of violence took place in a high school in Taber, Alberta, and hundreds of threats of violence involving bombs and guns were made in schools around Canada and the United States, causing evacuations and class cancellations. In the year and a half preceding the Littleton incident, six mass murders took place in American high schools (Phillips, 1999), and several have occurred each year since.

What can be said about elements common to this rash of mass murders in high schools? First, they all occurred in large high schools, with student populations ranging from 600 to 1900. Second, all shooters were young males between the ages of 11 and 18. Third, all had easy access to firearms. Fourth, all were deeply affected by corporate-marketed youth culture in some way, including movies like *Natural Born Killers*, video games like *Mortal Kombat*, and death-themed music like that produced by Marilyn Manson. Fifth, all were experiencing some psychological difficulties, especially depression. And, sixth, all were triggered by something related to peer involvements, like being excessively teased or having a girlfriend break up with them (Cloud, 1999).

The two Littleton murderers, Harris and Klebold, were both from middle-class, two-parent families, and were apparently fairly intelligent. However, they had no active religious involvements, and it appears that their parents were "distant" in the sense that they did not talk with them much, or monitor their behaviour, otherwise they would have seen the guns in the basements of their homes and noticed that their sons were making bombs.

In comprehending the Littleton incident, one needs to understand how the "agency" of these two young men interacted with their particular social circumstances. Most prominent is the existence of large, factory-like schools that breed forms of alienation and resentment now widespread in the high school student population. These schools give rise to clique formation and the setting of peers against one another. That is the "keg." The "powder" seems to be the mass youth culture to which all were exposed, but which some take so seriously that they alter their identity formation to incorporate it. This mass culture provides ample fodder for hate and alienation in the name of entertainment, and it shows people how to take revenge for perceived personal injustices, from point-and-shoot video games to instructions on bomb-making over the Internet. Harris and Klebold had even made a video for a class project in which they dress-rehearsed their carnage, and they customized a video game (*Doom*) that "computer-modelled their crime" (Pooley, 1999, p. 20). In fact, both had been through an anger management course at their high school, apparently receiving passing grades (Phillips, 1999, p. 20). Furthermore, no adult authority figures in their lives took a serious look at where these two young men were heading, and there were no buffers to keep them from going over the edge: There were no adult figures from their family, from a religion, or from a school who seriously attempted to bring them back from the edge, or who even saw them on the edge.

Although this may be an extreme example of how the forces involved in the manufacture of consent can go wrong in intermingling to produce horrific manifestation of dissent, extreme cases do shed light on what is otherwise taken for granted as harmless in small doses.

Youth Gangs The above examples show how dissent can be inadvertently manufactured among mainstream youth. While this form of dissent may be more difficult to discern among the more affluent segment of the youth population, it is more obvious among the less affluent segment, especially as it is manifested in gang formation. In societies where consent is manufactured to increase consumptive behaviour, it is appropriate to examine how this influences those who do not have the means to consume at the advertised rates. Most generally, one would expect that considerable resentment would build against the mainstream society that denies them consumer affluence while flaunting it in their faces in the daily stream of media messages and marketing campaigns. And this resentment can build. Historically, revolutions follow when a sufficient proportion of the disenfranchised organize themselves around this resentment.

However, it is also the case that the self-destructive behaviours of certain youth gangs from economically disadvantaged ethnic groups (e.g., violence, racism, sexism, and homophobia), serve the purpose of fracturing potential unity among this group as a whole. Such behaviours also limit the potential effectiveness that they could have as a youth bloc if they were to demand decent jobs and housing, relevant educational and training programs, social justice, responsible government, and so on. Responding to their personal situations of extreme marginalization and powerlessness, lacking formal educational credentials and skills, and being denied social legitimacy at every turn, the frustrations among these economically disadvantaged youth can mount and they can respond in two seemingly contradictory ways: (a) they might seek to acquire illegitimately the material trappings of success defined as acceptable by the status quo; and (b) like the countercultural generation of the sixties, they could attempt to reject the system altogether by proposing an alternative culture that makes the establishment sit up and take notice.

This would not be entirely unlike the situation described by Frantz Fanon in *The Wretched of the Earth*, where he discusses Black-on-Black violence in the colonial context as stemming from the extreme frustration experienced by the colonized person who cannot easily strike out at the colonial master, and who instead turns his or her venom on fellow colonized sisters and brothers:

> The colonized man will first manifest this aggressiveness which has been deposited in his bones against his own people. This is the period when the niggers beat each other up, and the police and magistrates do not know which way to turn. (Fanon, 1963, p. 52).

Thus, in both Europe and North America, whether organized or not, it is possible to find separate youth gangs of underclass Whites, Skinheads, Blacks, Sri Lankans, Jamaicans, and Vietnamese, among others. In Los Angeles, Hispanic and Black gangs such as "Los Diablos" and the "Bloods" can go after one another in the most murderous of ways. At the same time, the racially homogeneous Black gangs "Bloods" and "Crips" represent extremely vicious Black-on-Black violence,[3] while the "Zulu Nation" is an equally violent, but racially integrated gang that boasts Black, Hispanic, and White membership. More recent additions to the scene are the equally violent Asian-American and South Asian youth gangs.

When the young members of these gangs fight it out with each other, both on the streets and in prisons, the main problem goes unnoticed, as does the failure of the larger social system, and those who benefit from its maintenance, to acknowledge their part in the manufacture of dissent and to do something about it. The dominant ideologies of racism and individualism can render them so blind to their particular interests as underclass youth that they fail to grasp them as class interests, while simultaneously embracing as their own the contradictory interests of their oppressors; for example, competition and consumerism. As a result, more hip-hop and designer clothes, jewellery, running shoes, and DVDs are sold, each tailored to a different age and ethnic segment of the youth population. The clothing name brand FUBU (For Us By Us), which is associated almost exclusively with Black youth and Black street culture, is a case in point.

"Rock On" or Riot On? One final illustration of how the manufacture of consent and dissent have affected the youth period is in a comparison of the three Woodstock music festivals that have been staged since the 1960s. The first Woodstock in 1969 was largely a grass-roots event in which the organizers lost money. However, its impact on the music industry and youth culture was largely positive, and it will be remembered as a landmark cultural event.

The next Woodstock, held in 1994, has been called "history's largest convergence of the mass market" (Lacayo, 1994, p. 48). This time, the organizers test-marketed the lineup of entertainers, engaged in "merchandising" (like selling official condoms, T-shirts, and refrigerator magnets), and several transnational corporations sponsored the event. Plenty of profits were made, but there was no lasting impact on youth culture and no lasting cultural statement. The 30-million-dollar fixed cost of the event was underwritten by a large multinational corporation and a number of large corporations came to peddle their wares. As a journalist covering the story at the time for the *New York Times* noted, "in an adjacent field where hippies might have staged a nude happening in 1969, Apple Computer Inc. and Philips have erected air-conditioned tents to demonstrate their latest electronic toys" (Passell, 1994).

Woodstock '99 also made lots of money but will be remembered for the violence, including several rapes, but especially the riot in which a dozen transport containers of official merchandise were set on fire. The press was largely silent on the implications of the desecration of this symbol of youth culture as a peaceful revolutionary force, but the dissent that emerged in aggression and violence can be clearly understood in terms of the young people there expressing their revulsion at being exploited by the organizers (e.g., paying $4 for a Coke), not to mention the exploitation they face in their daily lives. Clearly, some attempts to induce conformity can backfire.

CONCLUSION

The net effect of these various manipulation efforts is that billions of dollars flow from the youth segment to the adult segment of society, particularly to the adult élite, either in the form of consumer purchases or profit made from low wages. The ideological defence against this charge is becoming increasingly untenable as more people wake up to how the transition to adulthood has changed. Moreover, it is clear that the consumption and production roles of young people today are largely social-structural in origin, and the attempt to portray them as biologically determined is ideological.

ENDNOTES

1. For a recent account of the public relations industry see Stauber and Rampton's *Toxic Sludge Is Good for You: Trust Us, We're Experts* (1995) and for films on the manufacture of consent, the public relations industry, and related analyses of the corrosive influences of the mass media, visit the website of the Media Education Foundation (**www.mediaed.org**).

2. For impassioned critiques of these practices, which have also been questioned by the American Psychological Association and the American Academy of Pediatrics, we recommend Schor's *Born to Buy: The Commercialized Child and the New Consumer Culture* (2004) and Linn's *Consuming Kids: The Hostile Takeover of Childhood* (2004). For a more general treatment of this problem see Bakan's (2004) *The Corporation: The Pathological Pursuit of Profit and Power*.

3. It is worth pointing out that as a result of the riots in Los Angeles in the early 1990s, members of these two gangs came together, made a truce, and agreed that their problems were not really with one another, but rather were systemic. They agreed that their immediate problems were related to racism, economic deprivation, and social exclusion, and as such they identified the predominantly White police force, which was acting on behalf of the government and leading economic interests, as the prime enemy on which they were going to focus. Unhappily, however, the truce was very short-lived.

Complementarity and the Social Control of Youth Dissent

INTRODUCTION

Building directly on the previous chapter's concern with the manufacture of consent, this chapter explores the ideological dimensions of social control as they might be applied to a given society generally and to the youth segment of the population in particular. In other words, we take lessons from social control measures at the most macro level of political control of entire societies in order to understand the more micro level of manipulation of youth cohorts. Because social control is generally believed to be highest in communist and non-liberal societies where individual freedoms are virtually nonexistent, and where governments are forcibly imposed on citizens, we will use an unconventional device in developing our argument. That is, given its seeming transparency, this chapter will look at selected aspects of contemporary Western societies using the insights provided by George Orwell in his dystopia, *Nineteen Eighty-Four*, in addition to those in Huxley's *Brave New World*, as was done in Chapter 5. This device is useful in providing analogies to highlight what is otherwise accepted as normal and inevitable in contemporary societies.

IDEOLOGICAL CONTROL

As noted earlier, the wider public generally equates totalitarian society with communist society and, among those who are familiar with *Nineteen Eighty-Four*, most presume that

Orwell's fictitious totalitarian society, Oceania, was really based on the Soviet Union. After all, the absence of individual liberty and choice among the inhabitants of Oceania, and the menacing intrusiveness of the government of Big Brother, square very well with the widely disseminated images of life in the Soviet Union that were common in the West. Interestingly, however, and with slight licence, Orwell may very well be seen to have been speaking of the West in his condemnation of Oceania as a totalitarian society. His words are clear:

> With the absorption of Europe by Russia and the British Empire by the United States, two of the three existing powers, Eurasia and Oceania, were already effectively in being. . . . Oceania comprises the Americas, the Atlantic islands including the British Isles, Australasia, and the southern portion of Africa (1948, p. 153).

The thought that all those subtle and not-so-subtle forms of manipulation and control present in Oceania actually apply to the West has to be somewhat disconcerting to those who always equated totalitarianism and dictatorship with communist society. But, herein lies one of the principal benefits of ideological control: The controlled are not even aware of the fact that they are controlled, and as a consequence, they offer little or no resistance to it. In other words, it is important, from the perspective of maintaining social order and the status quo, for the disenfranchised segments of Western society to continue to entertain the fiction that they are free while others are manipulated and unfree. This is particularly evident in a foreign policy such as that of the United States with its stated goals of establishing democracy and spreading freedom to non-democratic and unfree peoples everywhere.

Given the actions of the George W. Bush regime in the United States, however, the smugness of many westerners would be shaken if they read Orwell as speaking about them and if they were made aware of the fact that Aldous Huxley could very well have been talking about young people in contemporary Western culture when he observed in *Brave New World* that

> a really efficient totalitarian state would be one in which the all-powerful executive of political bosses and their army of managers control a population of slaves who do not have to be coerced, because they love their servitude. (Huxley, 1958, p. 12)

The apathy, alienation, and disaffection that can be found among many of today's youth combine to make them unwitting pawns in a system that does not have much respect for them. And the same may be said of those who, imbued with a sense of patriotism, are fighting wars and dying for a social order that has long accorded them scant regard. From the point of view of those who are in control, however, the secret is to not have the young people realize their servitude as servitude, or their apathy as apathy. This touches on the earlier discussion of the politics of language; for in the consumerist vein, if servitude to the system could be defined as freedom to choose and to spend their money on an endless array of youth identity—items such as $200 running shoes, compact discs, and designer clothes—then there is no real need to resort to physical coercion. Furthermore, if apathy is defined as freedom not to participate meaningfully in the dominant institutions of their society, as in the case of the "moratorium period" discussed in Chapter 4, then the task of social control is complete. The controlled (youth) do not even perceive the extent of their manipulation and disenfranchisement.

But how is this acceptance of the status quo engineered? Huxley explains: "To make them love it is the task assigned, in present-day totalitarian states, to ministries of propaganda, newspaper editors and schoolteachers" (1958, p. 12). This form of social engineering is akin to the situation in Western, liberal democratic countries today. For those who live in the West are not without newspaper and TV editors who censor and sanitize the news; schoolteachers who indoctrinate students politically; public relations "ministries of propaganda" that package politicians; and a powerful entertainment industry that sells fictional encounters in fictional locations as "reality TV."

The point Huxley makes, then, is valid for totalitarian societies everywhere, and also in various Western societies where control and manipulation of the populations are more subtle, more cleverly disguised. That this is not usually seen to be applicable to the latter societies, however, testifies to the fact that it is ideologically masked in those societies. Huxley outlines the ease by which the Cold War was orchestrated following the Second World War:

> By simply not mentioning certain subjects, by lowering what Mr. Churchill calls an "iron curtain" between the masses and such facts or arguments as the political bosses regard as undesirable, totalitarian propagandists have influenced opinion much more effectively than they could have done by the most eloquent denunciations, the most compelling of logical rebuttals. (1958, p. 12)

Huxley could have taken lessons from Donald Rumsfeld, U.S. Secretary of Defense, during the war in Iraq. Speaking on the question of U.S. intelligence regarding weapons of mass destruction in Iraq, Rumsfeld seems to have perfected the art of "doublespeak" when he noted the following:

> As we know, there are known knowns. There are things we know we know. We also know there are known unknowns. That is to say we know there are some things we do not know. But there are also unknown unknowns, the ones we don't know we don't know. (SourceWatch, 2004)

And with specific reference to (a) the location of weapons of mass destruction (WMD), and (b) evidence of their existence, the secretary was boldest: "We know where [Iraq's WMD] are. They're in the area around Tikrit and Baghdad and east, west, south, and north somewhat" (SourceWatch, 2004). But when weapons inspectors in Iraq failed to turn up any evidence of weapons of mass destruction, he flippantly asserted that "the absence of evidence is not necessarily the evidence of absence" (Rumsfeld, quoted in Hylton, 2003).

The tragedy of this arrogance and doublespeak is that the United States and British attack, invasion, and occupation of Iraq were premised on the supposedly "clear evidence" that such weapons existed and that they could be deployed against the West in a matter of 45 minutes (Dodd, 2003). In spite of what the public had been saying all along, the existence of the "clear evidence" only now appears to have been a lie fabricated to justify a much earlier decision to go to war. Still resolute, however, as the facts come to light at the time of writing this book, the American and British administrations seem bent on playing semantic games by claiming that they had evidence of "weapons programs" as opposed to "weapons'" per se, that Iraq represented a "gathering threat" as opposed to a "threat" per se, and so on.

From the perspective of youth in contemporary capitalist society, the propagandists and opinion-makers are the same as those in the once-feared communist societies: politicians, news media, teachers, advertisers, and the massive entertainment industry. The social control imperative is clear: Disenfranchised and potentially disruptive groups must be distracted from a clear understanding of their situation. And the most efficient form of such distraction is ideological—whether one is dealing with ideologies of democracy and freedom, of patriotism and nationalism, racism, sexism, or any other such body of beliefs and ideas that appeal to people's emotions and stir them to action. In other words, a distracted population is beneficial or complementary to the interests of those who wish to rule. But what exactly does "complementary" mean in this context?

THE PRINCIPLE OF COMPLEMENTARITY

From the perspective of those who are in positions of control, it is always important to use force only as a last resort. This stands to reason, since force produces resentment and could potentially lead to a rule that is continually contested, whether in an overt or a clandestine manner. The challenge for the successful rulers, then, is to secure the consent of the ruled, especially in situations where the latter do not stand to benefit. In Huxley's terms, it involves the political question of getting the slaves to love their servitude; or, as Marx would argue, the creation of a false consciousness (Allahar, 2004) whereby the slaves do not even realize that they are slaves.

To fully understand the manner in which this is effected, we need to examine the concept of complementarity. This concept is elaborated in the writings of Baldus (1975, 1977), and is closely related to the concerns with social control and legitimacy discussed above. Baldus argues that social control can be effected in one of two ways: either physically, via the deliberate intervention of some body or agency, or more subtly and ideologically by the manipulation of what he calls "complementary conditions." Physical and ideological control differ in both form and content. Ideological control is slower to effect, more indirect, less easily resisted, but more difficult to escape once it is established. Similarly, those who are subject to ideological control tend to be less aware of the fact that they are controlled than those who are subject to physical control. This makes ideological control more effective in the long run—it is less likely to produce protest on the part of the controlled, while those in control do not generally suffer a loss of legitimacy.

As a strategy of control, the manipulation of "complementary conditions" involves either the use of existing patterns of behaviour within the population and society at large, or the deliberate creation of such behaviour patterns. More concretely, those in control observe specific types of behaviour engaged in by the "target" population, noting whether or not such behaviour complements or furthers their interests. Where it is complementary it will be encouraged, used, or exploited; and where such patterns of behaviour do not exist beforehand, those who stand to benefit will attempt to ascertain the possibilities of creating them. This is the model of social control portrayed by Huxley. On the other hand, where a pattern of behaviour exists that appears inimical to the dominant interests, steps will be taken to modify or eliminate it; but this is often more related to the question of physical force. This is the model of social control portrayed by both Orwell and Huxley.

An example of the deliberate use of complementarity is reported to us by Baldus, based on his reading of Agee's *Inside the Company* (Agee, 1975). As an ex-CIA agent, Agee was in a position to give incisive insights into the daily operations of the American Central Intelligence Agency. The CIA, we are told, was very calculating in its search for pre-existing complementary conditions such as conservative, anti-civil rights sentiments in the population at large. And having discovered them, the agency was forthcoming with financial support for conservative parties, it fed false information to local mass media concerning the "true" aims of leftist political movements, and covered up the real identities of those who were behind the bombings of Black churches. This sort of activity, Baldus contends, was conducted "in such a way that it is likely to be attributed to 'radical subversives,' [and] takes advantage of existing conditions which are favourable to the Agency's goals" (Baldus, 1977, p. 250-251).

Thus, playing upon the fundamental conservatism of a significant proportion of the American people, the CIA was able to use their fear and suspicion of radical politics to discredit the civil rights movement and other political causes that were critical of the establishment. But while the CIA did not directly create the climate of fear and suspicion, its prior existence represented "important complements essential to the success of the Agency's operations" by contributing to the delegitimization of such movements and causes.

We may also refer to Orwell's *Nineteen Eighty Four* for another example of the use of complementarity. Among the so called "proles" (proletariat, or working class) of Oceania, who made up 85 percent of the total population of three hundred million, Orwell tells us that there existed a fairly high level of apathetic behaviour. Even the mass rallies were very carefully orchestrated and had a clear superficiality to them. The proles were fatalistic, apolitical, and largely resigned to their lots in life. They were mostly interested only in the most petty and irrelevant details of daily life. In fact, as Winston (the main protagonist) remarked after an aborted conversation with one of them, "The old man's memory was nothing but a rubbish heap of details. One could question him all day without getting any real information" (Orwell, 1948, p. 82).

A more practical example of this may be seen in the youth apathy alluded to above. If there is pre-existing, widespread apathy and distraction, the controllers may seek to perpetuate it. This is the case with many university students who each year are faced with rising tuition fees, increasingly expensive textbooks, overpriced junk food in the cafeterias, steep rents in the residences, and the like. It is not a common occurrence, however, to see students organizing politically over such issues. While protests against tuition hikes occur occasionally in Canada, other protests are limited to such trivial matters as the number of days of orientation (party) they are permitted, availability of student parking, and the provision of recreational and student services. In the event that such apathy and distraction are not present, they are created by the authorities via the active promotion of varsity sports leagues, student clubs, fraternity and sorority memberships, and so on (Collins, 1979).

The key question to be posed here is, how different are the average citizens in Western societies today from the proles of Oceania? Certainly, the prevalent indifference to social and political issues among young people can be seen as complementary to the interests of the dominant class, for the rule of the latter is seldom seriously challenged by them.[1] During the 1980s there was much talk of the so-called "Me Generation," which refers to an ascendance of the ideology of individualism and the primacy of financial well-being. Unlike the 1960s when a large segment of youth sought to find meaning in relationships with others and to explore alternative philosophies of life, we have witnessed over the last twenty years a progressive disengagement of youth as a group from a concern with these existential issues in their lives (cf. The CIRP Freshman Survey, CIRP, 2004). Although the reasons for this are currently being debated, the trend of disengagement from adult society among those under 30 is clear (cf. Kimberlee, 2002). A variety of examples of the use of complementary conditions in contributing to this disengagement is now presented.

COMPLEMENTARITY ILLUSTRATED

The Mass Media

Young people are enthusiastic consumers of the mass media. Recent estimates indicate that the average American teen spends between 6 and 7 hours per day with some form of mass media (Brown & Witherspoon, 2002), some spending as many as 55 hours in front of a television set watching TV programs, recorded movies, or playing video games (Strasburger & Donnerstein, 1999). The average time spent with the mass media is more than the time spent in school, which is 6.5 hours for each of the five weekdays (Milner, 2004; Steinberg, 1996). Concerns over the content of the mass media messages date back to the introduction of novels, comic books, movies, popular music, magazines, and more recently video games. Most of this apprehension involved the fear that some sort of moral degeneration would take place when young people are exposed to "adult" themes. This book does not advocate simply shielding young people from "adult" material; rather, the concern is with how consumption of this material cultivates an ethos of consumerism, conformism, and immediate gratification. As argued earlier, dominant interests have shaped these media to produce such an ethos, at the expense of a critical consciousness among the young concerning larger issues of personal and social responsibility. And, to the extent that a critical consciousness was not in evidence among proportions of previous generations, dominant interests have no desire to cultivate it now on any basis, limited or widespread. Accordingly, those aspects of youth behaviour that are complementary to dominant economic interests are encouraged in the bulk of the messages transmitted, while those that threaten those interests are discouraged by the content of these media.

A good window into the media influence on young people is through "teenzines," which date back to the 1940s, shortly after the term "teenager" was coined by marketers (Quart, 2003). Teenzines are popular magazines directed at young women (and more recently young men, although without nearly the startup success or circulation). Critics argue that teenzines play on young women's insecurities about their appearance and sexuality, in effect socializing them to intensify their feminine characteristics with cosmetics and fashionable clothing, and do little to help them form identities related to long-term educational or career aspirations or to learn about political issues or social responsibility (e.g., Evans et al., 1991). It has been obvious to critics for some time that these were little more than dumbed-down versions of the fashion magazines aimed at adult women, whose primary purpose is to show women how they can enhance their position in life by manipulating their public presentations of sexuality. Not surprisingly, then, in the 1990s, several adult women's magazines (*Vogue*, *Cosmopolitan*, and *Elle*) launched their own teenzines (*Teen Vogue*, *Cosmo Girl!* and *Teen Elle*), which have been described as "training wheels of the glossies" (Quart, 2003, p. 4). And, while the pre-1990s teenzines were at least ostensibly designed to give sensible fashion advice, the new breed are pushing top-of-the-line designer clothes and expensive cosmetics, constructing "an unaffordable but palpable world of yearning for girls" (Quart, 2003, p. 5). Thus, while earlier teenzines simply undermined young women's body self-image, the latest breed also stirs the pot of status competition in terms of who can keep up with the most expensive ways to display their sexuality. Ads for breast augmentation and other forms of body alteration have also found their way into these teenzines, helping to explain why so many teenagers have suddenly been undergoing cosmetic surgery and taking weight-altering supplements to alter their appearance (Quart, 2003).

Of course, defenders of these magazines argue that they are simply meeting a market need because women want them. However, another response is that these magazines are specifically engineered to create a consciousness among young women that is only then defined as a need by adult women. As evidence of this latter position, we can examine the relationship between advertisers and publishers.

Most magazines depend upon advertising for their survival (this is the second of five filters in the manufacture of consent identified by Herman & Chomsky, 1988). In fashion magazines, it appears that advertisers call the shots. Basow (1992, p. 166) argues that in the case of adult women's magazines, advertisers "require a certain number of 'complementary copy'" items for each of their ads, such as an article about hairstyling to accompany advertising for hair products. This explains why up to 90 percent of such magazines as *Glamour* and *Family Circle* contain ads and ad-related copy. It is also common for advertisers to refuse to advertise if they feel articles are unsympathetic to their products. Basow cites several examples of this: "Clairol withdrew its advertising from *Ms.* magazine after *Ms.* reported on a congressional hearing into the carcinogenic potential of hair dyes, and Estée Lauder refused to advertise there because no articles on makeup appeared in the magazine." Thus, the content of women's magazines is largely dictated by the needs and whims of advertisers. If these magazines are to survive, they have little choice but to comply. One notable exception to this is *Ms.* magazine, which no longer finances itself with ads (Basow, 1992).

The control of advertisers over the various media varies by degree, but few would dispute that advertisers have an interest in producing an ethos of consumption. Some of these media do so as agents for other economic interests (e.g., television programs, teenzines, and fashion magazines) while others do it directly for themselves (e.g., the music industry, including MuchMusic and MTV—highly profitable channels devoted entirely to this task). But, at the heart of all of this activity is the fact that these media can be used to sell young people some element of an identity that they have also been encouraged to crave. As argued above, the cultivation of identity-based consumption is possible because the basis for a viable identity rooted in more meaningful activities has been taken away from young people through a series of laws, customs, and institutional practices. With this accomplished, "identity elements" are sold back to them as "identity products" that ostensibly provide a means of demonstrating "individuality." These media thus play an integral role in effecting social control by stifling dissent among a potentially powerful and disruptive segment of the population. They normally do this by providing harmless outlets for "dissent" that are actually profitable to the system, such as outrageous clothing, hairstyles, music, and the like. Some forms of "dissent" are now so commonplace—hence mainstream—that they are advertised on TV (e.g., tattoo parlours) or even praised in greeting cards (Niedzviecki, 2004, admits that his self-image as a rebel was shattered when his parents gave him a birthday card for his thirtieth birthday congratulating him for being a "non-conformist").

Advertisers must kowtow to dominant interests in ways that we often do not hear about. One occasion that got noticed was when the Moral Majority set its sights in the mid-1990s on the teenzine *Sassy* for being too "liberal" in its treatment of issues of sexuality, straight and gay. The Moral Majority pressured advertisers to boycott the magazine, which brought it to its knees within a few years of its launch in 1988 (Gardiner, 1995). A large media corporation bought it, the youthful staff was fired, and the content became indiscernible from other teenzines that encourage being boy-crazy in socially acceptable ways (by luring them with clothing and cosmetics, and by being slim and hard to get). As journalist Sue Gardiner reports in *The Globe and Mail*, "an unambiguous corporate vision guides the editorial content" of the new *Sassy*, namely, to be "a training ground in how to shop" (1995, p. F2). Gardiner laments the all-too-obvious consequence: "as a girl reduces her identity to an accumulation of consumer choices—cola, jeans, pressed powder—her inner self is correspondingly stunted" (1995, p. F2).

The media have also taken on a curious role in informing young people about the world and political affairs. While the entire population is now fed a diet of TV "news" channels such as CNN and Fox, and conservative talk-radio programs that package fluff and political rantings that are then sold as news, it appears that the social and political consciousness of young North Americans is increasingly affected by comedians. Some media observers are concerned that young people are getting much of their information about, and views of, the world from cynical comics like Jay Leno and David Letterman. Of course, these comedians simply mock politicians in terms of stereotypical public perceptions and the latest scandal, and do not provide any factual depth and insightful analysis. More recently, Jon Stewart in the United States and Rick Mercer in Canada have drawn large youth audiences, and part of their routine is political commentary. While the attention to politics is refreshing, the nihilistic cynicism of these comics can simply reinforce a sense of "righteous disengagement" and resignation that seems to have spread throughout the youth population in relation to the mainstream polity. And, while there is much to be cynical about in terms of how the present political process is constituted in North America, this disengagement also means that alternative political and economic systems are not considered, and the spiral of youth disenfranchisement continues as the young move further and further from the centres of political and economic power.

Mass Education

The principle of complementarity applied to the mass manipulation of youth is also clearly illustrated via an analysis of the public (mass) education system. Such an analysis shows that the public system was developed to suit the traditional interests of dominant economic and social groups, which simultaneously resisted and discouraged developments that went counter to their interests. Schools currently contain, shape, and cultivate behaviours in young people; this prepares a good proportion of them to be part of a passive and uncritical workforce, which is crucial to the functioning of industrial societies. In Canada, there is a tendency to accept mass education as inevitable and necessary, but such a view clearly plays into the hands of those managing the status quo; for if mass indoctrination and mass processing can pass for education, then the indoctrinators and processors will encounter little real challenge to their authority (cf. Bowles & Gintis, 1976).

Furthermore, Canadian society has unmistakably become one in which most occupational roles require credentials formally granted by specially designated bureaucracies. It is no longer considered appropriate that workers acquire their qualifications and skills in the workplace, except in a few surviving apprenticeships. At the same time, the primary reason for keeping students in school for longer periods of time is not solely to ensure that they are better trained in terms of advanced skills, except for the minority that goes on to highly specialized fields. It is just as much for the sake of others, namely, schools and their employees, professional associations, and dominant economic interests (Milner, 2004). A case can be made that most of the Canadian workforce is underemployed when the skills they actually use in their daily jobs are compared to the amount of schooling they have received (e.g., Livingstone, 1993, 1998). Thus, among other things, the sequestering of young people in schools protects the community from disruptions that might occur if young people were idle and it legitimately keeps them out of the labour force as potential competitors with older workers (cf. Lapsley, Enright, & Serlin, 1985).

It is evident that Canada's modern mass-educational system has benefited big business and big government far more than it has benefited the so-called "masses" who have been subjected to it. These élites have only had an interest in establishing the custodial function of educational institutions, not educational functions that would nurture all students' full potential, including a critical consciousness and moral sensibility. It is certainly not in their interests to use corporate tax dollars to improve these institutions, for this would take away from corporate profits. Hence, the progressive decline in educational funding in many areas as corporate taxation has also declined (cf. Klein, 2000).

As we saw in Chapter 3, over time the mass-educational system has become a monopoly that created an "education inflation" by which the value of lower levels of education decreases as more people obtain higher levels. So, as more university degrees have flooded the market, the value of these degrees has decreased, and increasing numbers of graduates have become underemployed. Consequently, professions have required increasingly higher qualifications for entrance without a proportionate increase in direct skill acquisition. In addition, the growing costs associated with entering professional programs has kept their enrolment levels low, and has enabled them to maintain their high prestige and income levels as more people are competing for educational credentials with less chance of success—particularly those not from middle or upper class backgrounds (Collins, 1979; cf. de Broucker & Lavallée, 1998).

Those who scramble for credentials must endure years of socialization to qualify as workers who are suited for jobs over which they have little or no control (i.e., they are prepared for alienated labour). Hence, the emphasis on rigid training for the requirements of the industrial and business workplace, which often require punctuality, self-discipline, and an uncritical willingness to do whatever is required, no matter how demeaning, mind-numbing, or unethical. Such training also requires of students the suppression of independent, critical thinking about corporate-capitalist society. Those who resist this socialization in educational settings generally find themselves excluded from all but the most menial workplace settings.

Distractions and False Hope: Lotteries and Sports

To return to the Orwellian analogy, it is complementary to those in power that the disenfranchised do not come to realize their true strengths and the constraints placed on them from exercising those strengths. As stated earlier, distraction is a powerful form of social control that leads directly to social "stability." Orwell spoke of how the government of Big Brother was able to use the pervasive mood of apathy and disinterestedness among the proles, who, he said, were "without general ideas," to realize its program of mass control. By staging certain public happenings such as the Lottery, which served further to distract them from the reality of their conditions of existence, the rule of Big Brother went largely unnoticed. The Lottery, with its weekly payout of enormous prizes, was one public event to which the proles paid serious attention. It was probable that, for a significant proportion of proles, the Lottery was the principal if not the only reason for remaining alive:

It was their delight, their folly, their anodyne, their intellectual stimulant. Where the Lottery was concerned, even people who could barely read or write were capable of intricate calculations and staggering feats of memory. There was a whole tribe of men who made a living simply by selling systems, forecasts and lucky amulets. (Orwell, 1948, p. 82)

In a sense, then, the proles of Oceania appear not to be very different from their counterparts in today's North America, where the lottery and casino gambling mentality is firmly entrenched among those who invest heavily, hoping to strike it rich overnight. But lotteries and casinos are not the only public happenings that serve to distract youth and other powerless segments of Western society. The sports and entertainment industries are able to maintain a level of hype and distraction that is almost perpetual. For quite apart from the video revolution in music and computer games, and the compact disc and Walkman gadgets (most recently MP3s and iPods) that enable the individual to insert tiny speakers into the ear and tune out the rest of the society, the public is fed a steady diet of flashy pop, hip hop, and rap concert tours that are matched in pomp and ceremony only by the highest levels of sporting rivalries: the Superbowl, the Grey Cup, the Stanley Cup, the World Series, the National Basketball Association (NBA) finals, and National Collegiate Amateur Athletic (NCAA) confrontations. These are featured year-round and serve as powerful distractions.

On the one hand, these activities can act as useful forms of relaxation and release. On the other hand, while great numbers of young males contribute to a multimillion-dollar industry that produces hockey, football, baseball, and basketball cards, and while they can recite the batting, catching, pitching, and scoring statistics of individual players, many of them do poorly in schools and cannot perform simple numeracy tasks like reciting multiplication tables or literacy tasks like writing coherent formal letters. And the same goes for those who know every lyric of the top ten hit songs in any given week, but who are unable to learn material from their school courses to pass tests.

With salaries that are many times that of the highest-paid teachers who have acted as role models in previous generations, movie stars and sporting figures assume cult-like stature that the average young person is able to identify with vicariously. It is a sort of make-believe world that the average individual can dream about and take comfort in the knowledge that he or she too could have made it; for the most commonly repeated stories about these superheroes stress their "rags to riches" ascent of the social and economic ladders.

This mythology is especially prevalent regarding black athletes. However, according to Sabo and Jansen (1992), in the United States "only about 3,000 blacks make their living at professional sports, [including] coaches and management personnel. Indeed, there is greater probability for a black high school athlete to become a doctor than a professional athlete." Sabo and Jansen go on to argue more generally that modern sports are the "real-life analogue . . . [of] capitalist ideology," where there is the belief that "all players begin the game at the same starting point, but the most talented finish first." The reality of capitalism, however, is that not everyone has "the same starting point, teams are not evenly matched, and the scoring system does not necessarily reward skill, training, intelligence, or determination" (Sabo & Jansen, 1992, pp. 182-183). Thus, sports rituals play a key role in sustaining a sense of fairness for the average individual in capitalist societies, by giving him or her the illusion that all is well, at least while "the game" is being played.

Those who are suitably distracted and uninformed are more easily persuaded to support certain policies and agendas and are more easily manipulated to engage in certain behaviour patterns. And because distraction and ignorance are largely complementary to the interests of those who are in control, it is easy to see why so much emphasis is placed on the entertainment and sporting industries: They serve to minimize potentially disruptive behaviour; they make billions of dollars for those concerned; they are politically useful as distractions; and they enable dreams even among the least fortunate members of society. This is not to say, however, that such things as sports and movies were designed specifically for this purpose; rather, they are examples of behaviours and practices that are in prior existence, and which are complementary to the interests of those in control. But conversely, if such conditions did not exist beforehand, they could be created via the manipulation of such institutions as public education systems and the mass media, as is the case with lotteries, which became legal in Canada as recently as the 1970s.

Gender Intensification

A prominent feature of socialization in many advanced industrial societies is the differential socialization of young males and females into the "ideology of gender." In speaking of the ideology of gender, it is the exaggerated notions associated with the different roles that continue to hold many men and women in separate spheres of endeavour that are referred to. While progress has been made in "desegregating" men and women in terms of private and public spheres (e.g., family versus the paid labour force), this progress has been relatively slow, and in some ways appears to be "stalled." Indeed, the remaining role segregation persists, in spite of the fact that there is no longer any historical necessity for many of these differential role allocations—as in the fact that physical strength is no longer relevant for most jobs in the advanced industrial economy—and in spite of the fact that we now know that there are few substantial biological differences between men and women with respect to cognitive abilities, personality traits, or behavioural dispositions (e.g., Basow, 1992).

Thirty years of research has revealed that most apparent gender differences statistically disappear when socialization factors are taken into account in quantitative empirical research. The few remaining differences could be biological in origin (the definitive study statistically controlling all social factors is yet to be conducted), but their origin is of little practical importance because the magnitude of these differences is so small. Variables like verbal and mathematic abilities, visual/spatial abilities, and aggression all remain statistically significant when males and females are compared, even when other variables are taken into account. However, it must be stressed that the substantive or meaningful difference between females and males as groups is in the magnitude of a few percentage points. In other words, knowing someone's score on, say, a mathematics test, gives virtually no clue as to whether or not the test writer was male or female (e.g., Mackie, 1991). Clearly, males and females are far more similar than they are different in terms of most abilities, traits, and behaviours. Moreover, even if the differences were greater than has been found on the basis of scientific investigation, these would not justify the fact, for example, that males hold most of the jobs in certain sectors of the economy. Besides, women come out of this research with slightly greater verbal abilities, but they certainly do not comprise most of writers, poets, broadcasters, politicians or other professions in which verbal abilities are key.

The most plausible explanation for the continued segregation of males and females is that an ideology of gender persists that sustains a false view that biological differences justify differential gender roles and the segregation of men and women into their culturally defined "proper" domains. As discussed above, ideologies emphasize some things and de-emphasize others. In the case of gender comparisons, these biases have been referred to as "alpha biases" and "beta biases" (Hare Mustin & Marecek, 1988). Alpha biases exaggerate differences between males and females (e.g., cognitive abilities), while beta biases minimize or deny differences (e.g., the extent of discrimination or segregation in the workplace). Together, these biases bolster the ideology that sustains traditional gender roles and block the progress toward full equality between men and women.

In fact, it appears that some of the stall in the progress toward full gender equality and desegregation can be found with what have been called "gender intensification" processes occurring during adolescence and youth. These processes involve the continued socialization of young people with attitudinal and behavioural "scripts" based on the ideology of gender (Huston & Alvarez, 1990). But this script is for a society that is largely obsolete or is simply no longer sustainable. At the peak of industrialization, the traditional nuclear family prevailed with its segregated gender roles. In advanced industrial society, this family structure is no longer sustainable as women are drawn into the paid labour force. Unfortunately, these outdated gendering processes are now exploited by various youth-oriented business enterprises, such as the mass media, fashion, sports, and music. The exploitation takes the form of an identity manipulation whereby females are "sold" goods and services based on exaggerations of the traditional ideal of the "feminine identity," and males are "sold" goods and services based on the ideals of the "masculine identity" (cf. Mandell & Crysdale, 1993). In short, gender is "big business," so big business (Capital) has a vested interest in exaggerating conceptions of gender in order to continue selling "genderized" products.

This orchestration follows the principles of identity manipulation outlined above, but in this case results in a differential exploitation of males and females, with females coming out somewhat worse economically than males. What distinguishes the gender intensification processes from other identity manipulation processes is that the former frequently stimulate a "flight into femininity" for young women, and a similar "flight into masculinity" for young men (cf. Douvan & Adelson, 1966). Ultimately, however, the outcome can be a reproduction of traditional or semitraditional gender roles during adulthood. Accordingly, there is a reproduction of the ideology of gender whereby males dominate major political and economic institutions, and females remain in supportive roles where their labour is either underrewarded (as a reserve army of cheap labour) or unrecognized (when they carry out the bulk of household labour). In both cases, Capital is the beneficiary in the maintenance of traditional gender roles to the extent that profits are increased.

The flight into femininity that many young women experience in early adolescence is troubling because it is associated with many personality attributes among young women that place them at a disadvantage if and when they attempt to move into productive and responsible roles associated with political and economic institutions. If men and women are to enjoy equality in Western societies, the socialization experienced before adulthood must be congruent with the roles and experiences that will be faced *during* adulthood. But, because the traditional female role requires noncompetitiveness with, and subordination to, men, young women caught in the "flight" often experience, relative to young men, a decline in school motivations and career aspirations, a narrowing of interests (Huston & Alvarez, 1990), a lower self-esteem than young men (e.g., Hill & Lynch, 1983; Holmes & Silverman, 1992), less confidence in their academic abilities, and a tendency to blame themselves for failures or shortcomings beyond their control (Nielsen, 1991). These things have been known for some time, and little has changed since in spite of this knowledge.

Lowered school and career expectations are especially disturbing, given the well-established finding that females obtain higher grades throughout primary and secondary school (Stockard & Johnson, 1992). Indeed, pressuring women to conform to the ideals of femininity appears to restrict their possible repertoire of socially approved behaviours to about 25% of human traits, but leaves men with the other 75% (Broverman et al., 1970). This "homogenization" of women (Bem & Bem, 1970) is intensified in adolescence and reinforced in adulthood, but appears to be crystallized during adolescence around the notion that women must primarily attend to their appearance and popularity (supposedly to attract the best mate, according to one version of the ideology of gender). As noted by Nielsen (1991, p. 195), research indicates that "adolescent girls base more of their self esteem on their appearance, their social standing, and on the approval of other people."

In spite of this intense attention to their physical self, however, adolescent females are more dissatisfied with their appearance than are adolescent males. In fact, research consistently reveals that most American teenaged women actually *dislike their bodies*, and many believe that they are overweight, even though they often are of average or below average weight. Finally, while teenaged boys are also under pressure from arbitrary appearance norms (e.g., to be tall, muscular, and "macho"), it does not appear to be "killing them" in the same way that young women "kill themselves" with the types of obsessive dieting associated with anorexia nervosa and bulimia (Nielsen, 1991). As we saw in Chapter 4, young men can take a more direct route to killing themselves.

Why is gender intensification complementary to the interest of certain élites? One very obvious reason pertains to the fact that marketers know very well that "gendering" products works to increase profits. Not only can two sets of products be sold if people believe that men and women *should* have different soaps, shampoos, cars, and so forth, but higher prices can be charged for these "specialized" products, especially for women's products. Marketers did not create these gender stereotypes, but they certainly capitalize on them. And, to the extent that they play on them, they reinforce and perpetuate them. Thus, capitalists have a vested interest in maintaining a basic division between men and women in terms of their very "essence." The more men and women are convinced that they are a different "species," the more they can be sold special products and services. According to Rushkoff (2001), marketers have recently collectively created two archetypes representing this intensification in youth culture: the "midriff" and the "mook." The midriff is modelled after Britney Spears and represents the use of sexuality as personal empowerment, even if that power is not understood by the young women. The mook is inspired by the likes of "shock jock" Howard Stern and represents a stereotypical dumbed-down, coarse, and vulgar slob who does not care what others think of him.

Moreover, much of this marketing plays on heterosexual attraction, with women and men sold billions of dollars in products and services that ostensibly give them the inside track in attracting desirable mates. In doing this, men and women are not only alienated from their sexuality, but women are set in competition with each other in attempting to look the most attractive according to the arbitrary and unrealistic standards set by marketers. These influences now begin in childhood, become intensified in adolescence, and continue into adulthood. While many individual women and men do resist and escape these influences, the ideology of gender constitutes a pervasive cultural force in people's lives that continues to be transmitted intergenerationally. Consequently, many individual lives are deeply affected, including those young women who invest more in their appearance than in their inner self and personal potential, with predictable consequences in later life (e.g., being unprepared for non-traditional jobs).

At another level of benefit the ideology of gender is good for capitalism because it induces male and female employees to fight with each other over scarce resources (jobs and wages), while élites maintain their advantage unchallenged. But why would the economic élite be interested in perpetuating a "gender war" among individual women and men? Surely, it can't matter that much to them, in the sense that they would derive some personal gratification from it. Well, probably most do not, but if they are to maintain their superior position and lifestyle, they need a capitalist economy that is maximally effective. And, the basic principle of capital accumulation is the extraction of profit from the labour of others. But, more importantly, the lower the wages paid to workers, the greater the profit the élites reap. Quite simply, if the élites want to maintain their high salaries and personal wealth, they need to find someone to work for low wages, and the lower the wages of workers, the greater the wealth of élites. This is an essential component of capitalism.

Obviously, few people would choose to work for low wages if they had the opportunity to receive higher ones, especially in doing the same job as the person working beside them. Accordingly, capitalists have found it convenient to use "complementary conditions" to recruit cheap labour. In this case, the complementary condition of late-modern society is the legacy of patriarchy and the ideology of gender. Accordingly, marketers in the employ of the élites simply find it expedient to play upon peoples' stereotypes about a "differentness" between men and women. In playing on these ideas, and convincing people (with varying degrees of success) about them, capitalists have succeeded in maintaining wage disparities and job segregation—getting women to work for lower wages in low-skilled jobs. Interestingly, to the extent that the struggle against this exploitation has been successful, capitalists have turned to another segment of the population for cheap labour— young people, as demonstrated in Chapter 3.

In reference to the bigger picture of gender inequality in the history of industrial capitalism, capitalist élites have been subsidized by women's free labour in the household. Without this free labour, which reproduces and maintains the paid-labour pool, the amount of profit extracted from wage earners would have been far less. In other words, if capitalists had to pay their fair share of the costs of bearing and raising the children who become their workers, their accumulation of profits would have been much more constricted over this whole period. Little wonder, then, that the various media and institutions controlled or influenced by wealthy capitalists have sustained the stereotypes about women and men and nurtured the ideology of gender in intensifying people's sense of "gender."

Political (Non)Participation

Finally, given all the distractions, mistrajectories, and manipulations, it is easier to understand the progressive disengagement of the youth population for the mainstream political process. There are various interpretations of this disengagement, with some arguing that young people have simply shifted their political concerns elsewhere (cf. CIRCLE Staff, 2004; Gidengil et al., 2003; Kimberlee, 2002), but on the issue of mainstream participation, it is clearly in the interests of those in power that the young do not involve themselves in political affairs. This leaves those in power free to do as they please: keep the minimum wage low,[2] raise tuition to replace government and corporate support of higher education, or send the young off to war. On this point—sending the young off to war—there was little opposition to the war in Iraq, both originally and after the reasons for doing so were revealed as fabrications. But, why was there no widespread opposition among those who would be most affected by the war in terms of having to go and fight it? Aside from political apathy regarding mainstream politics, there also appears to be widespread ignorance of world affairs among the youth population in the United States. As an illustration of this, in the fall of 2002, the National Geographic Society reported the results of a study of 18- to 24-year-olds, which found that only 13 percent of young Americans could locate Iraq on a map (National Geographic Education Foundation, 2002).

The survey presented in face-to-face interviews 56 questions related to world geography and current events. The geography questions involved identifying a country out of four choices spread over the globe. Answering the question on Iraq correctly simply required knowing: (a) that Iraq is in the Middle East and (b) where the Middle East is on a map of the world. In fact, more young Americans could locate the Marquesas Islands, most likely because the pop culture TV show *Survivor* had just presented a series of episodes there, each of which began with a map to show where they are located. This demonstrates the mass media's influence in shaping people's mental representations of the world (i.e., part of their consciousness), and suggests that few young people even pay attention to TV news, otherwise they would have seen the maps of Iraq that have been presented countless times during newscasts in the 1990s and 2000s.

Before Canadian readers feel complacent, they should know that young Canadians did only marginally better than Americans, correctly answering only 27 out of the 56 questions (versus 23 out of 56 for young Americans). Young Swedes performed the best out of the nine countries surveyed, answering 40 questions correctly (National Geographic Education Foundation, 2002, p. 17). Apparently, there are qualitatively better ways to inform and educate the young, and perhaps North Americans have something to learn from the Swedes (as we will see in Chapter 7). But, how does one understand this survey in terms of the big picture of the manufacture of consent? With respect to the mass media and popular culture, it is apparent that these constitute massive distractions from the issues that really matter concerning the future of the world. In terms of mass education, it would appear that those who control the curriculum and funding in many countries either do not care that the bulk of young people are "educated" to be politically ignorant, or they have no interest in removing the veils of ignorance that have been constructed by other consent-manufacturing influences.

CONCLUSION: THE "BENEFITS" OF COMPLEMENTARITY IN THE MANUFACTURE OF CONSENT

The use of complementarity as a strategy of social control, then, will yield two types of benefits to the dominant interests. The first concerns the question of cost, for it manages to secure needed behaviour at costs that are much lower than would be incurred if the same behaviour were to be created by force, using police, courts, prisons, or the military. Where costs do arise, they are normally minor and technical and limited to finding or stabilizing complementary behaviour. Clearly, social control agents face a dilemma if conventional methods were to break down, and force emerged as the only option. In Canada, the prospect of using security guards to keep order in secondary schools is still viewed as unpalatable and somewhat un-Canadian, although in many American schools it is now commonplace.

The second benefit of the complementarity approach to social control relates to the fact that the dominant interests are served while simultaneously permitting a wide range or variety of behaviours among the population at large to continue. This has the added social control benefit of creating the illusion of freedom and individual choice, for as Baldus observes, "complementary behaviour is judged primarily by its instrumentality or utility for dominant class interests" (1977, p. 251). Hence, it is of no immediate importance if the proles in Orwell's Oceania or the youth of today, for example, attributed meanings to their behaviour that are totally different from those assigned by the dominant interests, just so long as their behaviour does not run counter to those interests. Speaking of the proles, Orwell says that the mundane details of their daily lives were of no importance to Big Brother, provided that they did not conflict with the aims of the authorities. Thus, they were generally left to themselves, free to revert to a style of life that appeared to be natural to them:

> They were born, they grew up in the gutters, they went to work at twelve, they passed through a brief blossoming period of beauty and sexual desire, they married at twenty, they were middle aged at thirty, they died, for the most part, at sixty. Heavy physical work, the care of home and children, petty quarrels with neighbours, films, football, beer, and above all, gambling filled up the horizon of their minds. To keep them in control was not difficult. (Orwell 1948, p. 65)

Again, by extension to the situation facing the youths of today, what is important is not the subjective meanings attached to their behaviour or the illusion of "agency" in participating in consumer society; rather, it is the outcome. For example, if they think that their rap and punk music, which is critical of the system, provides some release and grants some satisfaction that they have "raged against the machine," that is fine. To the extent that their protests and rebellion go nowhere, they are left alone, recording companies produce and sell their records and reap huge profits, and everyone is content, except perhaps parents and teachers who put up with the acting out it can produce.

However, if the young performers of rap, punk, or the latest alternative music chose to act on the message of their lyrics, then it is a different matter, and force would be brought into the picture. Imbued with a sense of their liberal freedoms, which includes the freedom of speech, these young people claim the right to sing about any themes and to be as outrageous and violent as they wish in their lyrics. Their right to do so is even defended by the establishment's invoking of the freedom-of-speech guarantees that are part of all liberal democratic constitutions, and this is why occasional calls for censorship are seldom seriously heeded. The point, however, is that the illusion of "freedom" contained in the "right of free speech," distracts the youths in question from a clear realization of the fact that theirs is often an empty freedom. They may make as many critical records as they wish decrying the injustices of the system just so long as they do not endanger the right of others to pursue "life, liberty, and happiness." In other words, the notion of freedom that is contained in such "rights" as free speech, free association, and freedom of the press, merely placate the powerless by leading them to believe that they are indeed free and equal with all others in the society, when in actuality they are not. Freedom thus conceived is ideological.

Complementary behaviour, in sum, contributes to the preservation of social order by giving those without power, for example young people, the impression that they are indeed empowered, agentic, and can pursue goals of their own choosing, free from outside interference (cf. Furlong & Cartmel, 1997). It is important to cultivate this appearance of freedom, for it leaves the power structure intact and says to the young people that they are personally responsible for their situations in life. If the overall system is portrayed as free, open, and fair, and individuals believe they make their own destinies, then there are no reasonable grounds on which youth and other disenfranchised groups can point accusing fingers at the system and its guardians. The legitimacy of the latter is secured on the basis of the very logic that says that order and control benefit everyone in the society. The less conscious that one is of being controlled or manipulated, and the more one feels in charge of one's destiny, the more effective is that control and the more secure that order. The very close relationship, then, among ideology, social control, and social order is evident.

We have also argued that since force, as a mechanism of control, is costly and presents many logistical problems to the controller, it is likely to be used in short-term situations and only as a last resort. Ideological control, on the other hand, is more subtle and less disruptive. It usually manages to effect compliance without at the same time producing feelings of resentment and resistance among the controlled. Thus, whether we are talking about a single population as in *Nineteen Eighty-Four*, or young people in the industrialized countries, the question of how to control the perceptions, sentiments, aspirations, personal preferences, and so on, of large numbers of citizens is ever present; and so too is the potential for social disorder. Power, therefore, must be transformed into authority. It must be viewed by the powerless as legitimate and as something that is used for the benefit of all citizens. To this end the discovery, utilization, and even the creation of complementary behaviour represent very effective means of social control. It is used either to make those who are controlled accept their social circumstances as natural, maybe even supernaturally ordained, or to have them accept the so-called "blame" for those circumstances.

ENDNOTES

1. In the 2004 U.S. presidential election, it appears that the youth vote increased somewhat (from about one third in the previous few elections to just over 40% of 18-24 year olds), perhaps because of the efforts of actors and pop stars to mobilize them to vote against the Bush administration and its war policies (CIRCLE Staff, 2004). In Canada, only about 25% of young people aged 18-30 voted in the 2000 federal election (representing a significant drop over the elections held over the last few decades), but this seems to have risen to about 40% in the 2004 election, showing a similar pattern to the U.S. election (CBC News Online, 2004; Pammett & LeDuc, 2003).

2. The minimum wage was originally intended to ensure that those earning it did not live in poverty; now it ensures that they will live in poverty.

chapter seven

Models of Social Justice for Youth

INTRODUCTION: A RECAP OF INSIGHTS

As noted in the introduction of this book, it is quite curious that more people have not expressed greater concern about how things have worked out with respect to the position of the young person in Canadian society. Presumably, there should have been more public outcry, marked by frequent demonstrations or some sort of political mobilization, as there has been over gender and race issues. Certainly, there has been disaffection, but there are few signs that there will be any concerted effort to remedy the situation. Instead of seeking remedies, it appears that the frustrations young people experience are either internalized (as manifested in rising problems associated with depression, anxiety, and eating disorders) or externalized (as evidenced in aggression, bullying, and other forms of violence, most of which is youth-on-youth in nature). When a public response is forthcoming to deteriorating youth conditions such as those described earlier, it often takes the form of victim blaming, whereby negative stereotypes about young people are used to "explain" their behaviours. In these cases, we can see the ideological nature of public perceptions concerning the nature of the problem. In pointing out these things, we are not complaining about "problem youth" or acting as curmudgeons fed up with young people. Rather, we have been pointing out how increasing problematic behaviours are socially produced and can therefore be *socially reduced* with appropriate measures.

A common public perception of the changing material conditions noted earlier is that they are historical inevitabilities. However, there is no one reason why the institutions reviewed had to change in the ways they did. Clearly, those who had the most say in these things influenced the direction of change and determined who benefited from the changes, namely, the managerial and administrative élite among the oldest age cohorts who control business and government. Yet, if we were to review media discussions of these issues, we would most likely see the problem framed as a Baby Boomer–Baby Buster conflict, with Baby Boomers portrayed as the greedy bad guys. As we saw in Chapter 3, however, it is the pre-Baby Boom cohorts who have benefited the most from changes over the past twenty years—Baby Boomers actually suffered losses as a cohort. But, even this media-produced distraction from the issues is only part of the story.

To gain a sense of how public perception about young people has changed, with the net effect of diminishing their status, it is also necessary to take a longer historical view, tracing the diminishing status of the young person to the negative stereotypes that have been perpetuated about him or her. The negative stereotypes gained scientific legitimacy in the early twentieth century, when the renowned psychologist G. Stanley Hall formulated the storm-stress model of adolescence. This marked a "discovery" of "adolescence" as a social problem by social scientists. Before this, "young people" were not as clearly distinguished from "older people" as they are now. In addition, Hall's work created the widespread belief that "adolescence" is a period distinct from both childhood and adulthood, characterized universally by a turmoil caused by hormonal instabilities stimulated at puberty. Moreover, Hall and others argued that it does not matter what experiences and opportunities are available to the young, for all must pass through this period of storm and stress.

It has been argued that this pathologization of "the adolescent" contributed to events during the twentieth century that helped marginalize the young person from North American adult society, affecting how the changing material conditions noted earlier played out in the workplace, the educational system, and the family. Viewed as inferior biologically and emotionally, and therefore in need of control and segregation, successive cohorts have increasingly been in holding patterns before gaining entry into adulthood and full productive participation in the community. Specifically, this ideology of "youth as an incapacity" has helped justify the disenfranchisement of this age group, particularly the teen segment. As this ideology has spread in the past few decades, those in their twenties have been increasingly treated the way teenagers used to be treated, especially as the bloated Canadian universities and colleges have become more like secondary schools. This has become so widespread that a new term has been coined to describe those affected—emerging adults (Arnett, 2000).

Unlike women and racial minorities, then, it is still considered legitimate to continue speaking of the young as somehow inferior, with inherent immaturities, and to use beliefs about forms of biological inferiority to justify their unequal treatment in society (the most recent claim of biological inferiority is incomplete brain development, as we saw in Chapter 2). These stereotypes serve to perpetuate their lower social status, so effectively that many young people believe those stereotypes themselves. Increasingly, youths' range of adult-appropriate behaviours became constricted by a loss of rights and respect in the community, the economy, and the polity. As young people have felt less welcome in the polity, they have disengaged accordingly. At the same time, governments have surrendered some ground to corporations as moral guardians of the young, a trend that clearly needs to be reversed, as argued in this chapter in comparing youth policies in Canada, the United States, the United Kingdom, and Sweden.

As a consequence of the events that played out in the twentieth century, it is now accepted by many adult Canadians that it is justified to deny young people—even those in their twenties—full membership in the adult community, especially the workplace, except as subordinate workers. The ideology supporting this practice nicely "complements" the fact that technological displacement has made it necessary to have a large pool of cheap labour to fill subordinate service positions, and because of the changing competition ratio, the young have the least bargaining power in terms of who does this labour. Thus, instead of having this segment of the population competing with older workers for the more valued and rewarding jobs, it is now accepted as "normal" for most people under 25 (and even 29) years of age to experience a delay in their transition to adulthood independence, such that elements of "adolescence" are now found among "emerging adults."

CYCLE OR TREND?

Some critics might read the above and argue that there have been periods when it was tough to be young in many societies, just as it has been tough to be any age, depending on the historical circumstances. For example, during the Great Depression in the 1930s, poverty and despair were widespread, forcing many young people to move about the country looking for work, and during the two World Wars, thousands of young people lost their lives in international conflicts. Indeed, young people have faced war and famine throughout history, and the physical consequences were far greater than what most young people face today. Critics might also add that the affluence of Canadian society makes the comparisons relative: Is it not much better to be non-affluent in contemporary Canada than in the Canada of two hundred years ago, or in a developing country somewhere else in the world? The answer to this last question is probably yes. But such a preemptive answer not only distracts us from problems with current circumstances, it also ignores the question of how things got this way, and why things did not work out more equally over this century. Such an answer is also insensitive to issues of social justice: It is likely better to be female or a member of a visible minority today, but that does not mean that their living conditions and opportunities are as good as men's or those among Canada's White majority. If we are supposedly working to improve the lives of women and minorities, why should young people be excluded from this reform agenda?

As for the future, it certainly holds promise for some; indeed, change can bring great benefits, as old interest groups lose their power and conventions change. However, a key issue for the future is whether the inequalities identified here constitute part of a cycle or part of a long-term trend. The bad news for the optimists is that a consensus is emerging that workplace changes are part of long-term structural changes. In fact, two long-term trends appear to be robust, one in the workplace and one in the education system. If current trends continue unabated in the workplace with respect to technological displacement, it is likely that we will see a continuing reduction in the size of the middle class in the next century, along with a continuing polarization of income.

One factor that may mitigate these long-term trends is demographic change. It is possible that we may witness another phase in a cycle where the fortunes of the young improve. This demographic change hinges on the movement of the Baby Boom cohort out of the labour force. The normal retirement period of the cohort will be 2010 through 2030, with a peak around 2020. The Baby Boomers as seniors will constitute a formidable market for goods and services, so the labour force will benefit in terms of providing these goods and services. However, it is also possible most of the jobs produced by this demographic shift will involve subordinate service delivery, as in senior homecare. However, there may also be a greater demand for higher-level financial, information, and health care services that would offset this trend (see Foot, 1996, for predictions regarding which occupations will experience growth in the future). Regardless, because of improved health care and the consequent increased human longevity, it is unlikely that the competition ratio will ever favour the young worker again.[1]

What lies beyond these demographic trends is difficult to say. Exactly how much more technological displacement will take place, and how much educational credentials will continue to inflate, is also difficult to say. Certainly, there will be peaks and plateaus to these trends. But the danger with trends like technological displacement is that one company's employee is another company's consumer. As Rifkin (1995) argues, when one company lays off one of its employees, it is also laying off another company's customer. In spite of the ability of capitalism to survive such crises in the past, this can only go on so long before companies collapse due to overproduction; if this becomes widespread, the entire economy can collapse. If that happens, the cleavages and fractures that underlie Canadian society will likely come to the surface, and the advantages that age now gives to the older portion of the citizenry may well come back to haunt them (cf. Lee, 1996).

INTERGENERATIONAL JUSTICE AND THE REVOLT OF THE ÉLITES

The foregoing has been underlining intergenerational relations and the responsibilities generations have for each other's welfare and the sharing of collective resources. Lee (1996) argues that there is a serious generation gap; not in the simple sense of parents and their children not understanding each other, but in terms of intercohort hostilities based on perceived self-interest. Indeed, in-group cohort identifications in the form of "us-them" antagonisms seem to be growing, and age-based blame and recrimination are now widespread. Thus, we have entered a new era of intergroup relations where many people, not just teens, are politically asserting identities based on a shared sense of oppression. This form of identity politics, resembling a form of "tribalization," gives people a sense of "rightness" in terms of their privilege or oppression as against the privilege or oppression of people from other groups.

Intergenerational tensions are familiar media favourites, especially on the evening news. Two in particular have been (a) the elderly, who fear and loathe teens for their violence and disrespect, and (b) so-called Generation Xers (or Baby Busters born between 1965 and 1975) who dismiss Baby Boomers as greedy and self-indulgent. From his study of intergenerational justice in the United States, Lee identifies the following tendencies to find fault with other generations that he believes are common to all generations:

> Members of older generations who came of age when good jobs with decent wages were readily available have little understanding of the job anxiety and economic insecurity experienced by many who are younger.

> Many members of all generations falsely assume that their experiences either have been or can be duplicated by members of other generations.

Many members of younger generations have high anger levels related to the taxes they pay to finance benefits for older generations. (1996, pp. 243-244)

However widespread these tensions might be, it is clear that from a social justice point of view, they must be set aside so that we can get down to the business of creating a more equitable society where age is not a basis for discrimination. This may sound idealistic in a society with a history of individualism, but a system of justice must be based on ideals. Given their economic underpinnings, Lee believes these generation gaps are more serious than any we have seen in the past, and the issues they raise cannot be casually postponed. In his view, "the years to come will be disastrous if we plunge headlong into the chasm of a war between the generations" (Lee, 1996, p. xii).

In sum, what we are witnessing now may be the beginnings of serious intergenerational animosities. Yet, in blaming each other, people miss the real cause of their financial troubles: a social and economic system in which 20% of the population controls 70% of the wealth, while 10% controls 53% (Kerstetter, 2002; Davies, 1993). For reasons of social control and political order, it is very useful for the wealthiest 20% of the population to have the other 80% distracted and fighting over their 30% share of the wealth. This 20% of the population includes the adult élite that has made the decisions adversely affecting the youth segment (cf. Lasch, 1995). At the same time, there is evidence that this élite has turned its back on the remainder of the population, contributing to a decline in the middle class and a polarization of wages (e.g., Rifkin, 1995). While the children of this élite have been affected, they are in a much better position to negotiate the longer transition to adulthood, especially in terms of having their longer schooling financed and using their parents' networks to help them enter the labour force.

STRUCTURAL SOLUTIONS: INTERNATIONAL COMPARISONS OF ECONOMIC PROSPECTS AND GOVERNMENT POLICIES

The roots of youth disenfranchisement appear to lie with transformations in industrial-capitalist economies, particularly the growth of the subordinate service sector and the parallel decline of the agricultural sector. However, the current economic system maintaining this disenfranchisement involves the corporate-capitalist neo-liberal economy, where big business has increasingly trumped government (a) regulation of the economy, (b) maintenance of social programs, and (c) control of the agenda for social reform.

It is important to note, however, that while the transformations of the industrial capitalist economy constitute *necessary* causes for the disenfranchisement of youth, it was the emergence of corporate hegemony that constitutes the *sufficient* cause. In other words, a change in industrial capitalism alone did not cause the disenfranchisement. Rather, recent economic changes since have conditioned the development of this problem. In particular, corporate interests have exploited the labour of young people to increase their profits and have also nurtured them as a principal market for their products. At the same time, to contain the fall-out from this decline in social status, several "custodial professions" like education and mental health care have found an increasing number of youth as their "clients" to be serviced and counselled for an ever-increasing period of time. Meanwhile, governments have gone along with corporate interests when drafting policies about issues (like keeping the minimum wage low) and implementing education "reforms" (like raising tuitions while lowering corporate taxes).

Because we have been dealing with liberal democracies, where politicians—and their policies—can be voted in and out of office, we will now focus on government-led initiatives regarding youth policies. The purpose is to draw attention to a policy model that is more welcoming to young people than is the case in Canada and the United States. It is in the public policy arena that a "re-enfranchising" of the young can be most immediately stimulated; if the State supports the re-enfranchisement of youth, other sectors of society will be more likely to follow.

Countries like Canada and the United States do not have comprehensive youth policies that inform the political agenda of adult leaders (e.g., Lerner, 2000). In fact, the federal government in Canada has not seriously considered developing policies to address youth employment problems since the early 1980s. Promises to do so during the 1984 election amounted to rhetoric and hollow promises (Coutts, 1987). James Coutts, the former principal secretary to Prime Minister Trudeau, noted in the late 1980s that policy-makers were struggling with three concerns involving youth employment in 1984: (1) the fact that almost one half of the new jobs created at the time paid only poverty-level wages, but there were no programs to help young people deal with the changing structure of the North American economy and the collapse of the youth labour market; (2) schools and training programs were not in step with the job market; and (3) there were inadequate supports for school leavers in terms of job placement and on-the-job training. Coutts went on to note that after the 1984 election, the proposals disappeared for measures like massive apprenticeship and co-op education programs, and the recognition for integration efforts among educators, employers, counsellors, and public policy-makers. Since then, efforts in Canada to assist young people have been sporadic and reactive, and dependent on local and regional resources, like tax bases and voluntary service groups. Indeed, the Canadian government has done little more than to continue its summer job programs for students and perfunctory job-placement programs.

As for the United States, there are numerous examples of "worst practices"—community practices that are "toxic" and to be avoided (e.g., conditions that promote youth violence and conflict). For example, Damon (2004) points out that what young people need for positive development stands in stark contrast to the situation faced by many young people in the United States. In his words,

> the future of any society depends upon the character and competence of its young. In order to develop their competence, young people need guidance to provide them with direction and a sense of purpose. They need relationships that embody and communicate high standards. They need to experience activities that are challenging, inspiring, and educative. (p. 1)

Unfortunately, the institutions that would support the development of such character and competence in the United States have destructured in recent years as late-modern conditions have set in, with schools and communities deteriorating in quality and places of worship and families becoming less influential. Consequently, rather than finding clear normative guidance from the adult community, Damon submits that young Americans too often "encounter inattention, low expectations, cynicism, or community conflict" (p. 1).

To address this problem, Damon has outlined a "Youth Charter" that promises to help rebuild a society where young people can realize their potential, but unfortunately, as with much academic research in the United States, it has had little impact on political and community leaders who could formulate a youth policy that would provide the protective and proactive measures needed to enhance the positive development of *all* young Americans. The rampant individualism of the United States is well known internationally, and it holds the fascination of the world as presented in its media portrayals of life in America, especially the high-risk behaviours of its young people and macho men. Unfortunately, these portrayals are often taken as an unalterable reality to be faced by all young people around the world in the future.

The fields of developmental psychology and the sociology of youth have produced a wealth of theories about what communities can do to enhance (and maximize) the human development of all members. Most recently, "positive youth development" has become an objective among researchers who are interested in implementing and evaluating intervention programs that seek to provide resources for young people rather than to simply remedy resource deficiencies. Those who advocate measures supportive of positive youth development argue that it is not enough for government policies to be directed simply at addressing perceived "youth problems." As well-intentioned, or misguided, these measures might be, the exclusive reliance on them neglects the fact that the entire youth segment is in need of resources with which to make the transition to adulthood. To this end, Benson (1997) has developed a checklist of 40 developmental assets for children and adolescents, many of which can be provided by communities (i.e., internal and external resources involving social support, empowerment, boundaries and expectations, and constructive use of time). Indeed, empirical research reveals a linear relationship between the number of such resources a young person possesses, or has access to, and lower levels of risk (e.g., depression, suicide, violence; Leffert et al., 1998) as well as higher levels of "thriving" (e.g., school success, physical health, delay of gratification; Benson, Leffert, Scales, & Blyth, 1998).

To cite another academic example that moves from a problem focus to a positive resource focus, Lerner (2000) has outlined the ambitious Applied Developmental Science project, which directs research on positive youth development to include communities in the planning, interpretation, and use of evaluation studies of intervention programs. The objective is to influence individual development in ways that nurture participation in civil society from an early age.

These are all excellent ideas that policy-makers can use to both provide the proactive measures needed to enhance the welfare of future generations and protect these future generations from the corrosive effects of extreme individualism. To do this we need to explore the "best practices" found in some countries, and make those in countries with the "worst practices" aware that alternatives are available. For example, we can look to countries like Sweden that have well-thought-out youth policies, and bring them to the attention of people in other countries, like Canada and the United States, so they are aware of both the ill effects of their own "worst practices" and the potential benefits of alternatives.

THE UNITED KINGDOM: FIGHTING SOCIAL EXCLUSION AND PROMOTING CITIZENSHIP RIGHTS

In contrast to Canada and the United States, academics and politicians in the United Kingdom have been working for some time to address the problems faced by young people since the collapse of the youth labour market in the late 1970s and early 1980s. The British government and private foundations have been generously funding academics specializing in Youth Studies to conduct policy-relevant research, putting the British Youth Studies community at the forefront of youth-policy analysis (for recent reports based on funding from the Economic and Social Research Council and the Joseph Rowntree Foundation, see Bynner et al., 2002; Catan, 2004; Jones, 2002). A common theme in this research is with the "youth divide" (Jones, 2002), whereby the polarization of wealth in general (described earlier for Canada and the United States) is having an especially deleterious effect on young people at the disadvantaged side of this polarization. At the same time, the British government under the Labour Party has undertaken a number of policy initiatives (like the "New Deal") and established government departments (like the "Social Exclusion Unit") in recognition of the fact that the circumstances associated with the transition to adulthood have deteriorated over the past few decades.

Catan (2004) summarizes these changes as follows:

> Arguably the most consistent message to come from youth research . . . has been that youth transitions are lengthening and that consequently, young people remain, to varying extents, dependent on their families of origin and, where this is limited, in need of support and protection by the State. The trend towards spending greatly extended periods in education and training, coupled with the poor earning potential of part-time and entry-level jobs and rising housing costs, has resulted in *average* incomes which are insufficient to support independent living until young people reach their mid-twenties and beyond. (pp. 56-57)

Catan goes on to note that the changes associated with prolongation and dependency are now acknowledged to be affecting all young Britons, with variations in terms of the economic and social resources their family and ethnic backgrounds provide (as has been argued earlier is the case in Canada and the United States). In this regard, one focus of these research efforts has been to study the factors creating, maintaining, and exacerbating "social exclusion," namely, marginalization of some young people from the education system, labour market, and other mainstream institutions. This research has confirmed the fact that there is a socially excluded segment of British youth, but it is a fluid "group, " with 10-20% of young Britons being at some time "excluded" for a variety of reasons. However, the problem runs deeper than merely an association with intergeneration disadvantage or poverty. Jones (2002) summarizes this problem in her report of the findings of a major research initiative involving the co-ordination of some two-dozen focused studies:

> This report is titled *The Youth Divide* for a reason. Inequalities persist among young people and in some respects they have deepened. However, the polarisation described in this report hides a more complex and disturbing picture. In the social hierarchy of young people, between the "socially included" and the "socially excluded", there is a large (and largely invisible) group trying to survive on scarce resources, including their own resilience. The current emphasis of policy makers and indeed many researchers on the most socially excluded should be revised to consider the varying circumstances and needs of all young people. There is a danger that the proverbial iceberg will be overlooked if we focus only on the tip. (p. 44)

At the same time, Catan (2003, 2004) is critical of British policy-makers for not extending the official definition of "youth" beyond the age of 19 (as is the case in other countries). The British government's thinking on this issue is perhaps affected by the long-standing tradition for young people to leave the parental home as soon as they can, beginning at age 16 and ending by age 19 (Bynner et al., 2002). The failure to recognize the extension of the transition into the twenties means that the concern for the difficulties faced in the transition to adulthood in the United Kingdom will not translate into policies to aid those in need. As Catan (2003) notes, the success of policies that are in train . . . *depend profoundly on the capacity of young people to make use of the opportunities they offer.* Young people who are beset by anxiety about mounting debts while in further and higher education, and who take on large amounts of poorly paid work while in full time education, do not make the best students. . . . Without a consideration of the range of support needs for young adults living independently of families and communities, young people will not move away from localities with few prospects for stable, well-paid work. (emphasis added, para. 9)

The primary problem with U.K. youth policy efforts identified by Jones, Catan, and others is a lack of co-ordination among the various Departments and agencies attempting to tackle even those problems that are agreed upon as in need of addressing, like social exclusion. This "departmentalism" is not unique to the British government, nor is the issue of regional diversity and disparity (an integrated youth policy is hampered in any country that is regionally diverse, especially when each region has relative political autonomy, as is the case with the provinces of Canada and states in the United States). The catchword in British policy circles is "joined up policy" (i.e., an integrated policy shared by all government departments), but this seems to be hampered by a schism among policy-makers, where some glorify young people as incapable of doing any wrong, and others condemn young people as doing *only wrong*. Accordingly, some departments attempt advocacy-oriented policies, while others advocate problem-containing initiatives. As noted earlier, this polarized view of the young—advocacy versus judgmental approaches—can be found in other countries, in both government approaches and academic positions taken on youth issues. Unfortunately, as in any polarized situation, those who take a middle ground approach (as this book does, advocating benign guidance) find themselves criticized from two irreconcilable extremes.

Bynner et al. (2002) draw similar conclusions based on their longitudinal analysis of changing youth transitions in the United Kingdom:

> The complexity of modern life choices demands assistance from experienced adults in ensuring that the best choices are made. Failure to make the right choices can bring psychological distress. . . . parents are usually the first adults young people turn to for advice about jobs and emotional support. When parents are absent, ineffective or simply lacking the information young people need, they rely on the state to fill the gap. (p. 71)

Bynner et al. go on to urge the British government to learn from other European governments, which recognize that

> young people need an extended period of support in the first steps toward employment. . . . the critical period is between the ages 15-25, when laying the foundations for successful adaptation to the demands of adulthood is achieved. Certainly, youth transitions cannot just be left to happen, they need backup over the whole period. (p. 72)

We now turn to an example of how one government has managed to develop and sustain an integrated youth policy that is designed to meet the needs of all young people making the transition to adulthood, not just those who are most marginalized (as in the United Kingdom) or privileged (as in Canada and the United States).

SWEDEN AND THE FULLY FUNCTIONING HUMAN BEING

Generation on Hold discussed the youth policies that were in effect in Sweden until the late 1980s, offering it as a model for other countries to follow. Although Sweden suffered some economic setbacks in the early 1990s that increased unemployment among all age groups, Swedes have maintained their efforts to guide and nurture their young. For example, active employment policies have been maintained to help businesses and the public service recruit young people; all unemployed young people are eligible for training programs; and young Swedes generally work within the same job categories as other age groups. Moreover, local authorities and schools are required to work together to provide forms of co-operative education-work experiences. Teenagers over sixteen who remain in school receive a study allowance, and generous grants with low-interest student loans are available for those who want to undertake a postsecondary education. Those who cannot find work and who are not in school are guaranteed benefits. In other words, everyone is guaranteed some form of income (Swedish National Board for Youth Affairs, 1999a).

Adult Swedes have also seen to it that young Swedes have opportunities for growth-enhancing activities during their leisure time. Young Swedes have ample opportunities to develop skills through their local schools with respect to the arts and classical music, and 1500 youth recreation centres provide places for young people to meet who are not otherwise involved in clubs or sports organizations (Swedish Institute, 1993). At these centres, facilities are provided for rehearsing plays, dance, and music of various genres; about 25% of teens attend municipal music classes. Two thirds of males and one half of females are members of some sort of sports association (Swedish Institute, 1993). These are but a few examples of how the adult community provides resources for their young to engage in positive forms of development. Sweden is not a panacea for all of the problems facing young people around the world, but it does provide a model of what can be done when the adult community—especially the élite of adults making business and political decisions—attempts to establish a positive and nurturing environment for those making their way to adulthood.

Sweden is a capitalist, advanced-industrial society. In fact, it is one of the most prosperous in the world. As a capitalist society, the market transformations that have taken place in the world economy, and the processes that have disenfranchised the young, can also be found there. But the Swedish government has grappled with this problem in a way that one would expect of enlightened political leaders. While Sweden too has myriad competing economic interest groups, it has also been able to produce effective social policies aimed at those who have been disadvantaged by economic transformations. Thus, Sweden still provides other capitalist democracies with a model of what they can do to address the problems outlined earlier in this book.

This country's long history of experimentation with social policies prepared it well to respond to the processes disenfranchising its young. These policies have been designed to ensure that Swedish society provides all of its citizens with a high standard of living. Countries like the United States and Canada maintain a high standard overall, but with large—and growing—disparities among the population (Dayton-Johnson, 2001). In other words, Canadian and American social policies tend to be based more on a "win-lose" model, while Swedish social policy tends to be based more on a "win-win" one.

Clearly, Sweden (as well as the other Nordic countries) has been concerned with the welfare of all of its citizens for some time, and continues to take measures to protect its young people from the more corrosive influences of individualism. For instance, the Swedish government passed legislation limiting advertising to children with the intention of providing them with a "safety zone" (Jacobsson, 2002), protecting them from the marketing efforts associated with "branding," discussed in Chapter 4. At the same time, this protects parents from "pestering"—children pressuring parents to buy them things they see in ads and embedded in TV programs and movies (marketers in the United States and Canada continue to study how to teach young children in advertisements how to pester their parents to buy them things; e.g., Bakan, 2004; Linn, 2004; Nader & Coco, 1999).

More recently, the Swedish parliament updated the national youth policy based on the assumption that young Swedes "should enjoy the same rights and opportunities to participate in society as other groups and they should have good living conditions in all areas" (Swedish National Board for Youth Affairs, 2004, p. 2), with the following three main objectives:

Independence. Young people shall be given the preconditions for living an independent life. For example, the right to good education and the possibility of getting both a job and accommodation.

Influence. Young people shall have genuine opportunities for influence and participation. For example, in their municipality and in their school through access to public discussion.

Resource. Young people's commitment, creativity, and critical thinking shall be seen and utilized as a resource. (Swedish National Board for Youth Affairs, 2004, p. 2)

Built into this policy is an annual evaluation. Each year the Swedish National Board for Youth Affairs (SNBYA) reviews measurable sub-objectives of their national youth policy, using a "management by objectives" approach. Currently, there are 32 sub-objectives that are undergoing continual evaluation and revision, informed by seeing young people as a "resource" rather than a "problem," with special efforts directed at serious problems like extreme marginalization.

These activities cannot be carried out in a vacuum. Accordingly, the SNBYA works with government and other national bodies at all levels, including municipalities, to fulfill the objectives of the youth policy. They do so by conducting regular studies of young Swedes' attitudes and activities, supporting research initiatives that interface with practitioners involved with young people, and producing official reports based on input and feedback from young Swedes (SNBYA, 2004/2005).

To encourage positive forms of leisure and informal social activities, the SNBYA provides grant money to young people themselves to set up their own organizations as well as to various national youth organizations. The SNBYA also oversees international youth programs to foster both the inclusion of young Swedes in mainstream adult society and to encourage their understanding of different cultures. This includes grant allocation for exchange programs and Sweden's involvement in the European Union's "youth" program (Commission of the European Communities, 2004). Young Swedes are among the best travelled of the world's youth, in part because of the active encouragement and support of their government to spend time in other developed and developing countries. Less privileged young people are especially targeted for these eye-opening experiences (SNBYA, 2004).

Finally, the SNBYA works directly with municipalities to develop local youth policies that integrate with the national policy. This includes interorganization liaisons, regular conferences for information sharing, and the "Youth Municipality of the Year" award (SNBYA, 2004).

SWEDEN'S FIGHT AGAINST YOUTH DISENFRANCHISEMENT

Swedish youth have not escaped the worldwide trend toward the disenfranchisement of youth. The most direct evidence of the youth-disenfranchisement process in Sweden can be found with (a) unemployment, (b) wage declines, and (c) lowered labour-force participation rates.

With respect to increasing unemployment, historically, Sweden has enjoyed a general unemployment rate of around 1% to 3%, with the rate for 16- to 24-year-olds running between 4% and 6%. Sweden's long-standing policy of full employment (since the 1930s) is responsible for their very low rates compared to other industrialized countries. However, with the worldwide recession of the early 1990s the general unemployment rate rose to unprecedented levels (as much as 8% in some years), with youth unemployment hitting 18-19% in 1993 (Statistics Sweden, 2004, Table 328, p. 294) and running at 14-17% in the mid-1990s (Swedish Institute, 1999). Given their commitment to full employment, action was taken to wrestle the rate back down to acceptable levels. By 1999, the rate for 16- to 24-year-olds was down to 9-10% in 1999, and through the first three years of the 2000s ran at just over 9% for 16- to 19-year-olds and 7-8% for 20- to 24-year-olds. Meanwhile the rate for workers over 24 was between 2.5% and 3.8% in 2003 (Statistics Sweden, 2004, Table 328, p. 294). Recall from Chapter 3 that Canada's youth unemployment rate remains in the mid-teens, while the adult rate is about 6%.

Other evidence that the youth-disenfranchisement process has been at work in Sweden can be found with wage levels. During the 1980s, income increases for the 16-to-24 age group did not match those of other age groups. In manual occupations, young males earned only about 80% that of the average manual worker salary in that decade (Swedish Institute, 1993). This differential in earning power continued in the 1990s, largely because youth wages stagnated while adult wages rose (SNBYA, 1999a). Without keeping up with inflation, disposable income among 18- to 24-year-olds dropped between 25% and 40% during the 90s (SNBYA, 1999a, 1999b).

Finally, Swedish youth labour-force participation has declined. In the 1970s, one half of those in their late teens were in the labour force full-time; by the mid-1990s, this was down to one quarter (SNBYA, 1999a). Similarly, full-time employment of those in their early twenties declined from 71% in 1987 to 54% in 1998 (SNBYA, 1999a). As in other countries like Canada, lower labour-force participation has been attributed in part to young people staying in school longer; unlike other countries, however, there are more financial incentives for young Swedes to participate in higher education, as we will see. Still, young Swedes are more likely than young Canadians to work in the same sectors as older workers (SNBYA, 1999a), so there is not really a "youth labour market" as there is in Canada and the United States (Tannock, 2001). At the same time, however, young Swedes tend to hold more temporary jobs than do older Swedes (SNBYA, 1999a).

So what has the Swedish government done to fight the disenfranchisement processes affecting the young? It certainly did not ignore the problem or exacerbate it as other countries have done. With widespread popular support, the government experimented with measures during the 1990s to counteract these processes. It may not have been entirely successful, but it seems to have counteracted some of the more serious problems seen in countries like Canada and the United States.

For example, in comparison to 30 years ago, young Swedes are leaving home at an earlier age (SNBYA, 1999a). Although more young Swedes needed to remain longer in their
parents' home as a result of the economic downturn of the 1980s and 1990s, they are still
the most independent youth among the industrialized countries in this respect. In the
1980s, almost 50% of males and 25% of females aged 20 to 24 were living with their parents (Swedish Institute, 1993). By the late 1990s, these figures had increased slightly, but
those in their late twenties remained largely unaffected by this aspect of the prolonged transition found elsewhere, with fewer than 10% residing with their parents (SNBYA, 1999a).
If we compare these figures with those for Canadian youth, this manifestation of disenfranchisement has clearly been less severe in Sweden. As noted in Chapter 3, in Canada,
in the late 1990s among the unmarried, about 75% of males and 60% of females in their
early twenties were living with their parents, while a full one half of males in their late
twenties were also, along with over one third of females (Boyd & Norris, 1999). At the
same time, the United States and United Kingdom lay somewhere between Canada and
Sweden, with between one quarter and one third of those in their late twenties still living
in the parental home (Halperin, 1998; Bynner et al., 2002).

In addition to their unified youth policy, the Swedish government has engaged in a
number of exemplary initiatives to combat the disenfranchisement of youth that stand as
models for other countries, including higher educational reforms, guaranteed incomes for
those having difficulty integrating into the labour force, special programs for marginal
youth, and the provision of resources for positive development for all youth.

The Higher Education System

Young Swedes are eligible for study allowances when they are 16 and remain studying in
upper secondary schools (950 Swedish kronor per month—about 165 Canadian dollars).
The vast majority of young Swedes take advantage of this, accounting for the high reten-
tion rates in Swedish schools—over 90% of 18-year-olds are in some form of schooling in
Sweden (SNBYA, 1999b, p. 11), compared to about 75% in Canada (see Table 3.2). This
measure of providing study allowances goes some way in preventing the exploitative use
of youth labour, and helps prevent outside distractions like part-time jobs from diminishing the student's ability to benefit from what their schools have to offer them.

Vocational programs in upper secondary school provide basically what Canadians get
in community college—courses of study in hospitality, health care, media, child care, etc.
But these courses of study are also integrated with the local labour market and industry,
including job placement (Swedish Institute, 2000). As noted earlier, Swedish schools are
required to offer programs that have relevance in terms of the local economy.

No tuition is charged Swedish students who go on to a higher education. In addition,
students are entitled to generous grants. As of autumn 2004, study loan assistance was
1725 Swedish kronor per week for full-time students (about 300 Canadian dollars) for a
maximum of 240 weeks (Swedish Institute, 2004a). About one third (34.5%) is received as
a non-repayable grant that also counts as pensionable income. Parental or spousal income
does not affect the student's eligibility for the loan/grant program. Loans can be repaid at
4% of subsequent income (with a 2004 interest rate of 3.1%; Swedish Institute, 2004b).

All students of higher education are required to join a student union (Swedish Institute,
2004a). These unions in turn nominate student representatives to sit on the bodies governing the higher educational system, and all local student unions have a membership in the

National Association of Student Unions, guaranteeing that student voices are represented in decisions affecting them (Swedish Institute, 2004a).

Participation in higher education doubled in Sweden during the 1990s, and the expansion continues. Like other industrial countries, the goal of the government is to eventually encourage up to 50% of the youth population to obtain higher degrees (Swedish Institute, 2004c).

Guaranteed incomes

Young Swedes who find themselves unemployed have access to a general unemployment insurance scheme if they have a sufficient work history, as well as basic insurance if they do not meet the criteria of the general scheme (SNBYA, 1999a). Unemployment insurance can amount to 80% of the pre-unemployment income, while basic insurance is about 3000 Swedish kronor per month (about 500 Canadian dollars; the cost of living is about the same in Canada and Sweden). In addition, further supplemental benefits are available for those who fall through the cracks of the other two payment systems and who do not have sources of family income support (SNBYA, 1999a). Recently, programs have been launched to help those who are most in need to achieve a more stable economic self-sufficiency, as discussed below.

Special Programs for Marginal Youth Almost 30 000 young Swedes aged 16 to 24 were not in school, working, or seeking employment in the early 2000s (SNBYA, 2003a). Although this constitutes only about 3% of the youth population (in contrast to 10% in countries like Canada and the United States, and more in the United Kingdom), there is still a concern about taking proactive measures to integrate them. In addition, a "best practices" approach is explicitly taken by the Swedish National Board of Youth Affairs, for use locally and to share with other countries (see SNBYA, 2002).

A program was developed in 1998 to address this problem. The "Youth Guarantee" (previously, the Development Guarantee) is directed at 20- to 24-year-olds who are registered as unemployed for three months at their local employment office but are not eligible for unemployment benefits or the supplemental benefit. They are guaranteed a minimum of 1967 kronor per month tax-free. Those who are eligible for the supplemental benefit will receive an additional allowance equivalent to that benefit, and those who qualify for unemployment benefits can receive an equivalent study allowance so long as they are involved in work experience programs (SNBYA, 1998).

The intention of the Youth Guarantee is to break the cycle that some young people get caught in of being unemployed, collecting benefits, and being put on government work programs, only to find themselves unemployed when the work program ends. For these young people, traditional means of dealing with their marginality have not worked. In these cases, municipalities are given full freedom to individualize training, courses, and work experience to match the particular needs and talents of the unemployed person for up to one year (SNBYA, 2001b). The municipalities receive 150 kronor per day per person for participating in the program (SNBYA, 1999c).

In 2000, about one half of the 4000 chronically unemployed Swedes in their early twenties were involved in the Youth Guarantee (1% of this age group; SNBYA, 2000). The evaluation undertaken of this initiative included investigating how well the municipal apparatuses that were set up succeeded in meeting program goals. It found that those with

the most personal resources when they entered the program (e.g., those with more education and some established skill) were more likely to find permanent employment, while
those with emotional problems, serious problems in their daily lives, or incomplete upper
secondary education were less likely to find a job. Therapy sessions with social workers
are provided in these most at-risk cases. The evaluation also found widespread dissatis-
faction with the low amount of the guaranteed income (1967 kronor is roughly $350
Canadian). However, it appears most young people involved in the program are positive
about it, and are especially appreciative of the availability of mentors, advisors, and job-
placement officers who help them sort out their plans and identify their opportunities. The
evaluation of this program also found that those involved either obtained a job in one third
of the time that it took long-term unemployed youth who did not participate to find a job,
or they entered a course of studies in half the time that it took the chronically unemployed
outside the program to do so (SNBYA, 1999c).

Consistent with their long-standing philosophy of full employment, efforts continue in
Sweden to address youth unemployment, with the goal of finding work for all young people. In 2003, a special board of inquiry was struck to report to the government about what
policies and programs should be developed to help the most difficult cases among the
residual 3% of the youth population targeted by the Young Guarantee (SNBYA, 2003a).
This group has special needs not met by the school system. Indeed, most of those who are
in this category for two full years have not completed an average level of compulsory education, some with only 7 or 8 years of compulsory education. Moreover, retrospective
analysis indicates that this can become a permanent form of exclusion for about one third
(i.e., one third of those who were "outsiders" in the early 1990s were still so in the early
2000s). Their problems range from early traumatic school experiences (like bullying) to
learning disabilities. This special board of inquiry recommended that efforts be increased
to give each of these young people support and guidance in finding an occupation, and that
the future goal be that all in this group be guided to an occupation by age 20. This could
be accomplished, they reasoned, by budgeting "at least as much per person as the cost of
normal upper secondary school education" (SNBYA, 2003a).

Educationally, the board calls for individualized, compensation-based programs
geared to the specific needs of the individual, rather than the needs of school bureaucracies. This would include a "portfolio system" that gives credit for informal learning,
as in international exchange programs and involvement in activities that generate social
capital (clubs, organizations, unions, and the like). In conjunction with these efforts,
they recommend special apprenticeships in non-traditional areas to facilitate integration
into employment. Finally, they propose the implementation of "Navigation Centres" that
provide a knowledge bank of, and co-ordination for, local resources in order to provide
"young outsiders" with a hub from which to link with various facilitative networks
(SNBYA, 2003a).

Resources for Positive Development Among all Youth

The Swedish youth policy is directed at addressing the lives of all young Swedes, not just
those at risk of exclusion. This is an important advance beyond previous thinking, or thinking in other countries, where only "problem" youth are the target of government initiatives.
As noted earlier, the positive youth development movement makes the convincing argument
that an apparent absence of visible problems does not mean that young people are being well

served by government policies. Rather, all young persons need the appropriate support and resources to maximize their chances of reaching their full potential.

The results of the first evaluation of the 32 sub-objectives of the Swedish youth policy help us see this focus on the positive aspects of young people's lives and their potentials (SNBYA, 2002). Of the 20 sub-objectives related to the aforementioned "independence" objective significant advances were made in about one quarter of the cases (some objectives are more long-term, so cannot be achieved in this short time span). For example, more students have access to computers in school, as well as opportunities for vocational work during the summer, and fewer have been in need of long-term income support. Eight sub-objectives address the "influence" objective, two of which showed positive trends in the short period the youth policy has been in effect (i.e., more now feel that they have more real influence in their schools, and more municipalities have action plans for directly involving the young). However, little discernible progress has been made on the "resource" objective, primarily because these involve long-term goals, like increasing the number of young people as permanent employees in government and corporate management.

The SNBYA has also undertaken a review of the youth councils it funds. The youth councils are provided for all young people and have an explicit mandate of "promoting the influence of young people in local communities" (SNBYA, 1999d, p. 1). The view is taken that opportunities to influence the community through participation are crucial to the positive development of young people in that they can "boost self-confidence and self-esteem, and result in greater knowledge and competency levels" (SNBYA, 1999d, p. 1). At the same time, the SNBYA recognizes that there are gaps in the provisions for young people to be involved in governing Swedish communities and the society as a whole, especially in decision-making bodies.

Youth council members can be between the ages of 12 and 25, but most are 16 to 19 years old and more girls than boys participate. These councils meet regularly (every two weeks or monthly) to work collaboratively on projects related to local environmental, school, work, and leisure issues. Concrete projects include setting up youth centres and arranging festivals. Regular meetings are also held between the youth councils and local political authorities to discuss issues of concern.

The SNYBA evaluation of youth councils found that although there are predictable problems (associated with turnover because they are age-based organizations, so people leave as they get older and/or lose interest), these organizations are viewed favourably by young people and they help nurture an interest in politics and engaging in active forms of citizenship (SNBYA, 1999d).

Swedes are also distinguished by their use of "study circles," in which groups of people informally meet to exchange their views, knowledge, and skills. These have been popular among adults for the past century (Oliver, 1987), but now young people can apply for funding to set up study circles for activities like learning music skills (SNBYA, 2001a).

Outcomes

There is more to providing guidance and opportunity for the young than simply guaranteeing them incomes. The young must also derive a sense of fulfilment, which can come from participation in social activities, to give meaning to one's life. In this area as well, Swedes have established an exemplary system. For example, drug use is low in comparison with other European countries and with Canada and the United States (SNBYA, 2002, p. 14). Instead of using drugs for recreation and fulfilment, Swedish youth are more likely to have more positive avenues for self-development as a result of community initiatives. And here "community" is meant quite literally; much of the support for youth activity is at the municipal level. With just under one million citizens aged 16 to 24, there are about 1350 youth clubs in Sweden, down from about 1600 in the late 1980s (SNBYA, 2002; Swedish Institute, 1991). One half of those aged 16 to 25 belong to a union (compared with over 80% for older workers; SNBYA, 1999b, p. 50).[2]

The impact of these efforts can be seen in the involvement of young people in socio-cultural activities. For example, young Swedes are highly involved with music of various forms. One in five 15- to 25-year-olds plays an instrument; one in five females and one in ten males are active singers; and 25% of 10- to 20-year-olds attend municipal music classes (Swedish Institute, 1993). Those aged 15 to 24 are actually the most active readers of all age groups in Sweden, spending an average of about 3 hours per day in all forms, including magazines and newspapers (SNBYA, 1999b).

These sociocultural activities have contributed to a politically aware and socially con-scious youth generation. Although there have been slight declines since the 1980s in polit-ical engagement (but not as great as in most other countries), some 70-80% of 16- to 24-year-olds voted in elections held in the 1990s (SNBYA, 1999b); 70% regularly discuss politics (Swedish Institute, 1991; SNBYA, 1999b, p. 49; compare this to only about 40% of young Canadians who follow any politics at all, O'Neill, 2003); 70-80% would wear a badge to express a political opinion; 60% are or would be a member of a political party (SNBYA, 1999b, p. 49); 80% have or would contact a politician over an issue (SNBYA, 1999b, p. 49); and so forth.

The contrast with youth in many other advanced industrial countries is striking. As argued throughout this book, young people in many of these countries have been led by their adult "guardians" into mindless consumerism and unattainable materialism. The Swedish case demonstrates that when self-development and independent thinking are encouraged, young people will respond positively, and that the widespread civil and polit-ical disengagement of many young people in other advanced industrial societies is in many ways a reaction to the limited opportunities available to them, to the lack of respect accorded them, and to their resultant sense of alienation from adult society (cf. Kimberlee, 2002).

Still, some readers may feel that Swedish social policies are too expensive—too much of a burden on the taxpayer. However, when balanced against the long-term costs of a high crime rate, escalating prison and court costs, and poor-quality education found in other countries, Swedish policies are much more attractive. The voting public in other advanced industrial countries must learn that they can pay now, or they can pay later; but at some point they must pay to maintain their communities and to welcome new gener-ations. If they pay later, many people suffer needlessly. In contrast, Sweden is not plagued with rampant crime, violence, or drug abuse. Swedes have worked out a com-passionate system that is conducive to the psychological well being of *all* of its citizens, *and* it has a high material standard of living. As Hadenius and Lindgren (1990, pp. 74-75) note, "the number of telephones, VCRs, cars, boats, and second homes per person is among the world's highest." With five weeks per year minimum paid vacation, even "80% of blue collar workers can afford an annual vacation trip, and numerous Swedes travel to foreign countries."

According to a SNBYA study (2003b), young Swedes aged 16 to 29 overwhelmingly are optimistic about their futures, and there is a trend for more to feel this way. In 1997, over 70% were optimistic, while in 2002 more than 80% were optimistic. Moreover, almost 80% feel confident that they can "influence their life situation," and almost 40% feel that they participate in Swedish society. This book does not offer comparable statistics for Canadian youth because of the paucity of youth research conducted in Canada. Not only is there a wealth of information available about Swedish youth, but the Swedes even keep track of the quality of their youth research, as with a recent evaluation commissioned by The Swedish Council for Working Life and Social Research (Jonsson, Helve, & Wichström, 2003).

Clearly, the Swedish concern for their young has not been an unbearable burden, and there is no reason why other advanced industrial countries cannot take some lessons from Swedish policies.

PERSONAL SOLUTIONS: RECOMMENDATIONS TO THE INDIVIDUAL YOUNG PEOPLE

After the publication of *Generation on Hold*, the most common question we were asked by journalists was what solutions we could recommend to young people themselves, and to society as a whole, to remedy the incipient age-based inequalities experienced by young people. In that book, we offered some; here we offer more, after having had more time to reflect on matters.

For young people themselves, a number of personal adjustments can be made:

- Be informed about who benefits and who loses as a result of certain economic changes—this is an antidote for self-blame.
- Resist indoctrination pressures that draw one into the mindless consumer role (this ranges from peer pressure to marketing strategies and political propaganda).
- Work to develop a meaningful philosophy of life not solely predicated on consumerism, materialism, or hedonism; balance the "pleasure principle" and the "reality principle" (i.e., have fun, but realize there are real issues that affect your long-term happiness and well-being).
- Think about what constitutes "success" for you, rather than what other people think (there are non-status-seeking forms of success, like being good at caring for others, and contributing to the social capital of one's community).
- Discover your own "special competency," namely, what you are really good at and feel good doing (but don't worry if what you are good at is not part of middle-class definitions of success).
- Take advantage of the prolonged period of youth imposed on you to develop your "real" self, instead of the self others want you to be for them (i.e., be true to yourself, and don't try to please others just for the sake of it).
- If you are locked out of adult independence, make the best of it in a positive fashion that builds your life-chances and improves you in ways that help you reach your potentials.
- Consider the real possibility that your adulthood will not be predicated on the middle-class model of the mid-twentieth century (you may be ahead of the times because it is a real possibility that everyone is going to have to adopt sustainable lifestyles for a sustainable planet for ecological reasons).

- Above all, pay attention to the individualization process affecting your identity formation and build a sound *moral base for your identity* that you can live with throughout
  your life.
- At the same time, invest in identity capital—personal resources that help you move
  through an increasingly globalized world; do not settle for a career and lifestyle based
  on the exploitation and manipulation of others. Just as you would not want it done to
  you (and the children you may have now or eventually may have), do not do it to
  others—build a concern for the welfare of others into your own sense of who you are.

At the collective level, we recommend that young people themselves attempt the
following:

- Get involved in political lobbying (e.g., through student federations).
- Push for the formation of well-funded youth councils (as in Sweden).
- Form a political party that speaks to youth interests (this party could mobilize the
  18- to 29-year-old vote, which amounts to almost 30% of eligible voters—compare the
  Bloc Québécois, which is a single-interest party ostensibly representing 30% of
  Canadian voters, yet was for a time the official Opposition in Canada's Parliament).
- Boycott products, media, etc. that manipulate young people and children and attempt
  to penetrate their lives and cultivate identity formations based on preoccupation with
  consumption.

In the end, these mechanisms could have the effect of stimulating a youth movement
modelled after the "grey power" movement, the environmental movement, or the women's
movement. People over 50 have their own organizations (e.g., American Association of
Retired People, Canadian Association of Retired People) that lobby for them and provide
platforms for understanding common financial and health issues for people their age (mainly
magazines, but also websites). There is no reason why people (emerging adults) between the
ages of 18 and 30 could not organize in a similar way. In fact, this would provide both morally
sound entrepreneurial opportunities for the individual organizers and a morally based social
movement for young people in which they contribute to one another's welfare.

At the level of political economy, the State must be lobbied to reverse its long-standing neglect of youth issues by focusing on the following, especially modelling the Swedish
experience:

- Adopt active versus passive employment practices (the Canadian Youth Foundation,
  1995, put the hidden costs of youth inequality at 4.5 billion a year, which is doled out
  in unemployment benefits and social assistance).
- Build the social capital of communities—the so-called "third sector"—by providing
  social wages (e.g., for work with nonprofit, volunteer, and community organizations)
  and shadow wages (i.e., tax deduction for work in the social economy.
- In order to create jobs for young people, encourage job sharing and shorter work
  weeks with economic incentives (i.e., state subsidies topping up lower wages, which in
  turn save on unemployment benefits and social assistance).
- Tax profits from transnationals, so money is invested in the communities from which it
  is taken, especially in educational and community-based resources for children, adolescents, and emerging adults (see Rifkin's *The End of Work* for a detailed discussion
  of these options).

If all of these things were done many of the problems identified in *Critical Youth Studies* would be mitigated. However, they require individual initiative, political will, and a sense of moral-ethical obligation to others. It remains to be seen if Canadians, who are known for their passive acceptance of authority, can rise to the occasion.

CONCLUSION: CONFRONTING THE "CULT OF IMPOTENCE"[3]

There does not appear to be a political revolution on the horizon that would eradicate the problems facing contemporary youth. On the one hand, advanced industrial societies provide many people with abundant material rewards, making it unlikely that they would support a revolutionary movement of this nature. On the other hand, many of those who are not rewarded in these societies have been so mystified by consent-manufacturing enterprises that they would not know what to fight for or whom to fight against. These mystification enterprises help explain why the signs of dissent we are now witnessing among many young people are simply individualist forms of conformity to an anti-mainstream youth culture (Niedzviecki, 2004) or stylistic, self-enhancing statements of rebellion (Heath & Potter, 2004). There is little sense of how youth disenfranchisement is an issue of social justice and certainly no political platform upon which to proceed. As such, this dissent appears to actually feed the system exploiting young people (Heath & Potter, 2004) and is therefore unlikely to culminate in a political movement.

So, who should be held responsible and what should be done about the problems facing young people?

First, with respect to responsibility, the current state of affairs has slowly evolved over the past century as a result of countless individual political and economic decisions taken on a daily basis, largely by the managerial and professional élite (see the discussion of the "revolt of the élite" earlier, based on Lasch, 1995). Many of these decisions have been made on the basis of self-interest and the interests of the groups to which members of the élite belong or with which they identify. No claim is made here that members of the élite sat down and masterminded a conspiracy against young people. However, this book has documented the political neglect of young issues, and there is ample evidence of specific "schemes" by members of the business élite that have seriously hurt young people, as in the case of the lobbying efforts (to keep the minimum wage low), hiring policies, and attitudes toward young workers by those in charge of the fast food industry (Schlosser, 2001).

Second, in reference to what should be done about the situation, the place to begin is with the "ideology of youth." As argued, the ideology justifying the disenfranchisement of youth does not stand up against the evidence. For example, technology has de-skilled many jobs, and made human labour redundant in much of the advanced industrial economy—the facts show that only a small proportion of the population is actually needed to maintain the advanced technological component of the society. The rest of us are needed mainly as consumers of the technology—to play with it until we tire of it and crave greater sophistication, the satisfaction of which is either already in production or on the drawing board (there is no secret that this is how the electronics industry works in marketing cell phones, computers, music listening devices, and the like). At the same time, some two thirds of jobs in advanced industrial societies have not increased in complexity, so there is little justification in pretending that everyone must be pushed through a mass-educational system to train for them. While as many people as possible should be educated to their highest intellectual potential, this is not what the current system is doing. In fact, there should be *more* education, rather than less, and it should be a lifelong process. But this must begin with both the content of what is taught and the processes by which it is taught, such that false consciousness is not nurtured by biased content, and a love of learning is not stifled by mind-numbing, bureaucratized educational processes.

What is needed is a revolution in the way we think about youth and coming of age. We must realize, for example, that the ideology of youth is responsible for some of the identity-formation difficulties experienced by many young people. In many cases, much of their identity confusion is a product of the social environment to which the young are exposed, especially the manipulation of their identity formation by marketers. Moreover, many young people do not know they have identity problems, and neither do their elders. Rather, their troubles are thought to be "natural" for them, a result of an inevitable biological defi-ciency that passes with age.

Unfortunately, in individualistic societies we do not usually attempt to solve problems by getting at their root causes, especially when those causes are not obvious or are rooted in the wider social order from which most of the rest of the community benefits. Rather, we repeatedly apply "band-aid solutions" in an attempt to mask or ignore the problem, or treat the symptom rather than the cause. Instead, in individualistic societies we prefer solu-tions that place the responsibility or "blame" for a problem squarely on the shoulders of individuals—*they* must adjust. We leave it to the victims to remedy the problem.

In other words, the easy way out is to try to "adjust" people to their environment and to ignore the possibility of adjusting the environment to people, or to differentially adjust it to different types of people. But by adjusting people to alienating environments, we are simply exacerbating the problem by denying its reality. If we alter our way of thinking, fol-lowing, for instance, the Swedish model, we will begin to adjust our programs and institu-tions to young people. In doing so, we will award them greater respect as autonomous human beings, but we will also recognize that they do have special needs as they come of age and join the ranks of adult society.

A vision for a better future for young people is best informed with a set of humanistic values that place human well-being ahead of consumerism, materialism, and technologism. But what is lacking in many advanced industrial societies, in spite of their expensive edu-cation and health-care systems, is a model of a truly humanistic democracy. Countries like Canada and the United States may pretend to be democratic, but they perpetuate exploitation of, and inequality among, their citizens. What is needed is a model that is humanistic in ideal *and* democratic in practice. Again, Sweden appears to provide a model that is worth examining, and adapting to other countries (see Dayton-Johnson, 2001, for evidence of greater economic equality in countries that have greater levels of social cohe-sion, like Sweden).

Policies and programs that are informed by humanistic values take into account the experiences and perspectives of those they are ostensibly supposed to benefit. Too many programs become avenues of sinecure for those administering them, and their clientele becomes secondary. Too many programs and institutions operate in their separate and sometimes competitive spheres, so that there are great gaps that allow people to "fall through the cracks." Accountability and co-ordination among such schemes can eliminate much of the expense that has given government-sponsored programs a bad name in coun-tries like the United States. Again, the Swedish experience can provide other countries with a model of effective and rational service delivery. Consequently, rather than simply forc-ing young people to stay in school until they are 18 (as is suggested from time to time by politicians), programs directed at career counselling, co-operative work-school programs, and job placement, in conjunction with study-allowance incentives, could bolster an education system more rationally integrated with the workplace. Rather than forcing a large segment of youth into idleness, their energies could be directed in various ways that benefit the national economy, the local community, and themselves.

Finally, with or without action on the part of the "adult community," young people themselves must take more responsibility for their behaviours and their lives, and resist the attempts to control and subjugate them. Every time young people feed into negative stereotypes by acting irresponsibly or immaturely, this helps perpetuate the system that oppresses them. By confirming negative stereotypes, they simply give justifications to those holding those stereotypes. Instead, young people must realize that other young people share their own "personal troubles," and only by collectively acting to address the "public issues" surrounding those personal troubles will the situation be alleviated (Mills, 1959). This may sound high-handed, but it is clear that if young people do not initiate this type of action, few others will. Most advanced industrial societies are currently based on the principle of self-interest, so young people must mobilize as a group based on their common self-interests.

It may be trite to say that the best hope for the future lies with new generations, but unless the liabilities plaguing the current generation of young people are rectified, that hope is not accompanied by moral and political will. What is called for is renewed energy and vision among adults, for it will take energy and vision to turn the tide against the forces oppressing young people, and by implication oppressing future humans as they come of age. Canadian and American youths and adults must become aware of practicable alternatives, as in the case of Swedish social and economic policies. Indeed, part of the hype behind their false consciousness is that young people in Canada and the United States are told that they are the most fortunate in the world, when it becomes apparent that they are not if we take the time to look elsewhere.

ENDNOTES

1. Earlier predictions that the smaller "Baby Bust" cohort (born 1965–1975) would have been in greater demand in the labour market were not borne out, mainly because of technological displacement (cf. Morissette, Myles, & Picot, 1993; Myles, Picot, & Wannell, 1988). As well, when the Baby Boom cohort passes through, the population "pyramid" will more closely resemble a vase than a pyramid, especially if fertility remains low. Indeed, by 2030 the median population age will be somewhere around 45, depending on fertility patterns (cf. McKie, 1993).

2. Very few young workers are in unions in the United States—only about 6% of 16- to 24-year-olds compared with about 15% of the overall labour force is, despite the fact that union members make about 30% more than do non-members (U.S. Census Bureau, 2001, p. 411). In Canada, about 40% of all workers are union members, and they too earn substantially more than non-union members (Jackson, 2003). Antiunionism among workers is an indication of false consciousness, as discussed in Chapter 5, and the widespread antiunionism in the United States testifies to the success of business interests there in cultivating that false consciousness (see Caldicott, 1992, for a detailed history of these cultivation strategies and programs in the United States that date back to the early twentieth century).

3. The expression is from McQuaig (1998).

References

Agee, P. (1975). *Inside the company: The CIA diary.* Harmondsworth, England: Penguin.

Akyeampong, E. B. (1992, Autumn). Discouraged workers—where have they gone? *Perspectives on Labour and Income,* pp. 38-44.

Allahar, A. (1995). *Sociology and the periphery: Theories and issues* (2nd ed.). Toronto: Garamond.

Allahar, A. (2004). False consciousness, class consciousness and nationalism. *Social and Economic Studies, 53*(1), 95-124.

Allahar, A. L., & Côté, J. E. (1998). *Richer and poorer: The structure of social inequality in Canada.* Toronto: Lorimer.

Allen, M., Harris, S., & Butlin, G. (2001). *Finding their way: A profile of young Canadian graduates* (Education, skills and learning—Research papers). Ottawa: Statistics Canada.

Almey, M., & Normand, J. (2002). *Youth in Canada* (3rd ed.). Ottawa: Minister of Industry.

Andres, L., Anisef, P., Krahn, H., Looker, D., & Thiessen, V. (1999). The persistence of social structure: Cohort, class, and gender effects on the occupational aspirations and expectations of Canadian youth. *Journal of Youth Studies, 2*(3), 261-282.

Anisef, P., & Axelrod, P. (2001). Baby boomers in transition: Life-course experiences of the "Class of '73." In V. W. Marshall, W. R. Heinz, H. Kruger & A. Verma (Eds.), *Restructuring work and the life course* (pp. 473-488*).* Toronto: University of Toronto Press.

Anisef, P., & Kilbride, K. M. (2003). *Managing two worlds: The experiences and concerns of immigrant youth in Ontario.* Toronto: Canadian Scholars Press.

Aries, P. (1962). *Centuries of childhood.* New York: Random House.

Arnett, J. J. (1992). Reckless behavior in adolescence: A developmental perspective. *Developmental Review, 12*(4), 339-373.

Arnett, J. J. (1999). Adolescent storm and stress reconsidered. *American Psychologist, 54,* 317-326.

Arnett, J. J. (2000). Emerging adulthood: A theory of development from the late teens through the twenties. *American Psychologist, 55,* 469-480.

Arnett, J. J. (2002). Adolescents in Western countries in the 21st century: Vast opportunities—for all? In B. B. Brown, R. W. Larson & T. S. Saraswathi (Eds.), *The world's youth: Adolescence in eight regions of the globe* (pp. 307-343). Cambridge, UK: Cambridge University Press.

Arnett, J. J. (2004). *Adolescence and emerging adulthood: A cultural approach.* Upper Saddle River, NJ: Prentice Hall.

Arnett, J. J., & Taber, S. (1994). Adolescence terminable and interminable: When does adolescence end? *Journal of Youth & Adolescence, 23,* 517-537.

Artz, S. (1998). *Sex, power and the violent schoolgirl.* Toronto: Trifolium Books.

Association of Universities and Colleges in Canada (AUCC). (2002). *Trends in higher education.* Ottawa: Author.

Bailey, G., & Gayle, N. (2003). *Ideology: Structuring identities in contemporary life.* Peterborough, Ontario: Broadview Press.

Bakan, J. (2004). *The corporation: The pathological pursuit of profit and power*. Toronto: Viking Canada.

Baldus, B. (1975). The study of power: Suggestions for an alternative. *Canadian Journal of Sociology, 1*, 179-201.

Baldus, B. (1977). Social control in capitalist societies: An examination of the problem of order in liberal democracies. *Canadian Journal of Sociology, 2*, 37-52.

Basow, S. A. (1992). *Gender: Stereotypes and roles* (3rd ed.). Pacific Grove, CA: Brooks/Cole.

Baumeister, R. F., & Tice, D. M. (1986). How adolescence became the struggle for self: A historical transformation of psychological development. In J. Suls & A. G. Greenwood (Eds.), *Psychological perspectives on the self* (Vol. 3, pp. 183-201). Hillsdale, NJ: Lawrence Erlbaum Associates.

Beaujot, R. (2004). *Delayed life transitions: Trends and implications*. Ottawa: Vanier Institute of the Family.

Berg, I. (1970). *Education and jobs: The great training robbery*. New York: Praeger Publishers for the Center for Urban Education.

Bem, S. L., & Bem, D. J. (1970). Homogenizing the American woman: The power of an unconscious ideology. In D. J. Bem (Ed.), *Beliefs, attitudes, and human affairs*. Belmont, CA: Brooks/Cole.

Beneteau, R. (1988, Winter). Trends in suicide. *Canadian Social Trends*, pp. 22-24.

Benson, P. (1997). *All kids are our kids: What communities must do to raise caring and responsible children and adolescents*. San Francisco: Jossey-Bass.

Benson, P., Leffert, N., Scales, P. C., & Blyth, D. A. (1998). Beyond the "village" rhetoric: Creating healthy communities for children and adolescents. *Applied Developmental Science, 2*(3), 138-159.

Bergman, G. (1951). Ideology. *Ethics, 61*, 210.

Berman, S., Montgomery, M., & Kurtines, W. (2004). The development and validation of a measure of identity distress. *Identity: An International Journal of Theory and Research, 4*(1), 1-8.

Bernard, J. (1981). The good-provider role: Its rise and fall. *American Psychologist, 36*, 1-12.

Bernays, E. (1955). *The engineering of consent*. Norman: University of Oklahoma Press.

Betcherman, G., & Morissette, R. (1994). *Recent youth labour market experiences in Canada* (Analytic studies branch research paper series No. 63). Ottawa: Statistics Canada.

Betts, J., Ferrall, C., & Finnie, R. (2000). *The transition to work for Canadian university graduates: Time to first job, 1982-1990* (Analytic studies branch research paper series No.141). Ottawa: Statistics Canada.

Bibby, R. W., & Posterski, D. C. (1992). *Teen trends: A nation in motion*. Toronto: Stoddart.

Birmaher, B., Ryan, N. D., Williamson, D. E., Brent, D. A., Kaufman, J., Dahl, R. E., Perel, J. & Nelson, B. (1996). Childhood and adolescent depression: Part I. A review of the past 10 years. *Journal of the American Academy of Child and Adolescent Psychiatry, 35*, 1427-1439.

Bourrie, M. (1995, Oct. 21). How Canada's rich stay rich. *The London Free Press*, p. E1.

Bowlby, G. B. (2000, Spring). The school-to-work transition. *Perspectives*, 43-48.

Bowlby, G. B., & McMullen, K. (2002). *At the crossroads: First results for the 18- to 29-year-old cohort of the Youth in Transition Survey*. Ottawa: Human Resources Development Canada.

Bowles, S., & Gintis, H. (1976). *Schooling in capitalist America*. New York: Basic.

Boyd, M., & Norris, D. (1999, Spring). The crowded nest: Young adults at home. *Canadian Social Trends*, pp. 2-5.

Broad, W., & Wade, N. (1982). *Betrayers of the truth: Fraud and deceit in the halls of science*. New York: Simon & Schuster.

Broverman, I., Broverman, D. M., Clarkson, F. E., Rosenkrantz, P. S., & Vogel, S. R. (1970). Sex-role stereotypes and clinical judgments of mental health. *Journal of Consulting and Clinical Psychology, 34,* 1-7.

Brown, B. B., Larson, R. W., & Saraswathi, T. S. (Eds.). (2002). *The world's youth: Adolescence in eight regions of the globe*. Cambridge: Cambridge University Press.

Brown, J. B., & Larson, R. W. (2002). The kaleidoscope of adolescence: Experiences of the world's youth at the beginning of the 21st century. In B. B. Brown, R. W. Larson & T. S. Saraswathi (Eds.), *The world's youth: Adolescence in eight regions of the globe* (pp. 1-20). Cambridge: Cambridge University Press.

Brown, J. D., & Witherspoon, E. M. (2002). The mass media and American adolescents' health. *Journal of Adolescent Health, 31,* 153-170.

Buchanan, C. M., Eccles, J. S., & Becker, J. B. (1992). Are adolescents the victims of raging hormones: Evidence for activational effects of hormones on moods and behavior at adolescence. *Psychological Bulletin, 111,* 2-107.

Bureau of Agriculture and Statistics, CD. (1863). *Census of Canada. 1860-61 Personal census* (Vol. I). Mountain Hill, Quebec: S. B. Foote.

Bynner, J., Elias, P., McKnight, A., Pan., & Pierre, G. (2002). *Young people's changing routes to independence*. York, UK: Joseph Rowntree Foundation.

Calcutt, A. (1998). *Arrested development: Pop culture and the erosion of adulthood*. London: Cassell.

Caldicott, H. (1992). *If you love this planet: A plan to heal the earth*. New York: Norton.

Call, K. T., Riedel, A. A., Hein, K., McLoyd, V., Petersen, A., & Kipke, M. (2002). Adolescent health and well-being in the twenty-first century: A global perspective. *Journal of Research on Adolescence, 12*(1), 69-98. .

Canadian Association of University Teachers (2004). *CAUT almanac of post-secondary education in Canada*. Ottawa: Author.

Canadian Youth Foundation (1995). *Youth unemployment: Canada's rite of passage*. Ottawa: Author.

Cassidy, S. (2004, May 11). Parents must drop prejudices to make apprenticeship scheme work, says CBI. *The Independent,* p. 16.

Catalano, R. F., Berglund, M. L., Ryan, J. A. M., Lonczak, H. S., & Hawkins, D. (2002). Positive youth development in the United States: Research findings on evaluations of positive youth development programs. *Prevention & Treatment, 5*(15), 1-111.

Catan, L. (2003). *Youth, Citizenship, and Social Change: Background to the youth research programme*. Retrieved March 3, 2005, from **http://www.tsa.uk.com/ YCSC/backg.html**

Catan, L. (2004). *Becoming adult: Changing youth transitions in the 21st century*. Brighton, UK: Trust for the Study of Adolescence.

CBC (2004). *CBC News Online*. Retrieved October 22, 2004, from **www.cbc.ca/ story/canada/national/2004/10/22/ youngvoters_041022.html**

Center for Information & Research on Civic Learning and Engagement. (2004). *Civic engagement index* (pp. 1-4). College Park, MD: Author. Retrieved December 12, 2004, from **www.civicyouth.org**

Chandler, M. (2001). The time of our lives: Self-continuity in Native and non-Native youth. In W. Reese (Ed.), *Advances in child development and behavior* (pp. 175-221). New York: Academic Press.

Charbonneau, L. (2004, December). University enrolment continues to surprise. *University Affairs*, p. 28.

CIRCLE Staff (2004). *Youth voting in the 2004 election* (Fact sheet Nov. 8). College Park, MD: The Center for Information & Research on Civic Learning & Engagement.

Clark, W. (1999, Autumn). University graduates at college. *Canadian Social Trends*, pp. 18-19.

Cloud, J. (1999, May 31). Just a routine school shooting. *Time*, pp. 14-21.

Cole, D. A. (1991). Adolescent suicide. In R. M. Lerner, A. C. Petersen & J. Brooks-Gunn (Eds.), *Encyclopedia of adolescence* (pp. 1113-1116). New York: Garland.

Coleman, J. C. (1978). Current contradictions in adolescent theory. *Journal of Youth & Adolescence*, *7*(1), 1-11.

Collins, R. (1979). *The credential society: A historical sociology of education and stratification*. New York: Academic Press.

Commission of the European Communities (2004). *European Youth Portal*. Retrieved December 28, 2004, from **www.europa.eu.int/youth/index_en.html**

Condon, R. G. (1987). *Inuit youth: Growth and change in the Canadian Arctic*. New Brunswick, NJ: Rutgers University Press.

Cook, T. D., & Furstenberg, F. E. (2002). Explaining aspects of the transition to adulthood in Italy, Sweden, Germany, and the United States: A cross-disciplinary, case synthesis approach. *The Annals of the American Academy of Political and Social Science*, *580*, 257-287.

Cooke-Reynolds, M., & Zukewich, N. (2004, Spring). The feminization of work. *Canadian Social Trends*, pp. 24-29.

Cooperative Institutional Research Program (CIRP) (2004). *CIRP Freshman Survey*.

Retrieved December 28, 2004, from **www.gseis.ucla.edu/heri/freshman.html**

Corak, M., & Zhao, J. (2003, October 3). Family income and participation in post-secondary education. *The Daily*. Ottawa: Statistics Canada. Retrieved March 7, 2005, from **http://www.statcan.ca/Daily/English/d031003b.htm**

Côté, J. E. (1992). Was Mead wrong about coming of age in Samoa? An analysis of the Mead/Freeman controversy for scholars of adolescence and human development. *Journal of Youth and Adolescence*, *21*(5), 1-29.

Côté, J. E. (1994). *Adolescent storm and stress: An evaluation of the Mead/Freeman controversy*. Hillsdale, NJ: Lawrence Erlbaum.

Côté, J. E. (1996). Sociological perspectives on identity formation: The culture-identity link and identity capital. *Journal of Adolescence*, *19*, 419-430.

Côté, J. E. (1997). An empirical test of the identity capital model. *Journal of Adolescence*, *20*, 577-597.

Côté, J. E. (2000). *Arrested adulthood: The changing nature of maturity and identity*. New York: New York University Press.

Côté, J. E. (in press). Emerging adulthood as an institutionalized moratorium: Risks and benefits to identity formation. In J. J. Arnett & J. Tanner (Eds.), *Emerging adults in America: Coming of age in the 21st century*. Washington, DC: American Psychological Association.

Côté, J. E., & Allahar, A. (1994). *Generation on hold: Coming of age in the late twentieth century*. Toronto: Stoddart.

Côté, J. E., & Levine, C. (1987). A formulation of Erikson's theory of ego identity formation. *Developmental Review*, *7*, 273-325.

Coupland, D. (1991). *Generation X: Tales for an accelerated culture*. New York: St. Martin's Press.

Coutts, J. (1987, February 8). Politicians turn silent on jobless youth. *The Toronto Star*, p. F3.

Cox, W. (1997, November 27). Girls hit with violent message. *Canadian Press*. Retrieved January 9, 1998, from **http://www.canoe.com/CNEWSFeaturesArchive/nov27_teens.html**

Crompton, S. (1996). Employment prospects for high school graduates. *Education Quarterly Review*, *3*, 8-19.

Crompton, S. (2002, Winter). I still feel overqualified for my job. *Canadian Social Trends*, pp. 23-26.

Cultice, W. W. (1992). *Youth's battle for the ballot: A history of voting age in America*. New York: Greenwood Press.

D'Emilio, F. (1996, April 20). Mamma mia! Gen X clings to home in Italy. *The Ottawa Citizen*, p. B1.

Damon, W. (2004). *The youth charter: How communities can work together to raise standards for all our children*. Stanford, CA: Stanford Center on Adolescence. Retrieved December 28, 2004, from **www.stanford.edu/group/adolescent.ctr/index.html**

Danesi, M. (1994). *The signs and meanings of adolescence*. Toronto: University of Toronto Press.

Danesi, M. (2003). *Forever young: The "teen-aging" of modern culture*. Toronto: University of Toronto Press.

Darroch, G. (2001). Home and away: Patterns of residence, schooling, and work among children and never-married young adults. Canada, 1871 and 1901. *Journal of Family History*, *26*, 220-250.

Davies, J. (1993). The distribution of wealth and inequality. In J. Curtis, E. Grabb, & N. Guppy (Eds.), *Social inequality in Canada: Patterns, problems, policies* (2nd ed.). Toronto: Prentice Hall.

Davies, S., Mosher, C., & O'Grady, B. (1994). Trends in labour market outcomes of Canadian post-secondary graduates, 1978-1988. In L. Erwin & D. MacLennan (Eds.), *Sociology of education in Canada*. Toronto: Copp Clark Longman Ltd.

Dayton-Johnson, J. (2001). *Social cohesion and economic prosperity*. Toronto: James Lorimer.

de Broucker, P., & Lavallee, L. (1998, Summer). Does your parents' education count? *Canadian Social Trends*, pp. 11-15.

De Graaf, J., Wann, D., & Naylor, T. (2001). *Affluenza: The all-consuming epidemic*. San Francisco: Berrett-Koehler.

Dei, G. (1996). *Anti-racism education: Theory and practice*. Halifax: Fernwood Publishing.

Denton, F. T. (1970). *The growth of manpower in Canada*. Ottawa: Dominion Bureau of Statistics.

Dittmar, H., & Dickinson, J. (1993). The perceived relationship between the belief in a just world and sociopolitical ideology. *Social Justice Research*, *6*, 257-272.

Dodd, V. (2003, August 16). 45-minute claim on Iraq was hearsay. *The Guardian*. Retrieved December 15, 2004, from **http://politics.guardian.co.uk/iraq/story/0,12956,1020033,00.html**

Douvan, E., & Adelson, J. (1966). *The adolescent experience*. New York: John Wiley.

Dryfoos, J. G. (1998). *Safe passage: Making it through adolescence in a risky society*. New York: Oxford University Press.

Dumas, C. (1996, Spring). The labour market: Year-end review. *Perspectives on Labour and Income*, pp. 9-15.

Eisenstadt, S. N. (1961). Archetypal patterns of youth. In E. Erikson (Ed.), *The challenge of youth* (pp. 29-50). Garden City: Doubleday Anchor.

Emirbayer, M., & Mische, A. (1998). What is agency? *American Journal of Sociology, 103*, 962-1023.

Erikson, E. H. (1963). *Childhood and society* (2nd ed.). New York: Norton.

Erikson, E. H. (1968). *Identity: Youth and crisis*. New York: Norton.

Erikson, E. H. (1970). Reflections on the dissent of contemporary youth. *Daedalus, 99*(1), 154-176.

Erikson, E. H., & Erikson, K. T. (1957). On the confirmation of the delinquent. *Chicago Review, 10*, 15-23.

Esterlin, R. A. (1978). What will 1984 be like? Socioeconomic implications of recent twists in age structure. *Demography, 15*, 397-432.

European Group for Integrated Social Research (EGRIS). (2001). Misleading trajectories: Transition dilemmas of youth adults in Europe. *Journal of Youth Studies, 4*, 101-118.

Evans, E. D., Rutberg, J., Sather, C., & Turner, C. (1991). Content analysis of contemporary teen magazines for adolescent females. *Youth & Society, 23*(1), 99-120.

Evans, K. (2002). Taking control of their lives? Agency in young adult transitions in England and the new Germany. *Journal of Youth Studies, 5*(3), 245-269.

Evans, K., & Heinz, W. R. (1994). *Becoming adults in England and Germany*. London: Anglo-German Foundation.

Fanon, F. (1963). *The wretched of the earth*. New York: Grove Press.

Fast, J., Frederick, J., Zukewich, N., & Franke, S. (2001, Winter). The time of our lives . . . *Canadian Social Trends*, pp. 20-23.

Fine, G. A., Mortimer, J. T., & Roberts, D. F. (1990). Leisure, work, and the mass media. In S. S. Feldman & G. R. Elliott (Eds.), *At the threshold: The developing adolescent* (pp. 225-252). Cambridge, MA: Harvard University Press.

Finnie, R., Lascelles, E., & Sweetman, A. (2005). *Who goes? The direct and indirect effects of family background on access to post-secondary education* (Analytical Studies—Research Paper Series No. 237). Ottawa: Statistics Canada.

Flannery, D. J., Hussey, D. L., Biebelhausen, L., & Wester, K. L. (2003). Crime, delinquency, and youth gangs. In G. R. Adams & M. Berzonsky (Eds.), *Blackwell handbook of adolescence* (pp. 502-522). Malden, MA: Blackwell.

Fleras, A., & Elliott, J. L. (2002). *Engaging diversity: Multiculturalism in Canada*. Toronto: Nelson.

Fombonne, E. (1994). Increased rates of depression: Updates of epidemiological findings and analytical problems. *Acta Psychiatrica Scandinavia, 90*, 145-156.

Foot, D. K. (1996). *Boom, bust & echo: How to profit from the coming demographic shift*. Toronto: Macfarlane Walter & Rose.

Fournier, E., Butlin, G., & Giles, P. (1994). Intergenerational change in the education of Canadians. Report 1994 *Dynamics* (Statistics Canada), pp. 24-30.

Frank, J. (1992, Autumn). Violent youth crime. *Canadian Social Trends*, pp. 2-9.

Frank, T. (1997a). *The conquest of cool: Business culture, counterculture, and the rise of hip consumerism*. Chicago: The University of Chicago Press.

Frank, T. (1997b, November-December). Let them eat lifestyle: From hip to hype—the ultimate corporate takeover. *Utne Reader*, pp. 43-47.

Frenette, M. (2000). Overqualified? Recent graduates and the needs of their employers. *Education Quarterly Review, 7*(1), 6-20.

Frenette, M. (2001, Spring). Overqualified? Recent graduates, employer needs. *Perspectives* (Statistics Canada), 45-53.

Fromm, E. (1955). *The sane society*. Greenwich, CT: Fawcett Publications.

Furlong, A., & Cartmel, F. (1997). *Young people and social change: Individualization and risk in late modernity*. Buckingham, UK: Open University Press.

Furstenberg, F. E., Cook, T. D., Sampson, R., & Slap, G. (2002). Preface: International perspectives on the transition to adulthood. *The Annals of the American Academy of Political and Social Science, 580*, 6-15.

Galambos, N. L., & Kolaric, G. C. (1994). Adolescence in Canada. In K. Hurrelmann (Ed.), *International handbook of adolescence*. Westport, CT: Greenwood Press.

Galaway, B., & Hudson, J. (1996). *Youth in transition: Perspectives on research and policy*. Toronto: Thompson.

Gardiner, S. (1995, March 18). Sassy loses its sass in editorial takeover. *The Globe and Mail*, pp. F1-F2.

Gauthier, M., & Pacom, D. (2001). *Spotlight on . . . Canadian youth research*. Quebec City: Les Presses de l'Université Laval.

Gidengil, E., Blais, A., Nevitte, N., & Nadeau, N. (2003). Turned off or tuned out? Youth participation in politics. *Electoral Insight, 5*(2), 9-14.

Giles, P., & Drewes, T. (2001, Autumn). Liberal arts degrees and the labour market. *Perspectives (Statistics Canada)*, pp. 27-33.

Gillis, J. R. (1974). *Youth and history: Tradition and change in European age relations: 1770-present*. New York: Academic Press.

Goode, W. (1980). Why men resist. *Dissent, 27*, 181-193.

Goffman, E. (1952). Cooling out the mark: Some aspects of adaptation to failure. *Psychiatry, 40*, 451-463.

Graham, L., & Hamdan, L. (1989). *Youthtrends: Capturing the $200 billion youth market*. Toronto: McClelland and Stewart.

Gregor, A. D., & Jasmin, G. (1992). *Higher education in Canada*. Ottawa: Minister of Supply and Service.

Hadenius, S., & Lindgren, A. (1990). *On Sweden*. Stockholm: The Swedish Institute.

Hagell, A. (2004). *Time trends in adolescent well-being*. London: The Nuffield Foundation.

Hall, G. S. (1904). *Adolescence*. New York: Appleton.

Halperin, S. (1998). Today's forgotten half: Still losing ground. In S. Halperin (Ed.), *The forgotten half revisited: American youth and young families, 1998-2008* (pp. 1-26). Washington: American Youth Policy Forum.

Hamilton, S. F., & Hamilton, M. A. (in press). *School, work, and emerging adulthood*. In J. J. Arnett & J. Tanner (Eds.), *Emerging adults in America: Coming of age in the 21st century*. Washington, DC: American Psychological Association.

Hare-Mustin, R. T., & Marecek, J. (1988). The meaning of difference: Gender theory, postmodernism, and psychology. *American Psychologist, 43*, 455-464.

Harris, M. (1983). Margaret and the giant-killer: It doesn't matter a whit who's right. *The Sciences, 23*(4), 18-21.

Heath, J., & Potter, A. (2004). *The rebel sell: Why the culture can't be jammed*. Toronto: Harper Collins.

Heath-Rawlins, J. (2005, February 4). We need more black teachers. *Toronto Star*, p. A15.

Heinz, W. (2002). Self-socialization and post-traditional society. *Advances in life course research, 7*, 41-64.

Hellman, H. (1998). *Great feuds in science: The ten liveliest disputes ever*. New York: Wiley.

Herman, E. S., & Chomsky, N. (1988). *Manufacturing consent: The political economy of the mass media.* New York: Pantheon.

Hess, M. (1991). Sinful wages. *Perception* (Canadian Council on Social Development), 15(3), 29-32.

Hill, R. F. & Fortenberry, J. D. (1992). Adolescence as a culture-bound syndrome. *Social Science & Medicine, 35*, 73-80.

Hill, J. P., & Lynch, M. E. (1983). The intensification of gender-related role expectations during early adolescence. In J. Brooks-Gunn & A. C. Petersen (Eds.), *Girls at puberty: Biological and psychological perspectives (pp. 201-228).* New York: Plenum.

Hoffman, A. M., & Summers, R. W. (2001). *Teen violence: A global view.* Westport, CT: Greenwood Press.

Hollands, R. (2001). (Re)presenting Canadian youth: Challenge or opportunity? In M. Gauthier & D. Pacom (Eds.), *Spotlight on . . . Canadian youth research* (pp. 97-133). Quebec City: Les Presses de l'Université Laval.

Hollingshead, A. B. (1949). *Elmtown's youth: The impact of social class on adolescents.* New York: John Wiley & Sons.

Hollingsworth, L. S. (1928). *The psychology of the adolescent.* Englewood Cliffs, NJ: Prentice Hall.

Holmes, J., & Silverman, E. L. (1992). *We're here, listen to us! A survey of young women in Canada.* Ottawa: Canadian Advisory Council on the Status of Women.

Howe, N., & Strauss, B. (1993). *13th GEN: Abort, retry, ignore, fail?* New York: Vintage Books.

Human Resources Development Canada (2000a). *Profile of Canadian youth in the labour market.* Hull, Quebec: Author.

Human Resources Development Canada (2000b). *The transition from initial education to working life: A Canadian Report*

for an OECD thematic review. Hull, Quebec: Author.

Hunter, A. A., & McKenzie Leiper, J. (1993). On formal education, skills and earnings: The role of educational certificates in earnings determination. *Canadian Journal of Sociology, 18,* 21-42.

Huston, A. C., & Alvarez, M. M. (1990). The socialization context of gender role development in early adolescence. In G. R. Adams, R. Montemayor, & T. P. Gullotta (Eds.), *Biology of adolescent behavior and development* (pp. 156-179). Newbury Park, CA: Sage.

Huxley, A. (1932). *Brave new world.* London: Triad Grafton.

Huxley, A. (1958). *Brave new world revisited.* New York: Harper & Row.

Hylton, F. (2003) *Dispatch from the Bolivian War: "Like animals they kill us."* Retrieved December 15, 2004, from **www.americas.org/Clippings/ 2003-10-15-Counterpunch**

International Labour Office (2004). *Global employment trends for youth.* Geneva: Author.

Isajiw, W. (1999). *Understanding diversity: Ethnicity and race in the Canadian context.* Toronto: Thompson Educational Publishing.

Jackson, A. (2003). *Canada beats USA—but loses gold to Sweden.* Ottawa: Canadian Council on Social Development. Retrieved October, 20, 2004, from **www.ccsd.ca/ pubs/2002/olympic/ind**

Jacobsson, I. (2002). *Advertising ban and children: "Children have the right to safe zones."* Stockholm: Swedish Institute.

Jhally, S. (Producer). (1997). *Advertising and the end of the world* [video cassette]. Northhampton, MA: Media Education Foundation.

Jones, G. (2002). *The youth divide: Diverging paths to adulthood*. York, UK: Joseph Rowntree Foundation.

Jonsson, J. O., Helve, H., & Wichström, L. (2003). *Youth research in Sweden, 1995-2001: An evaluation report*. Stockholm: FAS.

Kaplan, H. (1997). The evolution of the human life course. In K. Wachter & C. Finch (Eds.), *Between Zeus and the Salmon: The biodemography of longevity* (pp. 175-211). Washington: National Academy Press.

Katz, M. B. (1975). *The people of Hamilton, Canada West: Family and class in a mid-nineteenth-century city*. Harvard University Press: Cambridge, MA.

Kelleher, K. J., McInerny, T. K., Gardner, W. P., Childs, G. E., & Wasserman, R. C. (2000). Increasing identification of psychosocial problems: 1979-1996. *Pediatrics, 105*, 1313-1321.

Kelly, K., Howatson-Leo, L., & Clark, W. (1997, Winter). I feel overqualified for my job. *Canadian Social Trends*, pp. 11-16.

Kerstetter, S. (2002). Top 50% of Canadians hold 94.4% of wealth, bottom half 5.6%. *The CCPA Monitor, 9*(6), 1, 7.

Kimberlee, R. H. (2002). Why don't British young people vote at general elections? *Journal of Youth Studies, 5*, 85-98.

Klein, N. (2000). *No logo: Taking aim at the brand bullies*. Toronto: Knopf.

Korenblum, M. (1986, March 24). Canada's troubled youth the real victim of society? *The Globe and Mail*, p. A7.

Krahn, H., Lowe, G., & Lehmann, W. (2002). Acquisition of employability skills by high school students. *Canadian Public Policy, 28*(2), 275-296.

Lacayo, R. (1994, August 8). If everyone is hip, is anyone hip? *Time*, pp. 48-55.

Langlois, S., & Morrison, P. (2002, Autumn). Suicide deaths and attempts. *Canadian Social Trends*, pp. 20-25.

Lapsley, D. K., Enright, R. D., & Serlin, R. C. (1985). Toward a theoretical perspective on the legislation of adolescence. *Journal of Early Adolescence, 4*, 441-466.

Lasch, C. (1995). *The revolt of the elites: The betrayal of democracy*. New York: Norton.

Lavoie, Y., & Oderkirk, J. (1993, Winter). Social consequences of demographic change. *Canadian Social Trends*, pp. 2-5.

Lee, D. E. (1996). *Generations and the challenge of justice*. Lanham: University Press of America, Inc.

Leffert, N., Benson, P., Scales, P., Sharma, A., Drake, D., & Blyth, D. (1998). Developmental assets: Measurement and prediction of risks behaviors among adolescents. *Applied Developmental Science, 2*, 209-230.

Lerner, R. M. (1995). *America's youth in crisis: Challenges and options for programs and policies*. Thousand Oaks: Sage.

Lerner, R. M. (2000). *Positive youth development and civil society: A vision for youth development policy in the United States*. Paper presented at the Jacobs Foundation Conference, Marbach Castle, Germany.

Lerner, R. M. (2004). *Adolescence: Development, diversity, context, and application*. Upper Saddle River, NJ: Prentice Hall.

Lerner, R. M., Brown, J. D., & Kier, C. (2005). *Adolescence: Development, diversity, context, and application* (Canadian ed.). Toronto: Pearson.

Lerner, R. M., & Galambos, N. L. (1998). Adolescent development: Challenges and opportunities for research, programs, and policies. *Annual Review of Psychology, 49*, 413-446.

Levine, A., & Cureton, J. S. (1998). *When hope and fear collide: A portrait of today's college student*. San Francisco: Jossey-Bass.

Levine, S. (1984). *Radical departures: Desperate detours to growing up.* New York: Harcourt, Brace, Jovanovich.

Levitt, C. (1984). *Children of privilege: Student revolt in the sixties.* Toronto: University of Toronto Press.

Li, P. (2003). *Destination Canada: Immigration debates and issues.* Toronto: Oxford University Press.

Lindsay, C., Devereaux, M. S., & Bergob, M. (1994). *Youth in Canada* (2nd ed.). Ottawa: Minister of Industry, Science and Technology.

Linn, S. (2004). *Consuming kids: The hostile takeover of childhood.* New York: The New Press.

Little, B. (1995, January 9). Why it's not so wonderful to be young. *The Globe and Mail*, A9.

Livingstone, D. W. (1993). Lifelong education and chronic underemployment: Exploring the contradiction. In P. Anisef & P. Axelrod (Eds.), *Transitions: Schooling and employment in Canada.* Toronto: Thompson Educational Publishing.

Livingstone, D. W. (1998). *The education—jobs gap: Underemployment or economic democracy.* Boulder, CO: Westview Press.

Lockhart, A. (1975). Future failure: The unanticipated consequences of educational planning. In R. M. Pike & E. Zureik (Eds.), *Socialization and values in Canadian society* (pp. 196-214). Toronto: McClelland & Stewart.

Lockhart, A. (1978). *Future failure: A systematic analysis of changing middle class opportunities in Canada.* University of Essex: Unpublished Doctoral Dissertation.

Lowe, G. S. (2001). Youth, transitions, and the new world of work. In V. W. Marshall, W. R. Heinz, H. Kruger & A. Verma (Eds.), *Restructuring work and the life course* (pp. 29-43). Toronto: University of Toronto Press.

Mackie, M. (1991). *Gender relations in Canada: Further explorations.* Toronto: Butterworths.

Males, M. A. (1996). *The scapegoat generation: America's war on adolescents.* Monroe, ME: Common Courage Press.

Mandell, N., & Crysdale, S. (1993). Gender tracks: Male-female perceptions of home-school-work transitions. In P. Anisef & P. Axelrod (Eds.), *Schooling and employment in Canada* (pp. 21-41). Toronto: Thompson Educational Publishing.

Manning, M. L. (1983). Three myths concerning adolescence. *Adolescence, 18,* 823-829.

Marcuse, H. (1964). *One dimensional man.* Boston: Beacon Press.

Marcuse, H. (1969). *An essay on liberation.* Boston: Beacon Press.

Marcuse, H. (1972). *Counter-revolution and revolt.* Boston: Beacon Press.

Marney, J. (1991, December 9). Teen market offers growing opportunities. *Marketing,* p. 14.

Marx, K., & Engels, F. (1969). *The German ideology.* New York: International Publishers.

McCain, G., & Segal, E. M. (1969). *The game of science.* Belmont, California: Brooks/Cole.

McDonald, L., & Chen, M. Y. T. (1993). The youth freeze and the retirement bulge: Older workers and the impending labour shortage. *Journal of Canadian Studies, 28,* 75-101.

McGee, T. (1997, January). Getting inside kids' heads. *American Demographics,* 21-24.

McKie, C. (1993, Summer). Population aging: Baby boomers into the 21st century. *Canadian Social Trends*, pp. 2-6.

McQuaig, L. (1998). *The cult of impotence: Selling the myth of powerlessness in the global economy*. Toronto: Viking.

McVey, W. W. J., & Kalbach, W. E. (1995). *Canadian population*. Toronto: Nelson Canada.

McWhirter, J. J., McWhirter, B. T., McWhirter, A. M., & McWhirter, E. H. (1998). *At-risk youth: A comprehensive response* (2nd ed.). Pacific Grove, CA: Brooks/Cole.

Mead, M. (1928). *Coming of age in Samoa: A psychological study of primitive youth for Western Civilization*. New York: Morrow Quill Paperbacks.

Mead, M. (1970). *Culture and commitment*. Garden City, NJ: Doubleday.

Media Awareness Network. (2004). *Gender and tobacco: Women and girls*. Retrieved on December 13, 2004, from **www.media.awareness.ca**

Melton, G. B. (1991). Rights of adolescents. In R. M. Lerner, A. C. Petersen & J. Brooks-Gunn (Eds.), *Encyclopedia of adolescence*. (pp. 930-933). New York: Garland.

Mills, C. W. (1959). *The sociological imagination*. New York: Oxford University Press.

Milner, M., Jr. (2004). *Freaks, geeks, and cool kids: American teenagers, schools, and the culture of consumption*. New York: Routledge.

Modell, J., Furstenberg, F. F., & Hershberg, T. (1976). Social change and transitions to adulthood in historical perspective. *Journal of Family History, 1*, 7-31.

Mohr, P., & Luscri, G. (1995). Blame and punishment: Attitudes to juvenile and criminal offending. *Psychological Reports, 77*, 1091-1096.

Montgomery, M., & Côté, J. E. (2003). The transition to university: Outcomes and adjustments. In G. Adams & M. Berzonsky (Eds.), *The Blackwell handbook of adolescence* (pp. 149-172). Oxford: Blackwell.

Mørch, S. (1995). Culture and the challenge of adaptation: Foreign youth in Denmark. *International Journal of Comparative Race and Ethnic Studies, 2*(1), 102-115.

Morissette, R., Myles, J., & Picot, G. (1993). *What is happening to earnings inequality in Canada?* (Analytic studies branch research papers series No. 60). Ottawa: Statistics Canada.

Morissette, R., Zhang, X., & Drolet, M. (2002, Autumn). Are families getting richer? *Canadian Social Trends*, pp. 15-19.

Morris, M., & Western, B. (1999). Inequality in earnings at the close of the twentieth century. *Annual Review of Sociology, 25*, 623-657.

Mumford, L. (1944). *The condition of man*. New York: Harcourt, Brace & World.

Muuss, R. (1996). *Theories of adolescence* (6th ed.). New York: McGraw-Hill.

Myles, J., Picot, W. G., & Wannell, T. (1988). *Wages and jobs in the 1980s: Changing youth wages and the declining middle*. Ottawa: Statistics Canada: Social and Economic Studies Division.

Nader, R., & Coco, L. (1999, January). The corporate exploitation of children. *The CCPA Monitor*, pp. 12-14.

National Geographic Education Foundation (2002). *National Geographic—Roper 2002 Global Geographic Literacy Survey*. Retrieved December 28, 2004, from **www.nationalgeographic.com/geosurvey/ download/RoperSurvey.pdf: RoperASW**

Niedzviecki, H. (2004). *Hello, I'm special: How individuality became the new conformity*. Toronto: Penguin Canada.

Nielsen, L. (1991). *Adolescence: A contemporary view* (2nd ed.). Fort Worth, Texas: Harcourt Brace Jovanovich.

Nightingale, D. S., & Fix, M. (2004). Economic and labor market trends. *Children of Immigrant Families, 14*(2), 49-59.

Nobert, L., McDowell, R., & Goulet, D. (1992). *Profile of higher education in Canada: 1991 edition*. Ottawa: Ministry of Supply and Services.

Normand, J. (1995, Winter). Education of women in Canada. *Canadian Social Trends*, pp. 17-21.

O'Neill, J. (1991, Winter). Changing occupational structure. *Canadian Social Trends*, pp. 8-12.

O'Neill, B. (2003). Examining declining electoral turnout among Canada's youth. *Electoral Insight, 5*(2), 15-19. (Ottawa: Elections Canada)

Offer, D., & Church, R. B. (1991). Adolescent turmoil. In R. M. Lerner, A. C. Petersen & J. Brooks-Gunn (Eds.), *Encyclopedia of adolescence* (pp. 513-517). New York: Garland.

Offer, D., & Offer, J. B. (1975). *From teenage to young manhood: A psychological study*. New York: Basic Books.

Offer, D., & Sabshin, M. (1984). *Normality and the life cycle: A critical integration*. New York: Basic Books.

Oliver, L. P. (1987). *Study circles: Coming together for personal growth and social change*. Washington, DC: Seven Locks Press.

Ortiz, A. (2003). *Adolescent brain development and legal culpability*. American Bar Association. Retrieved January 29, 2004 from **www.abanet.org/crimjust/juvjus/factsheets_brain_development.pdf**

Orwell, G. (1948). *Nineteen eighty-four*. New York: Penguin.

Owram, D. (1996). *Born at the right time: A history of the Baby Boom generation*. Toronto: University of Toronto Press.

Ozer, E. M., MacDonald, T., & Irwin, C. E. (2002). Adolescent health care in the United States: Implications and projections for the new millennium. In J. Mortimer & R. W. Larson (Eds.), *The changing adolescent experience: Societal trends and the transition to adulthood* (pp. 129-174). Cambridge, UK: Cambridge University Press.

Paikoff, R. L., & Brooks-Gunn, J. (1990). Physiological processes: What role do they play in the transition to adolescence? In R. Montemayor, G. R. Adams, & T. P. Gullotta (Eds.), *Advances in adolescent development: Vol 2. The transition from childhood to adolescence* (pp. 63-81). Beverly Hills, CA: Sage.

Palladino, G. (1996). *Teenagers: An American history*. New York: Basic Books.

Pammett, J. H., & LeDuc, L. (2003). Confronting the problem of declining voter turnout among youth. *Electoral Insight, 5*(2), 3-8.

Parsons, T. (1961). Youth in the context of American society. In E. H. Erikson (Ed.), *The challenge of youth* (pp. 110-141). Garden City, NY: Doubleday Anchor.

Passell, P. (1994, August 13). Peace, love and black ink. *The Globe and Mail*, p. B3.

Petersen, A. C. (1991). History of research on adolescence. In R. Lerner, A. C. Petersen & J. Brooks-Gunn (Eds.), *Encyclopedia of adolescence* (pp. 499-503). New York: Garland.

Petersen, A. C., & Taylor, B. (1980). The biological approach to adolescence: Biological change and psychological adaptation. In J. Adelson (Ed.), *Handbook of adolescent psychology* (pp. 117-155). New York: John Wiley and Sons.

Phillips, A. (1999, May 3). Lessons of Littleton. *MacLean's*, pp. 18-24.

Phillips, C. E. (1957). *The development of education in Canada*. Toronto: W. J. Gage and Company Ltd.

Picot, G., & Myles, J. (1996, Autumn). Children in low-income families. *Canadian Social Trends*, pp. 15-19.

Picot, G., Myles, J., & Wannell, T. (1990). *Good jobs/bad jobs and the declining middle: 1967-1986* (Analytic studies branch research paper series No. 028). Ottawa: Statistics Canada.

Pooley, E. (1999, May 10). Portrait of a deadly bond. *Time*, pp. 14-20.

Proefrock, D. W. (1981). Adolescence: Social fact and psychological concept. *Adolescence, 26*(64), 851-858.

Putnam, R. (2000). *Bowling alone: The collapse and revival of American community*. New York: Simon & Schuster.

Quart, A. (2003). *Branded: The buying and selling of teenagers*. New York: Perseus.

Randall, H. E., & Byers, E. S. (2003). What is sex? Students' definitions of having sex, sexual partner, and unfaithful sexual behaviour. *The Canadian Journal of Human Sexuality, 12*(2), 87-96.

Reinherz, H. Z., Giaconia, R. M., Carmola Hauf, A. M., Wasserman, M. S., & Silverman, A. B. (1999). Major depression in the transition to adulthood: Risks and impairments. *Journal of Abnormal Psychology, 108*, 500-510.

Rejai, M. (Ed.). (1971). *Decline of ideology?* Chicago: Aldine and Atherton Inc.

Rice, F. P (1992). *The adolescent: Development, relationships, and culture*. Boston: Allyn and Bacon.

Rich, G. J. (2003). The positive psychology of youth and adolescence. *Journal of Youth & Adolescence, 32*(1), 1-3.

Rifkin, J. (1995). *The end of work*. New York: G. P. Putnam's Sons.

Ritchie, K. (1995, April). Marketing to Generation X. *American Demographics*, 34-39.

Robins, L. N. & Regier, D. A. (1991). *Psychiatric disorders in America—The epidemiologic catchment area study*. New York: Free Press.

Ross, D. P., &Shillington, R., (1994). *The Canadian fact book on poverty—1994*. Ottawa: Canadian Council on Social Development.

Rowe, D. C., & Rodgers, J. L. (1990). Behavioral genetics, adolescence deviance, and "d": Contributions and issues. In G. R. Adams, R. Montemayor, & T. P. Gullotta (Eds.), *Biology of adolescent behavior and development* (pp. 38-67). Newbury Park, CA: Sage.

Rowntree, J., & Rowntree, M. (1968). The political economy of youth. *Our Generation, 6*(1-2), 155-190.

Rudd, P., & Evans, K. (1998). Structure and agency in youth transitions. *Journal of Youth Studies, 1*, 39-62.

Rushkoff, D. (Producer). (2001). *The merchants of cool* [video cassette]. Public Broadcasting System, *Frontline*, *www.pbs.org*.

Sabo, D., & Jansen, S. C. (1992). Images of men in sport media: The social reproduction of gender order. In S. Craig (Ed.), *Men, masculinity, and the media*. Newbury Park, CA: Sage.

Saunders, D. (1996, April 22). Graduates facing postponed beginnings. *The Globe and Mail*, pp. A1, A8.

Schlegel, A., & Barry, H. (1991). *Adolescence: An anthropological inquiry*. New York: Free Press.

Schlosser, E. (2001). *Fast food nation: The dark side of the all-American meal*. New York: Perennial.

Schoeni, R. F., & Ross, K. E. (2005). Material assistance received from families during the transition to adulthood. In R. A. Settersten, F. F. Furstenberg, & R. G. Rumbaut (Eds.), *On the frontier of adulthood: Theory, research, and public policy* (pp. 396–416). Chicago: University of Chicago Press.

Schor, J. B. (2004). *Born to buy: The commercialized child and the new consumer culture*. New York: Scribner.

Schuller, T. (2004). Three capitals: A framework. In T. Schuller & et al. (Eds.), *The benefits of learning: The impact of education on health, family life and social capital* (pp. 12-34). London: Routledge-Falmer.

Schuller, T., Hammond, C., & Preston, J. (2004). Reappraising benefits. In T. Schuller, Preston, J., Hammond, C., Brassett-Grundy, A., & Bynner, J. (Eds.), *The benefits of learning: the impact of education on health, family life and social capital* (pp. 179-193). London: Routledge-Falmer.

Schuller, T., Preston, J., Hammond, C., Brassett-Grundy, A., & Bynner, J. (2004). *The benefits of learning: The impact of education on health, family life and social capital*. London: Routledge-Falmer.

Schultze, Q. J., Anker, R. M., Bratt, J. D., Romanowski, W. D., Worst, J. W., & Zuidervaart, L. (1990). *Dancing in the dark: Youth, popular culture, and the electronic media*. Grand Rapids, Michigan: William B. Eerdmans.

Schwartz, B. (2000). Self-determination: The tyranny of freedom. *American Psychologist, 55*(1), 79-88.

Schwartz, B. (2004a). *The paradox of choice: Why more is less*. New York: Harper Collins.

Schwartz, B. (2004b). The tyranny of choice. *The Chronicle of Higher Education, 50*(20), B6.

Seligman, M. (1988, October). Boomer blues. *Psychology Today*, pp. 50-55.

Shanahan, M. J. (2000). Pathways to adulthood in changing societies: Variability and mechanisms in the life course perspective. *Annual Review of Sociology, 26*, 667-692.

SourceWatch (2004). *Donald Rumsfeld: Notable quotes*. Retrieved December 15, 2004, from **www.disinfopedia.org/ wiki.phtml?title=Donald_Rumsfeld**

Speer, T. L. (1998, March). College come-ons. *American Demographics*, pp. 41-45.

Spiegler, M. (1996, November). Marketing street culture: Bringing hip-hop style to the mainstream. *American Demographics*, pp. 29-34.

Springhall, J. (1986). *Coming of Age: Adolescence in Britain 1860-1960*. Dublin: Gill and MacMillan.

Sprinthall, N. A., & Collins, W. A. (1984). *Adolescent psychology: A developmental view*. Reading, Mass.: Addison-Wesley.

Statistics Canada. (1989). *Youth in Canada: Selected highlights* (Cat. No. 89-511). Ottawa: Housing, Family and Social Statistics Division.

Statistics Canada. (1994, Winter). Working teens. *Canadian Social Trends*, pp. 18-22.

Statistics Canada. (1995, Winter). Life expectancy. *Canadian Social Trends*, p. 36.

Statistics Canada. (2002). *Profile of the Canadian population by age and sex: Canada ages*. Ottawa: Author.

Statistics Canada. (2003a). *Education in Canada: Raising the standard. 2001 Census: Analysis series*. Ottawa: Minister of Industry.

Statistics Canada. (2003b). *Earning of Canadians: Making a living in the new economy. 2001 Census: Analysis series*. Ottawa: Minister of Industry.

Statistics Canada. (2003c). *Income of Canadian families. 2001 Census: Analysis series*. Ottawa: Minister of Industry.

Statistics Canada. (2003d). *Religions in Canada. 2001 Census: Analysis series*. Ottawa: Author.

Statistics Canada. (2003e). *The changing profile of Canada's labour force. 2001 Census: Analysis series*. Ottawa: Author.

Statistics Canada. (2004a, September 27). Deaths. *The Daily.* Ottawa: Statistics Canada. Retrieved October 13, 2004, from **www.statcan.ca/Daily/English/040927/ d040927a.htm**

Statistics Canada. (2004b, Summer). Social indicators. *Canadian Social Trends*, p. 31.

Statistics Sweden. (2004). *Statistical Yearbook of Sweden 2004*. Stockholm: Author.

Steinberg, L. (1990). Pubertal maturation and parent-adolescent distance: An evolutionary perspective. In G. R. Adams, R. Montemayor, & T. P. Gullotta (Eds.), *Biology of adolescent behavior and development* (pp. 71-97). Newbury Park, CA: Sage.

Steinberg, L. (1996). *Beyond the classroom: Why school reform has failed and what parents need to do about it.* New York: Simon & Schuster.

Stevenson, K., Tufts, J., Hendrick, D., & Kowalski, M. (1999, Summer). Youth and crime. *Canadian Social Trends*, pp. 17-21.

Stockard, J., & Johnson, M. M. (1992). *Sex and gender in society*. Englewood Cliffs, NJ: Prentice Hall.

Stockard, J. & O'Brien, R. M. (2002). Cohort effects on suicide rates: International variations. *American Sociological Review, 67*(6), 854-872.

Strang, S. P., & Orlofsky, J. L. (1990). Factors underlying suicidal ideation among college students: A test of Teicher and Jacobs' model. *Journal of Adolescence, 13,* 39-52.

Strasburger, V. C., & Donnerstein, E. (1999). Children, adolescents, and the media: Issues and solutions. *Pediatrics, 103,* 129-139.

Stauber, J. and Rampton, S. (1995). *Toxic sludge is good for you: Trust us, we're experts*. Munroe, ME: Common Courage Press.

Sunter, D. (1994, Spring). Youths—waiting it out. *Perspectives on Labour and Income*, pp. 31-36.   :

Sunter, D. (1994, Autumn). The labour market: Mid-year review. *Perspectives on Labour and Income*, pp. 2-10.

Swedish Institute. (1991). Facts and figures about youth in Sweden. *Fact sheets on Sweden.* Stockholm: Author.

Swedish Institute. (1993). Facts and figures about youth in Sweden. *Fact sheets on Sweden.* Stockholm: Author.

Swedish Institute. (1999). Swedish Labor Market Policy. *Fact sheets on Sweden.* Stockholm: Author.

Swedish Institute. (2000). Upper secondary and adult education in Sweden. *Fact sheets on Sweden.* Stockholm: Author.

Swedish Institute. (2004a). Higher education in Sweden. *Fact sheets on Sweden.* Stockholm: Author.

Swedish Institute. (2004b). Financial circumstances of Swedish households. *Fact sheets on Sweden.* Stockholm: Author.

Swedish Institute. (2004c). The Swedish economy. *Fact sheets on Sweden.* Stockholm: Author.

Swedish National Board for Youth Affairs. (1998). *Young Sweden.* Stockholm: Author.

Swedish National Board for Youth Affairs. (1999a). *Youth in progress: The transition to adulthood in Sweden in the 1990s.* Stockholm: Author.

Swedish National Board for Youth Affairs. (1999b). *Statistics on young people in Sweden—tables.* Stockholm: Author.

Swedish National Board for Youth Affairs. (1999c). *Thumbs up: The development guarantee from young people's perspectives* (Summary of report no. 17). Stockholm: Author. Retrieved December 28, 2004, from **www.ungdomsstyrelsen.se**

Swedish National Board for Youth Affairs. (1999d). *Democratic procedures or gobbledegook?* Stockholm: Author. Retrieved December 28, 2004, from **www.ungdomsstyrelsen.se**

Swedish National Board for Youth Affairs. (1999e). *Review of National Youth Policy* (Summary of the Swedish National Report). Stockholm: Author. Retrieved December 28, 2004, from **www.ungdomsstyrelsen.se**

Swedish National Board for Youth Affairs. (2000). *One in a hundred—the third year of the development guarantee* (Summary of report no. 23). Stockholm: Author. Retrieved December 28, 2004, from **www.ungdomsstyrelsen.se**

Swedish National Board for Youth Affairs. (2001a). *Career opportunities in music and the creative industries in Sweden* (Summary of report no. 25). Stockholm: Author. Retrieved December 28, 2004, from **www.ungdomsstyrelsen.se**

Swedish National Board for Youth Affairs. (2001b). *Young Sweden.* Stockholm: Author.

Swedish National Board for Youth Affairs. (2002). *Swedish Youth 2002—Second year follow-up of the National Youth Policy* (Summary of report 2002:5). Stockholm: Author. Retrieved December 28, 2004, from **www.ungdomsstyrelsen.se**

Swedish National Board for Youth Affairs. (2003a). *Young outsiders* (English summary of SOU 2003: 92). Stockholm: Author. Retrieved December 28, 2004, from **www.ungdomsstyrelsen.se**

Swedish National Board for Youth Affairs. (2003b). *They call us young* (Summary of report 2003:1). Stockholm: Author. Retrieved December 28, 2004, from **www.ungdomsstyrelsen.se**

Swedish National Board for Youth Affairs. (2004). *The Swedish National Board for Youth Affairs (2004/2005).* Stockholm:

Author. Retrieved December 28, 2004, from **www.ungdomsstyrelsen.se**

Synge, J. (1979). The transition from school to work: Growing up in early 20th century Hamilton, Ontario. In K. Ishwaran (Ed.), *Childhood and adolescence in Canada* (pp. 249-269). Toronto: McGraw-Hill Ryerson Ltd.

Tannock, S. (2001). *Youth at work: The unionized fast-food and grocery workplace.* Philadelphia: Temple University Press.

Teixeira, R. A., & Mishel, L. (1995). Skills shortages or management shortage? In D. Bills (Ed.), *The new modern times: Factors reshaping the world of work* (pp. 193-205). Albany, NY: State University of New York Press.

Thorndike, E. L. (1904). The newest psychology. *Educational Review, 28,* 217-227.

Tyyskä, V. (2001). *Long and winding road: Adolescents and youth in Canada today.* Toronto: Canadian Scholars Press.

U.S. Census Bureau. (1981). *Statistical Abstract of the United States.* Washington, DC: Author.

U.S. Census Bureau. (2001). *Statistical Abstract of the United States.* Washington, DC: Author.

Wallace, C. (1995*). How old is young and young is old? The restructuring of age and the life-course in Europe.* Paper presented at Youth 2000: An International Conference, Middlesborough, UK.

Wallace, C., & Kovatcheva, S. (1998). *Youth in society: The construction and deconstruction of youth in East and West Europe.* Houndmills, UK: MacMillan Press.

Wannell, T., & Caron, N. (1994). *The gender earnings gap among recent postsecondary graduates, 1984-92* (Analytic studies branch research paper series No. 68). Ottawa: Statistics Canada.

White, L. (1994). Coresidence and leaving home: Young adults and their parents. *Annual Review of Sociology, 20,* 81-102.

William T. Grant Foundation (1988). *The forgotten half: Non-college youth in America.* Washington: Author.

Willis, L. A., Coombs, D. W., Cockerham, W. C., & Frison, S. L. (2002). Ready to die: A postmodern interpretation of the increase of African-American adolescent male suicide. *Social Science & Medicine, 55,* 907-920.

Winnicott, D. W. (1971). Adolescence: struggling through the doldrums. *Adolescent Psychiatry, 1,* 40-51.

World Health Organization. (2004a). *Suicide prevention and special programmes.* Retrieved December 28, 2004, from **www.who.int/mental_health/ prevention/en**

World Health Organization. (2004b). *World report of violence and health E-book: First world report on violence and health.* Retrieved April 21, 2004, from

www.who.int/violence injury prevention/ violence/global campaign/en/chap7.pdf

Wrong, D. (1961). The over-socialized conception of man in modern sociology. *American Sociological Review, 2,* 188-192.

Wyn, J., & White, R. (1998). Young people, social problems and Australian youth studies. *Journal of Youth Studies, 1(1),* 23-38.

Zhao, J., & de Broucker, P. (2001, December 7). Participation in postsecondary education and family income. *The Daily,* Ottawa: Statistics Canada (Catalogue No. 11-001E).

Zollo, P. (1995, November). Talking to teens: The teenage market is free-spending and loaded with untapped potential. A veteran of teen marketing explains what's cool, what's not, and how to tell the difference. *American Demographics,* 22-28.

Index